[...] 30th : 1st in Denmark: 1383
Stuttgart 628   31st: 9th in W. Germany
Bremen 607   32nd: 10th in W. Germany
Liverpool 603   33rd: 4th in the UK: 1263
Dublin 566   34th: 1st in Ireland: 670
's-Gravenhage 551   35th: 3rd in Neth: 719
Sevilla 548   36th: 4th in Spain
Manchester 542   37th: 5th in the UK: 2394
Helsinki/Helsingfors 533   38th: 1st in Finland: 804
Lyon 528   39th: 3rd in France: 1075
Hannover 518   40th: 11th in W. Germany
Sheffield 516   41st: 6th in the UK
Leeds 501   42nd: 7th in the UK: 1736
Bologna 491   43rd: 7th in Italy
Oslo 487   44th: 1st in Norway: 579
Zaragoza 480   45th: 5th in Spain
Nürnberg 477   46th: 12th in W. Germany
Firenze 459   47th: 8th in Italy
Duisburg 458   48th: 13th in W. Germany
Edinburgh 453   49th: 8th in the UK
Göteborg 452   50th: 2nd in Sweden: 678
Bristol 426   51st: 9th in the UK
Zürich 423   52nd: 1st in Switzerland: 675
Wuppertal 415   53rd: 14th in W. Germany
Catània 413   54th: 9th in Italy
Bilbao 410   55th: 6th in Spain
Teesside 396   56th: 10th in the UK
Málaga 374   57th: 7th in Spain
Toulouse 371   58th: 4th in France: 440

[...] 68th: 2nd in Portugal: 836
Bonn 299   69th: 18th in W. Germany
Nottingham 297   70th: 13th in the UK
Bradford 295   71st: 14th in the UK
Las Palmas 287   72nd: 8th in Spain
Kingston upon Hull 285   73rd: 15th in the UK
Leicester 282   74th: 16th in the UK
Utrecht 279   75th: 4th in Neth: 455
Trieste 278   76th: 12th in Italy
Cardiff 277   77th: 17th in the UK
Kiel 277   78th: 19th in W. Germany
Messina 272   79th: 13th in Italy
Wolverhampton 268   80th: 18th in the UK
Bordeaux 267   81st: 6th in France: 555
Malmö 266   82nd: 3rd in Sweden: 445
Stoke on Trent 264   83rd: 19th in the UK
Wiesbaden 261   84th: 20th in W. Germany
Nantes 259   85th: 7th in France: 394
Verona 259   86th: 14th in Italy
Karlsruhe 257   87th: 21st in W. Germany
Strasbourg 249   88th: 8th in France: 355
Graz 249   89th: 2nd in Austria
Oberhausen 249   90th: 22nd in W. Germany
Plymouth 247   91st: 20th in the UK
Murcia 244   92nd: 9th in Spain
Lübeck 242   93rd: 23rd in W. Germany
Hospitalet 242   94th: 10th in Spain
Valladolid 236   95th: 11th in Spain
Córdoba 235   96th: 12th in Spain

[...] 111th: 29th in W. Germany
Le Havre 200   118th: 10th in France: 247
Vigo 197   119th: 14th in Spain
Mülheim a.d. Ruhr 191   120th: 30th in W. Germany
Lille 191   121st: 11th in France: 881
Granada 190   122nd: 15th in Spain
La Coruña 190   123rd: 16th in Spain
Eindhoven 189   124th: 5th in Neth: 335
Gijón 188   125th: 17th in Spain
Piraiévs/Piraeus 187   126th: 3rd in Greece
Dudley 185   127th: 26th in the UK
Alicante 185   128th: 18th in Spain
Walsall 184   129th: 27th in the UK
Dundee 183   130th: 28th in the UK
Aberdeen 182   131st: 29th in the UK
Rennes 181   132nd: 12th in France: 193
Aachen 178   133rd: 31st in W. Germany
Mainz 177   134th: 32nd in W. Germany
Solingen 176   135th: 33rd in W. Germany
Toulon 175   136th: 13th in France: 340
Ludwigshafen am Rhein 175   137th: 34th in W. Germany
Livorno 174   138th: 19th in Italy
Genève 174   139th: 3rd in Switz: 321
Parma 172   140th: 20th in Italy
Haarlem 172   141st: 6th in Neth: 239
Swansea 171   142nd: 30th in the UK
Bielefeld 169   143rd: 35th in W. Germany
Groningen 169   144th: 7th in Neth: 201
Modena 167   145th: 21st in Italy

Reims 153   167th: 17th in France: 168
Tilburg 153   168th: 8th in Neth: 202
Mönchengladbach 152   169th: 37th in W. Germany
Santa Cruz de Tenerife 151   170th: 23rd in Spain
Salerno 151   171st: 24th in Italy
Jerez de la Frontera 150   172nd: 24th in Spain
Blackpool 150   173rd: 37th in the UK
Santander 150   174th: 25th in Spain
Gent 149   175th: 3rd in Belgium: 226
Bournemouth 149   176th: 38th in the UK
Clermont-Ferrand 149   177th: 18th in France: 205
Bremerhaven 149   178th: 38th in W. Germany
Nijmegen 149   179th: 9th in Neth: 203
Liège 147   180th: 4th in Belgium: 444
Pamplona 147   181st: 26th in Spain
Cartagena 147   182nd: 27th in Spain
Dijon 145   183rd: 19th in France: 184
Le Mans 143   184th: 20th in France: 166
Darmstadt 141   185th: 39th in W. Germany
Osnabrück 141   186th: 40th in W. Germany
Foggia 140   187th: 25th in Italy
Prato 140   188th: 26th in Italy
Stockport 140   189th: 39th in the UK
Enschede 139   190th: 10th in Neth: 230
Tàrrasa 139   191st: 28th in Spain
Birkenhead 138   192nd: 40th in the UK
Lausanne 137   193rd: 5th in Switz: 219
Remscheid 137   194th: 41st in W. Germany

Trondheim 126   216th: 2nd in Norway
Recklinghausen 126   217th: 45th in W. Germany
Bergamo 125   218th: 31st in Italy
Salamanca 125   219th: 31st in Spain
Thurrock 125   220th: 46th in the UK
Apeldoorn 124   221st: 12th in Neth
Nancy 123   222nd: 24th in France: 258
Nîmes 123   223rd: 25th in France: 125
Ipswich 123   224th: 47th in the UK
Elche 123   225th: 32nd in Spain
Heidelberg 122   226th: 46th in W. Germany
Breda 121   227th: 13th in Neth: 147
Rouen 120   228th: 26th in France: 370
Würzburg 120   229th: 47th in W. Germany
Burgos 120   230th: 33rd in Spain
Villeurbanne 120   231st: 27th in France
Offenbach am Main 119   232nd: 48th in W. Germany
Peristérion 118   233rd: 4th in Greece
Salzgitter 118   234th: 49th in W. Germany
Amiens 118   235th: 28th in France: 137
Neuss 118   236th: 50th in W. Germany
Pescara 117   237th: 32nd in Italy
Rimini 117   238th: 33rd in Italy
Västerås 117   239th: 4th in Sweden
Mulhouse 116   240th: 29th in France: 199
Norrköping 116   241st: 5th in Sweden
Bergen 116   242nd: 6th in Norway
243rd: 3rd in Norway: 149

Sassari 107   265th: 37th in Italy
Santa Coloma de Gramanet 107   266th: 36th in Spain
Poole 107   267th: 53rd in the UK
Koblenz 106   268th: 54th in W. Germany
Terni 106   269th: 38th in Italy
Oldham 106   270th: 54th in the UK
León 105   271st: 37th in Spain
York 105   272nd: 55th in the UK
Torbay 105   273rd: 56th in the UK
Siracusa 105   274th: 39th in Italy
Bolzano/Bozen 105   275th: 40th in Italy
Linköping 105   276th: 9th in Sweden
Forlì 104   277th: 41st in Italy
Piacenza 104   278th: 42nd in Italy
St. Helens 104   279th: 57th in the UK
Trier 103   280th: 55th in W. Germany
Wilhelmshaven 103   281st: 56th in W. Germany
Pisa 103   282nd: 43rd in Italy
Meriden 102   283rd: 58th in the UK
Perpignan 102   284th: 35th in France: 107
Frederiksberg 102   285th: 5th in Denmark
Badajoz 102   286th: 38th in Spain
Leiden 101   287th: 14th in Neth
Blackburn 101   288th: 59th in the UK
Herne 101   289th: 57th in W. Germany
Rheydt 101   290th: 58th in W. Germany
Hälsingborg 101   291st: 6th in Sweden
South Shields 100   292nd: 60th in the UK

S

THE BARTHOLOMEW/SCRIBNER

Atlas of Europe

A PROFILE OF WESTERN EUROPE

Editorial Director: GEOFFREY S. BROWNE
President, The Economist Intelligence Unit

Executive Editor: ROBERT M. CROUCHER

Designer: RUFUS SEGAR

Cartographic Director: JOHN C. BARTHOLOMEW

Contributing Editor: JOHN McLACHLAN

Statistical Editor: MALCOLM C. MacDONALD

Educational Adviser: RAYMOND B. SALMON

THE BARTHOLOMEW/SCRIBNER

Atlas of Europe

A PROFILE OF WESTERN EUROPE

JOHN BARTHOLOMEW, EDINBURGH ◑ CHARLES SCRIBNER'S SONS, NEW YORK

Copyright © 1974 John Bartholomew & Son Ltd
and Frederick Warne & Co Ltd

Cartography by
John Bartholomew & Son Ltd and
David L. Fryer & Company
Henley-on-Thames

Diagrams by
Rufus Segar and
David L. Fryer & Company

Portraits on pages 20 and 21 by Rodney Shackell

1 3 5 7 9 11 13 15 17 19 I/C 20 18 16 14 12 10 8 6 4 2

Printed in Great Britain

Library of Congress Catalog Card Number 73-20985

ISBN 0-684-13806-9

Foreword

The years after the 1939/45 war have seen a transformation of Western Europe. Its countries have achieved marvels of recovery from the chaos and demoralization of war, and there have been astonishing records of economic growth and productivity. The wartime disruption of traditional trading and the decline of its old empires compelled Europe to look more towards its own self-sufficiency. More important, groups of nations looked towards the creation of a united Europe. From the inspiration of Winston Churchill and other leading statesmen there emerged a blueprint for economic and political co-operation, and foundations were laid for this in the late fifties. This was by no means the first attempt that Europeans had made to unite and, even now, unity means different things to different countries. To some, commercial interests dominate and there are widely differing views of political integration and national sovereignty. The final shape and size of the co-operative structure has yet to be seen and its strength to be fully tested. In this atlas we have described the main stages in the path towards unity but, naturally, we have made no predictions.

Whatever the results of the movement towards greater co-operation, the peoples of Europe outnumber those of either North America or the USSR and form a very large part of the world's wealthier citizens. They also form its largest trading group. Over the centuries they have penetrated all continents and have done much to mould the style of life, and influence the religions,

political systems, and social and legal codes of many countries. Much of this influence remains and, indeed, with greater economic and political co-operation within the continent, Western Europe has increased its help for the development of the poorer countries.

In these pages we have attempted to describe conditions and activities in eighteen countries of Western Europe, to compare their patterns of living and to show them in relation to North America and other areas. Also, as change has often been large and rapid, we have given comparisons over a decade or more for such topics as agricultural production, trade between countries and consumer spending. And wherever appropriate we have tried to show Europe's place and activities in a world context.

In his introduction the Executive Editor explains some of the problems met and techniques used in compiling this book. For my part, I have had the privilege of working with a very able and enthusiastic editorial team headed by Robert Croucher whose ideas and often complex material the designer and cartographers have illustrated in a way which I believe will appeal to the reader. We have all had the benefit of advice, suggestions and information from many people and organisations and we are very grateful to them for this help.

Geoffrey Browne
Editorial Director

Contents

Western Europe

Iceland
Finland
Norway
Sweden
Denmark
Republic of Ireland
United Kingdom
Netherlands
Belgium
Luxembourg
West Germany
Switzerland
France
Austria
Portugal
Spain
Italy
Greece

Eastern Europe

USSR
East Germany
Poland
Czechoslovakia
Hungary
Rumania
Yugoslavia
Bulgaria
Albania
Turkey
Malta
Cyprus

Introduction

This atlas aims to set out a series of clear, definitive statements about Western Europe and the quality of life that its people enjoy. The evidence presented is intended to provide insights that enable interested observer and serious student alike to make informed judgments about the kind of place Western Europe really is. The pages reveal interesting variations in economic and social patterns among the eighteen countries selected, affording an impartial basis for comparative studies. By the selection of statistics from a variety of international sources and by the reduction of textual explanation to a minimum we believe we have achieved a neutral and objective approach, leaving the reader free to make his own interpretations. Direct factual comparisons between countries are made easy by the provision of many graphs, diagrams and tabulations in addition to the maps.

This atlas breaks new ground in the way that geographical information is presented and the reader will find that many of the cartographic techniques used are helpful in dealing with the quantification that characterises geography today. A carefully made selection of ingredients for each page avoids the temptation to pile fact upon fact in a confusion of symbols. The use of an overall design covering colour, typography and drawing methods gives it a clear and rich visual consistency. From the point of view of scale Western Europe is an inconvenient shape and size for the mapping of economic and social themes and the problems are not made any easier by the tendency of Europeans to crowd into a relatively limited area of the continent. Sometimes, for the sake of clarity, graphs or diagrams have been preferred to maps. To give depth to some subjects deliberate use has been made of the case study approach, although this has been done with caution as it is easy to present

the reader with a summary picture of Western Europe that consists essentially of the industrial centres of the four biggest nations. A proper appreciation of the scale of economic and social activity in Western Europe can only effectively be made by reference to the wider total area and so normally all eighteen countries are shown as a whole.

To get this atlas prepared and published many individuals and organisations were consulted for information and advice. My thanks go to them all for the invaluable help which they so generously gave.

Robert M. Croucher
Executive Editor

Editorial Notes

Statistical Base: The frame of reference for this atlas is 1970 and statistics normally refer to that year. This permits the use of the decade 1960-70 for comparison purposes. Latest available figures will be found in the statistical profile.

Sources and Acknowledgements: These are listed on page 118.

Definitions: Throughout the atlas statistics referring to Spain include the Balearic Isles and the Canaries and Portugal include the Azores and Madeira, but the figures for Denmark exclude the Faeroes and Greenland.

Units: Metric measurements are used throughout.

Projections: The basic map projection used is the conical orthomorphic with origin at 7°E and standard parallels at 40° and 50°N. Where other projections have been used a reference is included on the map.

Scales: The standard scale for the thematic maps is 1:15 000 000.

Glossary: Specialized terms and abbreviations are used throughout without detailed explanation in the text and a glossary is provided for the reader seeking specific definitions.

Index: A general place name index is provided for the reference maps section and a separate subject index gives a quick reference to the main themes of the atlas.

The West Europeans

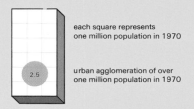

each square represents
one million population in 1970

2.5 urban agglomeration of over
one million population in 1970

In a demographic map, areas
are proportional to population
and not to the amount of
land. This map shows where
the 335 million people in our
eighteen countries are
concentrated and, except in
the relatively empty lands of
Scandinavia, Iceland, and
Ireland where excessive
shrinkage occurs, there is
little geographic distortion.

The concept of the
agglomeration is used to
identify and locate the
massive concentrations of
city-living people which
dominate the population
distribution of Western
Europe. Although this term
has no precise meaning, it does
define sufficiently for economic
planning purposes the urban
areas which typically spread
well beyond the official
boundaries of many cities.

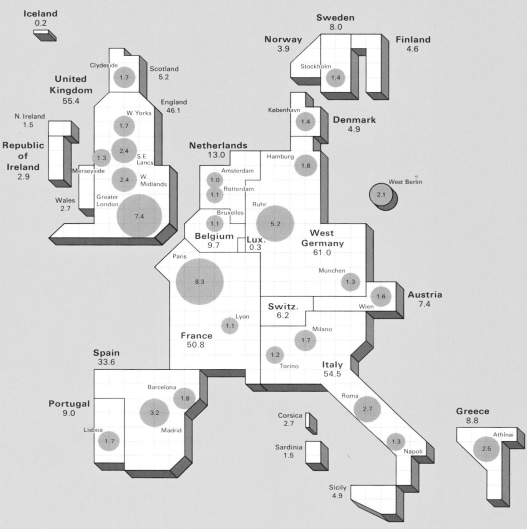

The Distribution of Population

	Population 1970[a] in thousands	Area in thousand km²	Population per km²	Km² per thousand population
West Germany	60 987	248	245	4
United Kingdom	55 375	244	227	4
Italy	54 504	301	181	6
France	50 776	544	93	11
Spain	33 646	505	67	15
Netherlands	13 039	41	319	3
Belgium	9 676	31	317	3
Portugal	8 950	92	97	10
Greece	8 793	132	67	15
Sweden	8 046	450	18	56
Austria	7 410	84	88	11
Switzerland	6 240	41	151	7
Denmark	4 921	43	114	9
Finland	4 629	337	14	73
Norway	3 879	324	12	83
Republic of Ireland	2 944	70	·42	24
Luxembourg	339	3	131	8
Iceland	204	103	2	505
The Eighteen	335 037	3 593	93	11

[a] estimated mid-year total

The Distribution of Urban Population
Urban population as a percentage of total population

Country	Percentage
West Germany	70
United Kingdom	77
Italy	64
France	70
Spain	51
Netherlands	80
Belgium	67
Portugal	24
Greece	53
Sweden	67
Austria	51
Switzerland	59
Denmark	45
Finland	51
Norway	43
Republic of Ireland	49
Luxembourg	62
Iceland	69
The Eighteen	65

Europe's Place in the World

By continental standards Europe is small in mass, but in terms of population and wealth it is one of the world's giants. This is explained partly by its central position in the land hemisphere, partly by the length of its historical perspective and partly by its encouraging environment, which has been a rich stimulus to man's restless initiatives. In such a situation, Europe has developed a pivotal role which has permitted an extension of its influence on the world out of proportion to its moderate size. For centuries now, by exploration and conquest, it has spread its inventions, technical skills and political ideas to all parts of the world.

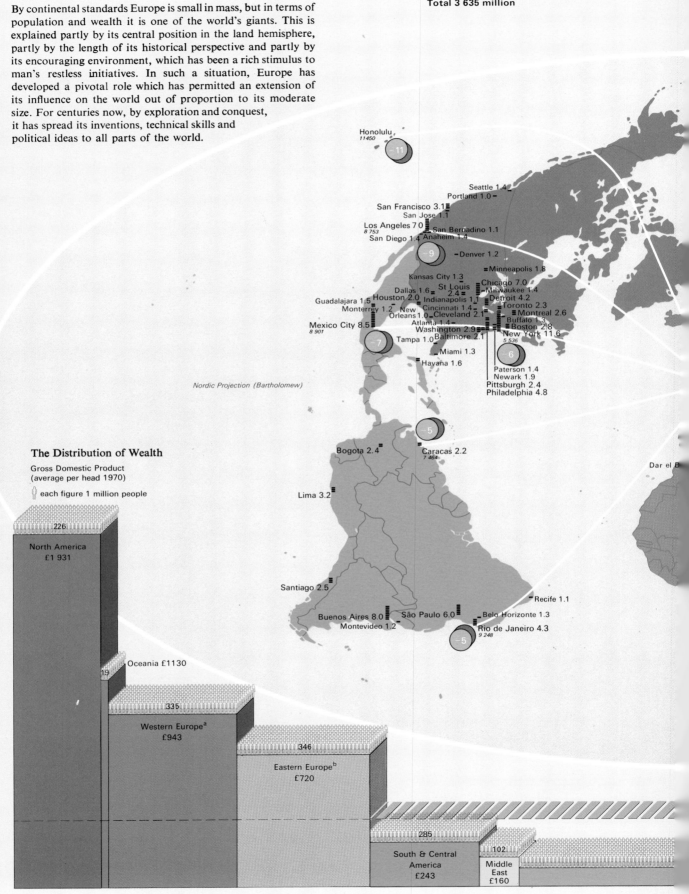

World Population
in millions 1970
Total 3 635 million

Asia 1 951

China 760

Nordic Projection (Bartholomew)

Honolulu
11450
-11

Seattle 1.4
Portland 1.0 -
San Francisco 3.1
San Jose 1.1
Los Angeles 7 0
8 753
San Diego 1.4
San Bernadino 1.1
Anaheim 1.4
-9
-Denver 1.2
Minneapolis 1.8
Kansas City 1.3
Chicago 7.0
Dallas 1.6
St Louis
2.4
Milwaukee 1.4
Guadalajara 1.5
Houston 2.0
Indianapolis 1.1
Detroit 4.2
Monterrey 1.2
New
Orleans 1.0
Cincinnati 1.4
Toronto 2.3
Cleveland 2.1
Montreal 2.6
Atlanta 1.4
Buffalo 1.3
Mexico City 8.5
8 901
Washington 2.9
Boston 2.8
-7
Tampa 1.0
Baltimore 2.1
New York 11.6
5 536
Miami 1.3
-6
Havana 1.6
Paterson 1.4
Newark 1.9
Pittsburgh 2.4
Philadelphia 4.8

-5
Bogota 2.4
Caracas 2.2
7 464
Dar el B

Lima 3.2

Santiago 2.5

Recife 1.1

Buenos Aires 8.0
São Paulo 6.0
Belo Horizonte 1.3
Montevideo 1.2
Rio de Janeiro 4.3
9 248
-5

The Distribution of Wealth

Gross Domestic Product
(average per head 1970)

each figure 1 million people

226
North America
£1 931

19
Oceania £1130

335
Western Europe[a]
£943

346
Eastern Europe[b]
£720

285
South & Central
America
£243

102
Middle
East
£160

[a] excludes Turkey and Yugoslavia

10

[b] including all USSR but not Albania

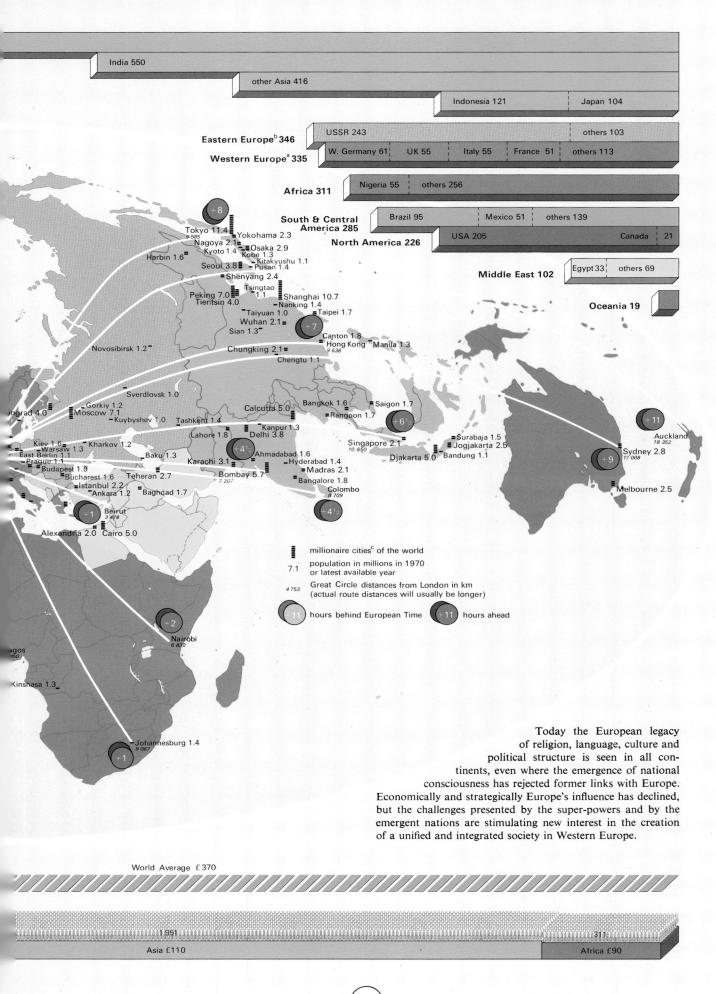

India 550

other Asia 416

Indonesia 121 | Japan 104

Eastern Europe[b] 346 — USSR 243 | others 103

Western Europe[a] 335 — W. Germany 61 | UK 55 | Italy 55 | France 51 | others 113

Africa 311 — Nigeria 55 | others 256

South & Central America 285 — Brazil 95 | Mexico 51 | others 139

North America 226 — USA 205 | Canada 21

Middle East 102 — Egypt 33 | others 69

Oceania 19

Tokyo 11.4 *9 585*
Yokohama 2.3
Nagoya 2.1
Kyoto 1.4 — Osaka 2.9
Kobe 1.3
Kitakyushu 1.1
Harbin 1.6
Seoul 3.8 — Pusan 1.4
Shenyang 2.4
Peking 7.0 — Tsingtao 1.1
Tientsin 4.0 — Shanghai 10.7
Nanking 1.4
Taiyuan 1.0 — Taipei 1.7
Wuhan 2.1
Sian 1.3 — Canton 1.8
Novosibirsk 1.2 — Hong Kong *9 638* — Manila 1.3
Chungking 2.1
Chengtu 1.1

Sverdlovsk 1.0
Gorkiy 1.2 — Bangkok 1.6 — Saigon 1.7
ingrad 4.0 — Moscow 7.1
Kuybyshev 1.0 — Calcutta 5.0 — Rangoon 1.7
Tashkent 1.4
Kiev 1.6 — Kharkov 1.2 — Kanpur 1.3
Lahore 1.8 — Delhi 3.8
East Berlin 1.1 — Baku 1.3 — Singapore 2.1 *10 850* — Surabaja 1.5
Prague 1.1 — Karachi 3.1 — Ahmadabad 1.6 — Jogjakarta 2.5
Budapest 1.9 — Hyderabad 1.4 — Djakarta 5.0 — Bandung 1.1
Bucharest 1.6 — Teheran 2.7 — Bombay 5.7 *7 207* — Madras 2.1
Istanbul 2.2 — Bangalore 1.8
Ankara 1.2 — Baghdad 1.7 — Colombo *8 709*

Auckland *18 352*

Sydney 2.8 *17 008*

Melbourne 2.5

Beirut *3 478*
Alexandria 2.0 — Cairo 5.0

Nairobi *6 830*

gos

Kinshasa 1.3

Johannesburg 1.4 *9 067*

millionaire cities[c] of the world

7.1 — population in millions in 1970 or latest available year

4 753 — Great Circle distances from London in km (actual route distances will usually be longer)

-11 — hours behind European Time   +11 — hours ahead

Today the European legacy of religion, language, culture and political structure is seen in all continents, even where the emergence of national consciousness has rejected former links with Europe. Economically and strategically Europe's influence has declined, but the challenges presented by the super-powers and by the emergent nations are stimulating new interest in the creation of a unified and integrated society in Western Europe.

World Average £370

1 951 — 311

Asia £110 — Africa £90

[c] generally includes suburbs and some agglomerations   **11**   © Bartholomew/Warne 1974

Vatna Jökull

ATLANTIC
OCEAN

Norwegian
Sea

K j ø l e

2470

North
Sea

Baltic
Sea

Elbe

Oder

Vistula

Limit of Quaternary

Rhein

1142

Seine

Bay
of
Biscay

Loire

Tatra
2663

C a r p a t h

Garonne

Mt.
Blanc
4810

A   l   p   s

Po

Rhône

Douro

P y r e n e e s
3404

Ebro

A p e n n i n e s

Adriatic
Sea

25

Danube

Tejo

2912

Tyrrhenian

Sea

P i n d h o s

2637

Olympus
2917

Ionian
Sea

M E D I T E R R A N E A N

Etna
3263

S E A

1:15 000 000

0   100   200   300   400   500   600   700   800   900   1000 km

© Bartholomew/Warne 1974

The Landscape of Europe

ICE CAP: A cold desert with below freezing temperatures all year. Little vegetation. **GLACIERS:** Individual ice masses formed by movement down valley from the permanent icefields above the snow line. Most of Europe's glaciers are in the Swiss Alps.

NORTH

TUNDRA: Low temperatures, virtually continuous daylight in summer, and darkness in winter, poor soils and permafrost. The growing season barely lasts four months. A bare, treeless landscape with a close cover of shallow-rooted shrubs, mosses, lichens, colourful flowers and berried plants. *Saxifrage, bilberry, dwarf willow, birch.*

see ALPINE below

BOREAL FOREST: The Taiga forms vast, unbroken stands of conifer forest. Unfavourable habitat, few species of tree. Major European source of softwoods. The poleward limits approximate to the 10°C summer isotherm. *Pine, spruce, firs, larch.*

see MOUNTAIN FOREST below

The natural vegetation cover in Europe reflects poleward variations in climate, although local conditions of soil and relief may influence particular plant distributions. A subsidiary control is the effect of continentality with reduced rainfall and extremes of temperature.

MIXED WOODLAND & GRASSLAND: Broad-leaved deciduous woodland with conifers in cooler locations and grassland in drier areas and on hillsides. Little original vegetation in the most densely peopled part of Western Europe because of long-established intensive cultivation. *Oak, beech, ash, elm.*

HEATH: Open ground with close growing herbage and scattered trees. Typically associated with sand dunes and glacial gravels. Often reclaimed by afforestation. *Ling, gorse, bracken, silver birch.*
MOORLAND: More frequent on high ground. Often waterlogged and exposed. Poor pastures and peat for fuel. *Heather, sedge, sphagnum moss, whortleberry.*

MEDITERRANEAN TYPE: Little original natural vegetation remains. The broad-leaved evergreen hardwoods well-adapted to the long, dry summers mostly replaced by scrubland (*maquis*). Grass uncommon in lowland areas. The poorest scrub (*garrigue*) common in dry limestone areas. *Cork, holm oak, wild olive, oleander, laurel.*

STEPPE: Plant growth limited by light summer rainfall and high evaporation. Much of the original grassland is now under the plough. In the wetter western area wheat and maize are extensively grown with cattle and sheep herding common in the drier eastern parts. *Wild grasses, xerophytic shrubs.*

SOUTH

DESERT: High temperatures and insufficient rainfall. Little or no vegetation. Typical plants are thorny succulents with long, water-seeking tap roots. Fringing SEMI ARID areas and oases have a permanent growth of low thorn scrub. Dormant seeds germinate and flower rapidly after occasional rain. *Cacti, date palm, acacia, coarse grasses.*

These levels represent average conditions and the actual zones are extremely fluid reflecting local conditions of aspect and form.

HIGH ALTITUDES

3000m — GLACIERS:
snow-line

ALPINE: Plant cover similar to Tundra but more vivid and varied. *Anemone, edelweiss, buttercup, crocus.*

2000m — tree-line

MOUNTAIN FOREST: Thick stands of conifers found in the zone of maximum precipitation. *Beech, spruce, pine, larch.*

1000m

MIXED & DECIDUOUS FOREST:

sea-level

Altitude mimics the climatic changes of higher latitude. Average temperatures decrease with height by 6.5°C per 1 000 m and there is a zone of increased precipitation before giving way to Alpine conditions.

Administrative Divisions

I: NORTHWEST EUROPE

Administrative Boundaries

International
Regional and other units

Semi-autonomous states and regions are
identified by colour and by name (e.g. **NORD**)

Administrative Centres
(non-agglomeration populations)[a]

Capitals		Regional Centres
	over 5 million	
	over 1 million	
	over 500 thousand	
	over 250 thousand	
	over 100 thousand	
	over 50 thousand	
	under 50 thousand	

a – latest available

ICELAND
23 sýslur

1 Gullbringusýsla
2 Kjósarsýsla
3 Borgarfjarðarsýsla
4 Mýrasýsla
5 Snaefellsnes-og-Hnappadalssýsla
6 Dalasýsla
7 Austur-Barðastrandarsýsla
8 Vestur-Barðastrandarsýsla
9 Vestur-Ísafjarðarsýsla
10 Norður-Ísafjarðarsýsla
11 Strandasýsla
12 Vestur-Húnavatnssýsla
13 Austur-Húnavatnssýsla
14 Skagafjarðarsýsla
15 Eyjafjarðarsýsla
16 Suður-Þingeyjarsýsla
17 Norður-Þingeyjarsýsla
18 Norður-Múlasýsla
19 Suður-Múlasýsla
20 Austur-Skaftafellssýsla
21 Vestur-Skaftafellssýsla
22 Rangárvallasýsla
23 Árnessýsla

UNITED KINGDOM
of Great Britain and N. Ireland

ENGLAND [a]
40 counties
6 metropolitan counties *

WALES [a]
8 counties

SCOTLAND [b]
12 regions

N. IRELAND
26 districts

ISLE OF MAN
(crown dependency)

CHANNEL ISLANDS
(crown dependency)

Jersey
Guernsey
Alderney
Sark, Is, etc.

(a) 1974

(b) 1975

Rep. of IRELAND
8 regions
26 counties

REYKJAVIK

FÆRØERNE — Thorshavn

Shetland

Orkney

Western Isles

Highland

SCOTLAND

Grampian

Tayside

Central

Fife

Edinburgh

Lothian

Strathclyde

Borders

Dumfries & Galloway

Northumberland

Tyne & Wear *

Cumbria

Durham

Cleveland

North Yorkshire

Lancs.

*Merseyside

*Gtr. Manc.

*W. Yorks.

*S. Yorks.

Humberside

Ches.

Derby

Notts

Lincoln

DON. Donegal

Leitrim

NORTHERN IRELAND — Belfast

NW

Sligo

Roscommon

Monaghan

Cavan

NE

Mayo

WEST

Galway

Longf'd

W'meath

Meath

Louth

Dublin

ISLE OF MAN — Douglas

MIDL

Offaly

Clare

MID W.

N. Rid'g

Laioighis

Kildare

EAST — DUBLIN

Wicklow

Limerick

Tipperary

S. Rid'g

Kilkenny

Carlow

Kerry

SW

Cork

SE

Wexford

Waterford

Gwynedd

Clwyd

WALES

Powys

Dyfed

Salop

Staffs

W. Midlands

Leics.

Cambridge

Norfolk

Suffolk

Hereford & Worcs.

Warwick

Northants

Beds

Herts

Essex

W. Mid

Glamorgan S.

Gwent

Gloucester

Oxford

Bucks

Gtr. London

LONDON

Cardiff

Avon

Wilts.

Berks

Surrey

Kent

Devon

Somerset

Dorset

Hants.

W. Sussex E.

Cornwall

I. of Wight

ENGLAND

Groningen

Friesland

Drente

Noord-Holland

AMSTERDAM

Overijssel

Osnat

Utrecht

Gelderland

Münste

Zuid-Holland

Zeeland

Noord-Brabant

West Vlaanderen

Oost-Vlaand

Antwerpen

Limburg

Düssel

NORDRH

Au

Hol

Longitude West of Greenwich

Longitude East of Greenwich

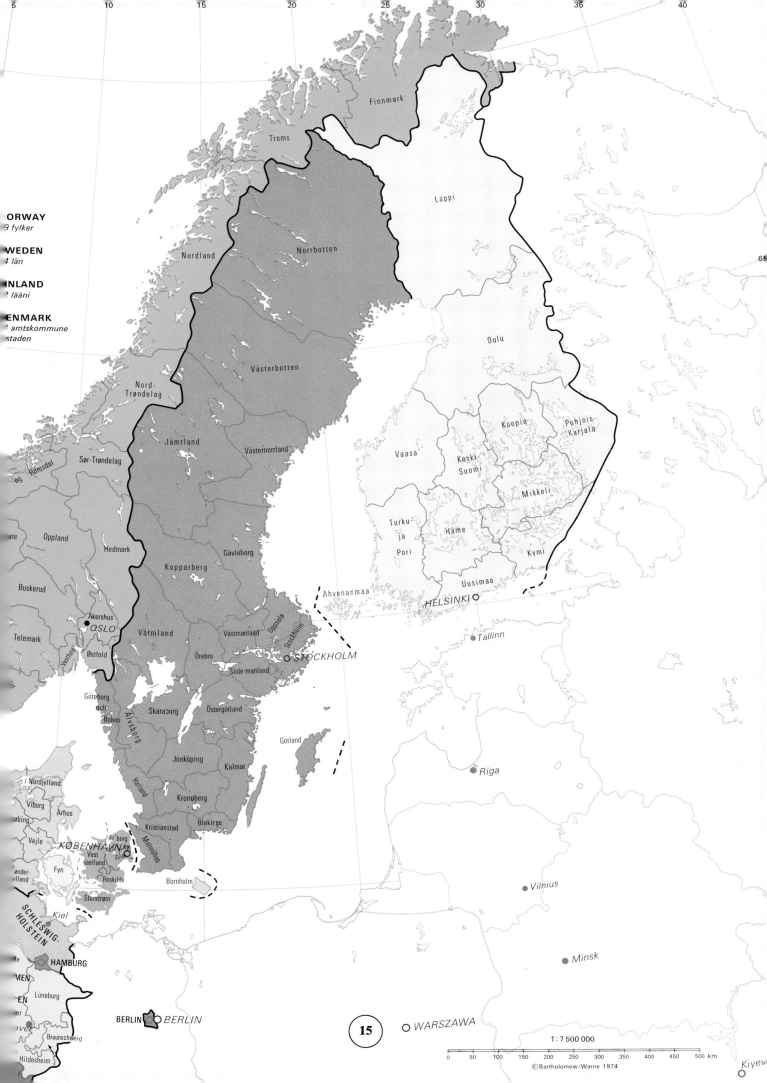

ORWAY
9 fylker

WEDEN
4 län

NLAND
? lääni

ENMARK
1 amtskommune
staden

Finnmark

Troms

Lappi

Nordland

Norrbotten

Oulu

Nord-
Trøndelag

Västerbotten

Sør-Trøndelag

Romsdal

Jämtland

Västernorrland

Kuopio

Pohjois-
Karjala

Vaasa

Keski-
Suomi

Mikkeli

Oppland

Hedmark

Gävleborg

Turku
ja
Pori

Häme

Buskerud

Kopparberg

Kymi

Telemark

Värmland

Västmanland

Uppsala

Ahvenanmaa

Uusimaa

HELSINKI

Akershus

OSLO

Vestfold

Østfold

Örebro

Stockholm

STOCKHOLM

Tallinn

Södermanland

Göteborg
och
Bohus

Skaraborg

Östergötland

Älvsborg

Gotland

Jönköping

Kalmar

Riga

I Nordjylland

Halland

Viborg

Kronoberg

Århus

Kristianstad

Blekinge

øbing

Vejle

KØBENHAVN

Fr'borg

Malmöhus

Vilnius

nder-
lland

Fyn

Vest
jælland

Fr

Roskilde

Bornholm

Storstrøm

SCHLESWIG-
HOLSTEIN

Kiel

Minsk

ME

Lüneburg

N

er

BERLIN

BERLIN

15

WARSZAWA

1 : 7 500 000

Braunschweig

0   50   100   150   200   250   300   350   400   450   500 km

Hildesheim

© Bartholomew/Warne 1974

Kiyev

Administrative Divisions

II: SOUTHWEST EUROPE

Administrative Boundaries

International

Regional and other units

Semi-autonomous states and regions are
identified by colour and by name (e.g. **NORD**)

Administrative Centres
(non-agglomeration populations)[a]

Capitals		Regional Centres
○	over 5 million	◎
○	over 1 million	◎
○	over 500 thousand	●
●	over 250 thousand	●
•	over 100 thousand	•
•	over 50 thousand	•
•	under 50 thousand	•

a – latest available

ITALY
20 regioni
94 provincie

GREECE
7 dhiamerisma
53 nomoi

1 : 7 500 000

0 50 100 150 200 250 300 350 400 450 500 km

© Bartholomew/Warne 1974

15 *Longitude East of Greenwich* 20

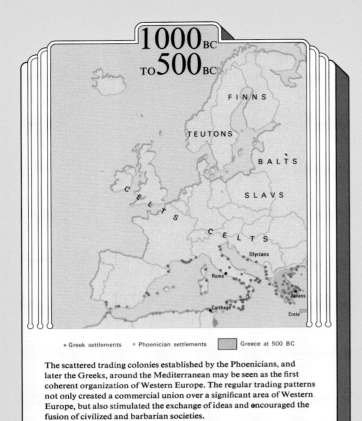

1000 BC TO 500 BC

FINNS

TEUTONS

BALTS

SLAVS

CELTS

CELTS

Illyrians

Rome

Athens

Carthage

Crete

● Greek settlements   ● Phoenician settlements   ▢ Greece at 500 BC

The scattered trading colonies established by the Phoenicians, and later the Greeks, around the Mediterranean may be seen as the first coherent organization of Western Europe. The regular trading patterns not only created a commercial union over a significant area of Western Europe, but also stimulated the exchange of ideas and encouraged the fusion of civilized and barbarian societies.

Changing Europe

1974 boundaries are shown on all maps

AD 117

Thule

Scandia

Caledonia

Oceanus Germanicum

Hibernia

Britannica

Germania

Sarmatia

Belgica

Mare Cantabricum

Gallia

Raetia Noricum
Pannonia

Dacia

Moesia

Illyricum

Thracia

Mare Hadriaticum

Italia

Macedonia

Hispania

Rome

Mare Tyrrhenum

Achaia

Mare Internum

Mauretania

Numidia

Africa

▢ Rome by 200 BC

▢ Territorial gains by 100 BC
At the death of Augustus AD 14
In the time of Trajan AD 98–117

Roman imperialism stretched its control in stages from the Mediterranean northwestwards to the Rhine and the British Isles, and introduced the conquered Celts to the material prosperity of a highly sophisticated urban society. Although this vast empire was to be in decline by the third century, the stamp of Roman culture continued to influence West European civilization in many ways.

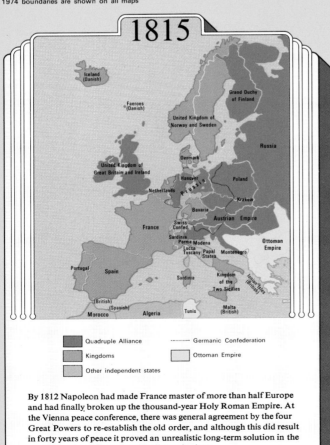

1815

Iceland (Danish)

Faeroes (Danish)

Grand Duchy of Finland

United Kingdom of Norway and Sweden

Russia

United Kingdom of Great Britain and Ireland

Denmark

Hanover

Poland

Netherlands

Prussia

Krakow

Bavaria

Austrian Empire

France

Swiss Confed.

Sardinia
Parma Modena
Lucca
Tuscany Papal States

Montenegro

Ottoman Empire

Portugal

Spain

Sardinia

Kingdom of the Two Sicilies

Ionian Isles (British)

(British)
(Spanish)
Morocco

Algeria

Tunis

Malta (British)

▢ Quadruple Alliance   ---- Germanic Confederation

▢ Kingdoms   ▢ Ottoman Empire

▢ Other independent states

By 1812 Napoleon had made France master of more than half Europe and had finally broken up the thousand-year Holy Roman Empire. At the Vienna peace conference, there was general agreement by the four Great Powers to re-establish the old order, and although this did result in forty years of peace it proved an unrealistic long-term solution in the prevailing atmosphere of nationalist aspirations.

1914

Iceland (Danish)

Faeroes (Danish)

Grand Duchy of Finland

Norway

Sweden

Russia

United Kingdom of Great Britain and Ireland

Denmark

Neths.
Belgium
Lux.

Germany

Austria
Hungary

Rumania

France

Switz.

Montenegro

Serbia

Bulgaria

Italy

Albania

Portugal

Spain

Greece

Gibraltar

Morocco (Fr.)

Algeria (French)

Tunis (French)

Malta (British)

▢ Entente Powers   ▢ Central Powers

▢ Neutral at first, later joined Entente Powers   ▢ Neutral at first, later joined Central Powers

▢ Neutral throughout the war

The social and economic optimism of the turn of the century was dashed by the news that Europe was at war. The long-drawn agony this created led yet again to a reshuffling of the European pack and the end of three great military monarchies. Europe's domination of world trade was critically damaged by the war and the 1919 peace settlement led to the creation of further new states in Eastern Europe.

800

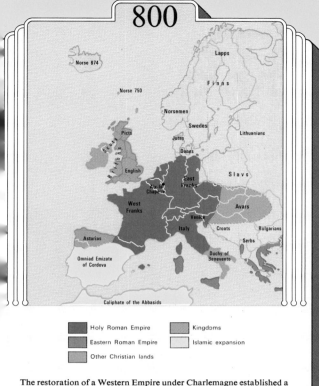

- ■ Holy Roman Empire
- ■ Eastern Roman Empire
- ■ Other Christian lands
- ■ Kingdoms
- ■ Islamic expansion

The restoration of a Western Empire under Charlemagne established a basis from which Europe emerged in its mediaeval shape. This revival of the imperial dignity was, however, a personal tribute to his authority in Western Christendom rather than recognition of a Frankish dynasty, and in the unsettled times following his death the legacy of his intellectual achievements far outlasted the Carolingian State itself.

1500

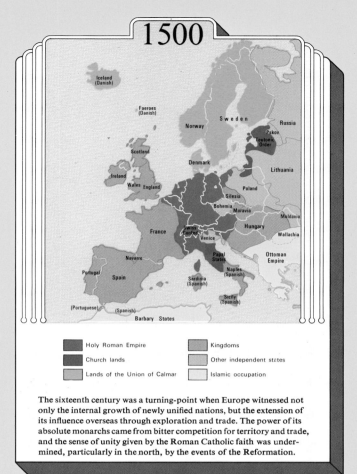

- ■ Holy Roman Empire
- ■ Church lands
- ■ Lands of the Union of Calmar
- ■ Kingdoms
- ■ Other independent states
- ■ Islamic occupation

The sixteenth century was a turning-point when Europe witnessed not only the internal growth of newly unified nations, but the extension of its influence overseas through exploration and trade. The power of its absolute monarchs came from bitter competition for territory and trade, and the sense of unity given by the Roman Catholic faith was undermined, particularly in the north, by the events of the Reformation.

1941

- ■ Germany 1937
- ■ German occupation
- ■ Italy 1937
- ■ Italian occupation
- ■ Neutral States
- ▨ Sympathisers with Axis Powers
- ▨ Axis occupation
- ■ Allied Powers
- ■ Territories occupied by Allied Powers

Europe once again witnessed temporary unification as a consequence of war. National boundaries had little relevance in the face of the high mobility possible in this conflict, and even neutral countries were forced into positions which presented some advantage to one or other of the participating powers. By the outcome in 1945 Western Europe faced a daunting problem of reconstruction.

1961

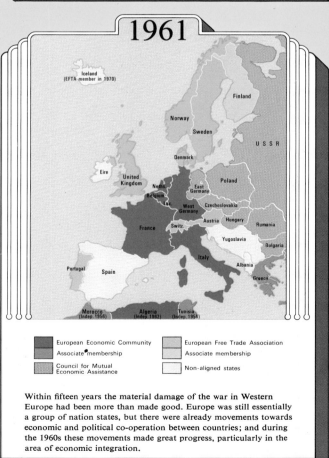

- ■ European Economic Community
- ■ Associate membership
- ▨ Council for Mutual Economic Assistance
- ■ European Free Trade Association
- ■ Associate membership
- □ Non-aligned states

Within fifteen years the material damage of the war in Western Europe had been more than made good. Europe was still essentially a group of nation states, but there were already movements towards economic and political co-operation between countries; and during the 1960s these movements made great progress, particularly in the area of economic integration.

Towards European Unity

Emperor Charlemagne 742-814

Europeans first set foot on the long road towards unity at least as far back as the early Middle Ages. When Charlemagne was crowned in AD800, he and the Papacy together exercised spiritual and temporal authority over virtually all of Western Europe, and in the process produced what was for those times an integrated civilization. By any standards, it was also remarkably durable. Before its final decline it had created moments of genuine popular co-operation in Europe as at the Council of Clermont in 1095, when Pope Urban II called the Western Christian world to unite in fighting to regain the Holy Land. But all of this came to very little. By the 16th century, the full emergence of the nation state had created a fragmented rather than an integrated Europe.

The period from the 16th to the 18th centuries was essentially one of nationalism throughout, but there was no lack of ideas or proposals for unity in one form or another. One of the earliest of these, and among the most important, was made by the Duc de Sully in 1630. The Duke had been a prominent minister under Henry IV, so there was particular force in his Grand Design for the modification of existing national boundaries to create fifteen new states of equal strength, to be controlled by a 40-member council, with a large army at its command to back up its decisions. Sully's scheme was especially significant for its enforceable supra-national nature.

William Penn 1621–1670

In 1693 a more sophisticated and innovatory plan was put forward by an Englishman, William Penn, who advocated a system of weighted voting in a European Diet to reflect existing national states' population and resources and so avoid the utopian ambition of Sully's plan to redraw the whole map of Europe. Penn even specified that debates would be in two 'official languages', French and Latin, and that a three-quarters majority should be required to reach binding decisions.

Other significant proponents of the European idea in those times included the Abbé de Saint-Pierre, whose primary aim was peace through unity—ironically to be secured if necessary by force. Immanuel Kant, the German philosopher, also saw the need for security as the main reason for unity in his *Philosophical Project for Perpetual Peace*, published in 1795.

But not until the French Revolution and Napoleon's Empire did there come any authoritative calls for a united Europe. The one that came from the Revolution Convention in 1792 was essentially ideological and a symptom of the new gospel of liberty and equality that was stirring the world. This revolutionary call for the peoples of Europe to unite failed, but it did serve to bring about a sense of common purpose among governments—particularly as it followed the almost successful attempt by Napoleon to unite Europe by force.

The 19th century saw a heightened awareness of the threat to Europe's progress and well-being posed by aggressive nationalism, but there were no early conceptual or long-lasting practical advances in thinking about European unity. Even the Congress System, conceived at Vienna in 1815, which held out the possibility of the major European powers working together for peace, failed to inspire mutual co-operation. The proposals of Saint-Simon for a united Europe built around the United Kingdom and France, and Auguste Comte's idea for a 'Republique Occidentale' grouping the United Kingdom, France,

Germany, Italy and Spain, with Greece, Portugal, Belgium, the Netherlands and the USA as associated states, were far removed from practical politics, or from anything that, in the context of the times, might have had the remotest chance of being implemented, even in part. Yet the 19th century can, just, claim the first concrete step towards European integration as we know it today. From the first international peace conference held at The Hague in 1899 came The Hague Tribunal, charged with resolving international disputes by arbitration; initially this organization was in practice European in conception and operation. However, this single step forward was all too soon followed by the devastating setback of the 1914–18 war which deeply divided Europe. And the consequences of that war, and of the Versailles peace settlement in particular, were even more divisive than the war itself.

The League of Nations, formed in the aftermath of 1914–1918, held out hopes for many that a new era of co-operation might be about to begin. For, as the USA and the USSR were not members, the League was in effect primarily concerned with Europe. But its record of achievements was not impressive.

Richard Coudenhove-Kalergi 1894-1972

Richard Coudenhove-Kalergi, who founded the Pan-European Union in 1923 was an energetic advocate of a federal Europe. He had a strong influence on Aristide Briand, who, as foreign minister of France, was well placed to put his own plans for a united federal Europe to the League of Nations assembly. This he did on September 5, 1929, and Gustav Stresemann, the former German Chancellor, and who was then foreign minister, gave Briand his full support.

Unfortunately, the League's members showed little enthusiasm. The United Kingdom, in particular, was discouraging. On September 14, 1930, two days before Briand's plan was due to be discussed by the League Assembly, the Nazis scored a major victory in the German national elections, making it plain that European union as envisaged by Briand, Stresemann and their supporters was not going to be achieved for a long time yet. And World War II made nonsense of any plans for peaceful unification of Europe.

At the end of the war, in 1945, Europe was economically devastated and socially exhausted, and was overwhelmingly preoccupied with the immediate problems of survival—economic first, political second. There was little time or energy for following through any of the plans for uniting Europe that had proliferated during the period between the wars. At best, there were two Europes and relations between the two were well summed up by those evocative phrases of the time: 'Cold War' and 'Iron Curtain'.

Although seen then as primarily communism against capitalism, the divisions in post-war Europe were essentially part of the historical continuity of European relationships. For, while the countries of Eastern Europe share essentially the same cultural inheritance with the West European nations, the two Europes' political cultures have for centuries—and not just since the Cold War—been far apart. The Iron Curtain of post-World War II is only the latest form—and the latest geographical location—of the historical boundary between the two traditions governing man's relationship to the state: the one authoritarian and closed, the other open.

This division into two Europes was made clear by the communist coup in Czechoslovakia in February, 1948, followed later that year by the Soviet Union's severance of the land and water routes to Berlin, the city in the heart of East Germany governed by four powers, the USA, Britain, France and the USSR.

At this time the USA, as well as the USSR, was a dominant influence in European affairs. Unlike the USSR in Eastern Europe, the USA backed and helped to sustain Western Europe, but it did not seek direct political control. Nevertheless, the USA had an important role and gave much of the initial momentum to the drive towards unity in Western Europe.

Harry S. Truman 1884-1972

The Truman doctrine of March, 1947, effectively committed the USA to the military defence of Western Europe, and later that year laid the way for the Marshall Plan. Through its administering group, the Organization for European Economic Co-operation, this plan was the first concrete move towards economic co-operation in Europe, pre-dating the formation of the Council for Mutual Economic Assistance (COMECON) in Eastern Europe by a year.

In March, 1948, the United Kingdom, France, Belgium, the Netherlands and Luxembourg signed the Treaty of Brussels, pledging themselves to a political, cultural, economic and military alliance. Then, in 1949, partly showing the momentum of the movement towards integration, partly to provide an organization with both far-reaching terms of reference and a broad membership, another most important new body, the Council of Europe, was formed to secure 'a greater measure of unity between the European countries'.

Jean Monnet 1888-

While providing new means of consultation and general co-operation, these new organizations fell short of the widely felt need among the continental nations of Western Europe for greater economic security and prosperity. For this they sought more effective ways of pooling their resources. The inspiration was to come from Jean Monnet, regarded by many as 'the father of the Common Market' and instigator of the plan to pool coal and steel in a new Community. The European Coal and Steel Community was formed in 1951, followed in 1957 by the signing of the Rome Treaties setting up the Common Market and the European Atomic Energy Community (Euratom). The founder members of all three communities were Belgium, France, Italy, Luxembourg, the Netherlands and West Germany, together comprising around 180 million people. Provision was made, too, for the overseas countries associated with the member states to have associate status within the Economic Community, with preferential advantages in the development of trade and aid.

Most of the other countries of Western Europe hesitated to take part in these developments which involved more far-reaching obligations than simple co-operation between governments and they formed a more united, but essentially parallel, European Free Trade Association, (see pages 22–23) the true long-term aim of which was to facilitate the majority of them eventually to join the European Communities. With the 'Six' becoming 'Nine' in 1973 this has now partly been achieved.

So, after much striving and many setbacks, European integration is on the way to becoming reality. The qualification must be made, however, that the great differences between the integration of Western Europe and of Eastern Europe, has only served to emphasize the wider Europe's fundamental disunity.

Winston Churchill 1874-1965

If Europe were once united in the sharing of its common inheritance, there would be no limit to the happiness, to the prosperity and glory which its three or four hundred million people would enjoy . . . We must build a kind of United States of Europe. In this way only will hundreds of millions of toilers be able to regain the simple joys and hopes which make life worth living . . .
WINSTON CHURCHILL
AT THE UNIVERSITY OF ZÜRICH
SEPTEMBER 19, 1946

Europe will not be built all at once, or through a single comprehensive plan. It will be built through concrete achievements, which will first create a de facto solidarity . . . These proposals will build the first solid foundations of the European federation which is indispensable to the preservation of peace.
ROBERT SCHUMAN
THEN FRENCH FOREIGN MINISTER, MAKING THE STATEMENT OF
MAY 9, 1950, WHICH LED TO THE SETTING UP OF THE ECSC

One thing is certain and we may as well face it. Our people are not going to hand to any supra-national authority the right to close down our pits or steelworks. We will allow no supra-national authority to put large masses of our people out of work in Durham, in the Midlands, in South Wales or in Scotland.
HAROLD MACMILLAN
COUNCIL OF EUROPE CONSULTATIVE ASSEMBLY, AUGUST 16, 1950,
ON THE EUROPEAN COAL AND STEEL COMMUNITY

Resolved to substitute for historic rivalries a fusion of their essential interests; to establish, by creating an economic community, the foundations of a broader and deeper community among peoples long divided by bloody conflicts: and to lay the bases of Institutions capable of guiding their future common destiny . . .
ECSC TREATY,
PARIS, APRIL 18, 1951

Determined to establish the foundations of an ever closer union among the European peoples . . . Resolved to strengthen the safeguards of peace and freedom by combining their resources in a single unit, and calling upon the other peoples of Europe who share their ideal to join in their effort, have decided to create a European Economic Community.
COMMON MARKET TREATY,
ROME, MARCH 25, 1957

Entry upon the final stage of the Common Market not only means confirming the irreversible nature of the work accomplished by the Communities, but also means paving the way for a united Europe capable of assuming its responsibilities in the world of tomorrow and of making a contribution commensurate with its traditions and its mission.
MEETING OF THE MEMBER STATES' HEADS OF STATE AND HEADS OF
GOVERNMENT
THE HAGUE
DECEMBER 1–2, 1969

The Member States of the Community, the driving force of European construction, affirm their intention to transform before the end of the present decade the whole complex of their relations into a European Union.
THE HEADS OF STATE AND HEADS OF GOVERNMENT OF THE
COUNTRIES OF THE ENLARGED COMMUNITY
MEETING FOR THE FIRST TIME
PARIS, OCTOBER 19 AND 20, 1972

Co-operation in Europe

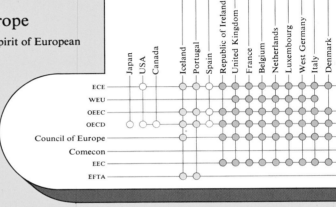

ECE
ECONOMIC COMMISSION FOR EUROPE

The ECE is today mainly significant as an organization that might have co-ordinated wider economic co-operation had Europe not separated soon after World War II into the politically and economically distinct Eastern Europe and Western Europe. The ECE originated as a regional organization of the United Nations Organization, created in 1947 to co-ordinate the economic reconstruction of Europe.

Its efforts at concerted regional action at a truly pan-European level came to very little and even the immediate task of helping to co-ordinate post-war economic reconstruction was never materially achieved. But the ECE is still the only organization in which there is any wider co-operation between the states of Eastern and Western Europe, even although at a relatively superficial level. Its reports on the European economy include considerable statistical data on Eastern Europe not readily available from any other sources.
HEADQUARTERS *Geneva*.

OECD
ORGANIZATION FOR ECONOMIC
CO-OPERATION AND DEVELOPMENT

Although the Organization for European Economic Co-operation, the parent of OECD, was concerned primarily with co-ordinating the administration of US aid to Europe after World War II, OECD's functions are very much wider, ranging from specialized scientific research to the international payments system. Because of its consultative rather than decision-making status, OECD is increasingly ill-equipped to co-ordinate members' economic policies as inter-relationships become more complex and less easily resolvable by consultation alone.

OECD's membership includes the US, Canada and Japan, with Australia and Yugoslavia participating in part of its work. But OECD is the one organization that has developed the means for economic co-ordination of all aspects of economic activity throughout Western Europe.
HQ *Paris*.

WEU
WESTERN EUROPEAN UNION

The WEU grew out of the Brussels Treaty Organization that was set up in 1948 by Belgium, France, Luxembourg, the Netherlands and the United Kingdom for joint defence and the promotion of economic, social and cultural co-operation. Its aims were widened in 1955 to include the task of fostering European integration. In 1960 the social and cultural activities of WEU were taken over by the Council of Europe, but the former continued to be of great importance as the only forum where the six countries of the EEC and the UK could discuss common political and economic problems prior to the enlargement of the Community.
HQ *London*.

Council of Europe

Founded in 1949 in a spirit of European unity and post-war reconciliation, the Council of Europe has since doubled its membership, although Greece resigned in 1969. Despite its founding hopes of a united continent, its membership clauses effectively debar communist states from joining.

Its most outstanding achievement has been the European Convention for the Protection of Human Rights and Fundamental Freedoms, which became operative in 1953. The Charter covers among other things working conditions, social and medical assistance and the protection of family life.
HQ *Strasbourg*.

Comecon
COUNCIL FOR MUTUAL
ECONOMIC ASSISTANCE

Comecon aims to co-ordinate and unite the efforts of member countries in order to promote economic development and progress, and specifically industrial development.

Comecon has been strongly affected by the radical changes that began in 1963 in the systems of economic management in the various countries of Eastern Europe. Though differing from country to country, the economic reforms share as a common characteristic the decentralization of decision-making. This means that Comecon has hardly progressed beyond the organization of a limited number of joint projects (such as an electricity grid) and technical exchanges between members. Development of trade has been hampered by artificial exchange rates between members.
HQ *Moscow*.

EEC
EUROPEAN ECONOMIC COMMUNITY

The primary objective set out in the Rome Treaty was to set up a Common Market among members by removing the existing obstacles to the free movement not only of goods, but also of people, firms, services and capital. An integral part of achieving the customs union was to harmonize conditions under which imports from non-members enter the Common Market by establishing a common external tariff.

Probably even more important in shaping the new Europe is the Rome Treaty's second aim. This is no less than to harmonize the national economic policies of all members, and particularly policies concerning agriculture, free competition in industry, transport, and trading with the rest of the world.
HQ *Brussels*.

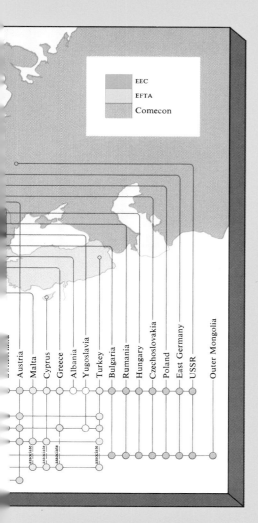

EEC
EFTA
Comecon

Austria
Malta
Cyprus
Greece
Albania
Yugoslavia
Turkey
Bulgaria
Rumania
Hungary
Czechoslovakia
Poland
East Germany
USSR
Outer Mongolia

ASSOCIATE
ASSOCIATE
ASSOCIATE

EFTA

EUROPEAN FREE TRADE ASSOCIATION

Set up by the Stockholm Convention in November, 1959, EFTA, unlike the EEC, aimed only at establishing free trade between members in industrial goods, and not at a customs union. The essential difference is that trade with non-members was not covered by the EFTA agreement.

EFTA was important mainly as a way of ensuring that the tariff and trade policies of its members could be co-ordinated and kept broadly in step with those of the EEC, which most EFTA members expected to join when agreement with the former could be reached. It therefore fulfilled a valuable function as a 'bridge' to the EEC, and can best be understood in this context.

The United Kingdom, Republic of Ireland and Denmark are now full members of the EEC. The Special Trade Agreements have been concluded between the rest of EFTA and the Enlarged Community. The European Free Trade Association continues functioning as a genuinely viable organization in its own right.
HQ *Geneva.*

Diary of Co-operation

1945: The War ends, but most of Europe is already dividing into the open society of the West and the closed society of the East. Governments are preoccupied with how to organize economic reconstruction and how to re-establish political stability.

1946: *September 19* At Zürich, Winston Churchill launches a campaign for a 'United States of Europe', giving the initial impetus to European integration. *June 5* General George E. Marshall, US Secretary of State, announces the intention of the US government to assist the recovery of Europe. (The Marshall Plan). *July* The Marshall Plan offer is rejected by the Soviet bloc. *October 29* Creation of Benelux—economic union of Belgium, Luxembourg and the Netherlands.

1948: *March 17* Belgium, the Netherlands, Luxembourg, France and the UK sign the Brussels Treaty, providing the basis for joint defence and economic, social and cultural co-operation. *April 16* The Convention for European Economic Co-operation signed, bringing into being the OEEC, which aims to free trade and get business moving.

1949: *January* Comecon is formed in response to the Marshall Plan. *April* The North Atlantic Treaty Organization, NATO, is set up, initially with plans to extend co-operation between members from defence matters to political and economic areas. *May 5* The Council of Europe established, but has no real authority.

1950: *May 9* Robert Schuman, then foreign minister of France, proposes that the French and West German coal and steel industries be placed under one authority. *September* The European Payments Union is formed, creating multilateral financial clearing arrangements, and extending credits to debtor countries.

1951: *April 18* The European Coal and Steel Community Treaty is signed by France, West Germany, Italy, Belgium, the Netherlands, Luxembourg. Thus the first federal-type authority with real powers comes into being.

1952: Nordic Council set up by Parliaments of Denmark, Norway, Sweden and Iceland.

1953: *February 10* A common market for coal, iron ore and scrap is opened.

1955: *June 1–3* The foreign ministers of the ECSC meet at the Messina Conference and propose further steps towards full economic integration. A British observer is present, but later withdraws.

1957: *March 25* As the outcome of the Messina Conference, the Rome Treaty is signed by the Six, setting up the Common Market and Euratom.

1958: *January 1* Rome Treaties come into force; the primary objective is to achieve a customs union by 1970.

1959: *January 1* First tariff reductions and quota changes in the Common Market. *November 20* The European Free Trade Association Convention is signed in Stockholm by Austria, Denmark, Norway, Portugal, Sweden, Switzerland and the UK.

1960: *December 14* Convention signed setting up the Organization for Economic Co-operation and Development, which, with a widened role, is to succeed the OEEC (its functions fulfilled).

1961: *July 18* The six EEC members issue a joint declaration aimed at political union. *August 1* The Republic of Ireland, the UK, Denmark and Norway apply for EEC membership. *December 15* Austria, Sweden and Switzerland apply for association with the EEC.

1963: *January 14* President de Gaulle states that the UK is not ready for membership of the EEC, and the negotiations with the applicants are broken off. *July 1* Yaoundé convention associates sixteen former French possessions in Africa (including Madagascar), Somalia (formerly Italian) and the former Belgian Congo (Zaire) with the EEC on advantageous terms.

1964: *May 4* Negotiations begun for General Agreements on Tariffs and Trade, GATT, inspired by President Kennedy's Trade Expansion Programme which aims to be the start of a partnership of equals between the US and Europe.

1965: France wishes to abandon majority voting within the EEC on matters which a member government considers vital to its interests, and withdraws from active participation in the Community.

1966: The other five members of the EEC are unable to resolve fully their disagreement with France, and though France resumes an active role in Community affairs it is clear that the EEC cannot, in the foreseeable future, exercise the truly supra-national authority implied by the Rome Treaty. *December 31* With few exceptions, quota restrictions and tariffs on trade in industrial goods between EFTA members are abolished, three years ahead of schedule.

1967: *May 11* The UK, Denmark and the Republic of Ireland re-submit formal applications for membership of the EEC. *May 15* 'Kennedy Round' negotiations end in agreement to make substantial cuts on tariffs on industrial goods. *July* The executive and decision-making bodies of the EEC, the ECSC and Euratom merge; a single Communities Commission takes office. *November 27* President de Gaulle reiterates his objections to British membership, and the negotiations end—but the applications remain effective. *December 13–14* EEC Council agrees on definite steps to implement common transport policy.

1968: *July 1* The EEC customs union is completed, ahead of schedule, and goods move freely between the Six in industrial goods and most farm products. *December 31* Free movement of labour within the EEC established.

1969: *December 1–2* At a summit meeting at The Hague, the heads of state of the Six decide to move forward from a customs union to a full economic and monetary union. Also, with de Gaulle no longer in power, they agree to reopen membership negotiations with the UK, Republic of Ireland, Denmark and Norway. *April 21* EEC Council of Ministers reaches agreement on a series of measures for financing EEC farm policy, setting up sources of independent community revenue and increasing the budgetary powers of the European Parliament. Thus, the Six complete the main commitments set out in the Rome Treaty.

1972: *January 22* With the entry negotiations successfully completed, the Treaty of Accession is signed by the four candidate members and the Six. *October 6* As a result of a national referendum Norway withdraws her application to join the EEC. *October 19–20*. European Summit meeting of the Heads of State or of Government of the countries of the enlarged Community agrees on common policies for money, social affairs, the environment, labour relations and aid to the underdeveloped regions.

1973: *January 1* The EEC of Six becomes the EEC of nine, and movement towards European integration enters a new and decisive phase. *April 1* The tariff reduction timetable on industrial goods between old and new members of the Community begins the 5-year transition period with a 20% cut.

The European Press

Newsprint Consumption

kg per person in 1970   in 1960

increase 1960 to 1970

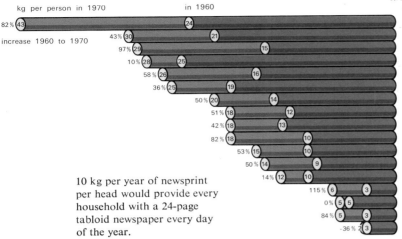

%	1970	1960
82%	43	24
43%	30	21
97%	29	15
10%	28	25
58%	26	16
36%	25	19
50%	20	14
51%	18	12
42%	18	13
82%	18	10
53%	15	10
50%	14	9
14%	12	10
115%	6	3
0%	5	5
84%	5	3
-36%	2	3

10 kg per year of newsprint
per head would provide every
household with a 24-page
tabloid newspaper every day
of the year.

Daily Newspapers in 1970[a]

Combined circulations millions	Average per 100 population	
4·3	53	Sweden
1·8	36	Denmark
3·9	31	Netherlands
25·6	46	United Kingdom
2·3	38	Switzerland
1·8	39	Finland
1·5	38	Norway
0·7	23	Republic of Ireland
2·6	27	Belgium/Luxembourg
19·7	32	West Germany
0·1	45	Iceland
2·0	27	Austria
12·0	24	France
3·5	10	Spain
6·8	13	Italy
0·7	7	Portugal
0·7	8	Greece

[a] or latest available

Books Published in 1970[a]

Total number of editions	Average per 100 000 population
7 709	96
5 052	103
11 159	86
32 826	59
8 321	133
3 520	76
3 935	102
615	21
4 646	48
45 369	74
683	337
4 781	65
22 935	45
19 717	59
8 615	16
5 340	60
1 946	22

The Major Newspapers
Circulations in thousands 1973

Daily Newspapers
*the largest five
in each country*

**Newspapers and periodicals
of international interest**
*some of the large dailies above
are in this category*

WEST GERMANY

4 700	Bild-Zeitung
649	Westdeutsche Allgemeine
400	Hamburger Morgenpost
372	Rheinische Post
353	Frankfurter Allgemeine Zeitung (FAZ)
340	Hamburger Abendblatt
296	BZ
263	Die Welt
236	Süddeutsche Zeitung
70	Handelsblatt
1 032	Der Spiegel (weekly)
324	Die Zeit (weekly)

UNITED KINGDOM

4 314	Daily Mirror
3 311	Daily Express
2 931	Sun
1 703	Daily Mail
1 423	Daily Telegraph
345	The Times
195	Financial Times
103	The Economist (weekly)

FRANCE

1 025	France-Soir
1 010	Le Parisien Libéré
787	Ouest-France
545	Le Progrès
509	Le Figaro
472	Le Monde
170	International Herald Tribune
853	Paris-Match (weekly)
510	L'Express (weekly)

AUSTRIA

679	Unabhängige Kronen-Zeitung
492	Kurier
106	Arbeiter-Zeitung
101	Kleine Zeitung
76	Die Neue Zeit
60	Die Presse
50	Wiener Zeitung

SWEDEN

588	Expressen
484	Aftonbladet
441	Dagens Nyheter
300	Göteborgs-Posten
149	Svenska Dagbladet
387	Vi (weekly)

NETHERLANDS

506	De Telegraaf
305	Algemeen Dagblad
200	De Volkskrant
177	De Courant Nieuws van de Dag
170	Het Parool
170	Haagsche Courant
92	NRC Handelsblad
101	Vrij Nederland (weekly)

ITALY

504	Corriere della Sera
450	L'Unità
404	La Stampa
309	Il Messaggero
257	Il Resto del Carlino
230	Il Giorno
90	Il Giornale d'Italia
70	Il Sole-24 Ore
24	Daily American (Rome)

BELGIUM

334	De Standaard (group)
306	Het Laatste Nieuws
271	Le Soir
218	Het Volk
208	Gazet van Antwerpen
160	La Libre Belgique

FINLAND

308	Helsingin Sanomat
123	Aamulehti
116	Turun Sanomat
86	Uusi Suomi
85	Ilta-Sanomat
28	Kauppalehti

SWITZERLAND

267	Blick
234	Tages Anzeiger
95	Neue Zürcher-Zeitung
93	Feuille d'Avis de Lausanne
88	National-Zeitung
18	Journal de Genève

DENMARK

244	Ekstra Bladet
233	B. T.
146	Berlingske Tidende
130	Politiken
81	Jyllands-Posten
21	Information

SPAIN

242	Pueblo
223	La Vanguardia Española
216	ABC
165	Ya
140	Marca
48	Diario de Barcelona

NORWAY

201	Aftenposten
130	Verdens Gang
125	Dagbladet
82	Bergens Tidende
74	Adresseavisen
69	Arbeiderbladet
47	Stavanger Aftenblad
14	Norges Handels- og Sjøfartstidende

PORTUGAL

200	Diário de Notícias
133	Diário Popular
90	O Século
90	Jornal de Notícias
50	O Primeiro de Janeiro
50	A Capital
32	República
15	Jornal do Comércio

REPUBLIC OF IRELAND

166	Irish Independent
152	Evening Press
138	Evening Herald
95	The Irish Press
68	The Irish Times

GREECE

164	Vradyni
113	Apogevmatini
108	Akropolis
58	Ta Nea
22	Naftemboriki
13	Eleftheros Kosmos
10	Athens Daily Post
6	Athens News

LUXEMBOURG

73	Luxemburger Wort
32	Tageblatt
25	Letzeburger Journal
24	Républicain Lorrain (Luxembourg ed.)
12	La Meuse (Luxembourg ed.)

ICELAND

40	Morgunbladid
20	Visir
19	Timinn
12	Althýdubladid
9	Thjódviljinn

USA

Approximate
European circulation

4 800	Reader's Digest (monthly)
750	Time (weekly)
320	Newsweek (weekly)

Television Networks 1972

communications satellite receiving station
international transmission terminal
national transmission terminal
Eurovision link
national contribution circuit
Intervision link

20 — television licences per 100 population 1970

colour television system 1972

PAL   SECAM   no colour transmission

18
ICELAND
Receives recorded material on film or tape only

From the map it looks as if there is close horizontal integration between the national television services of Europe. In practice, however, European-wide television mostly means general interest programmes such as international news and sporting events shown with their own national commentaries. Although it is possible to view television in every country of Europe, far more households own sets in north and west Europe than in the poorer south. Television is a short-range medium and the only truly European viewers are those living near national frontiers who can tune in to the overlapping networks of foreign programmes. Technical inconsistencies also work against European-wide television and the earlier confusion of different black and white line systems has now been replaced by incompatible colour systems—the German PAL and the French SECAM. The horizontal pattern of the Eurovision and Intervision networks shown here will in time be replaced by vertical links to a communications satellite in stationary orbit above Europe.

1:15 000 000
0 100 200 300 400 500 600 700 800 900 1000 km
© Bartholomew/Warne 1974

Density of Population

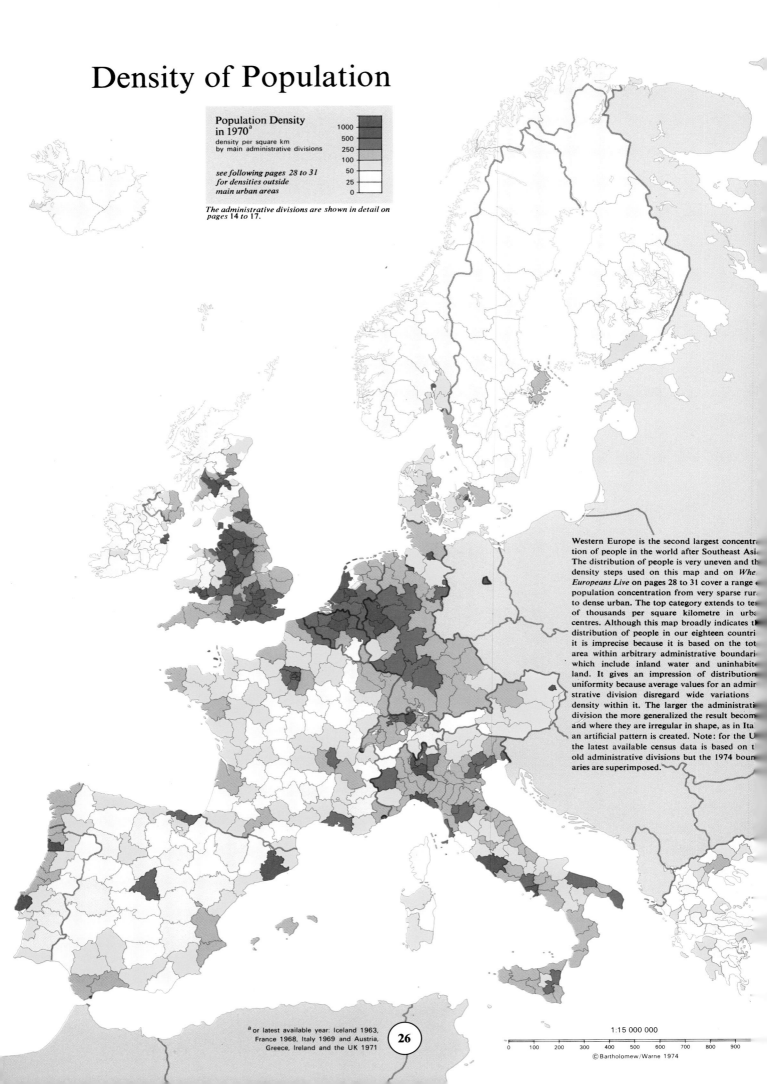

Population Density in 1970[a]

density per square km
by main administrative divisions

*see following pages 28 to 31
for densities outside
main urban areas*

	1000
	500
	250
	100
	50
	25
	0

The administrative divisions are shown in detail on pages 14 to 17.

Western Europe is the second largest concentration of people in the world after Southeast Asia. The distribution of people is very uneven and the density steps used on this map and on *Where Europeans Live* on pages 28 to 31 cover a range of population concentration from very sparse rural to dense urban. The top category extends to tens of thousands per square kilometre in urban centres. Although this map broadly indicates the distribution of people in our eighteen countries it is imprecise because it is based on the total area within arbitrary administrative boundaries which include inland water and uninhabited land. It gives an impression of distribution uniformity because average values for an administrative division disregard wide variations in density within it. The larger the administrative division the more generalized the result becomes and where they are irregular in shape, as in Italy, an artificial pattern is created. Note: for the UK the latest available census data is based on the old administrative divisions but the 1974 boundaries are superimposed.

[a] or latest available year: Iceland 1963, France 1968, Italy 1969 and Austria, Greece, Ireland and the UK 1971

1:15 000 000

0	100	200	300	400	500	600	700	800	900

© Bartholomew/Warne 1974

Growth of Population[a]

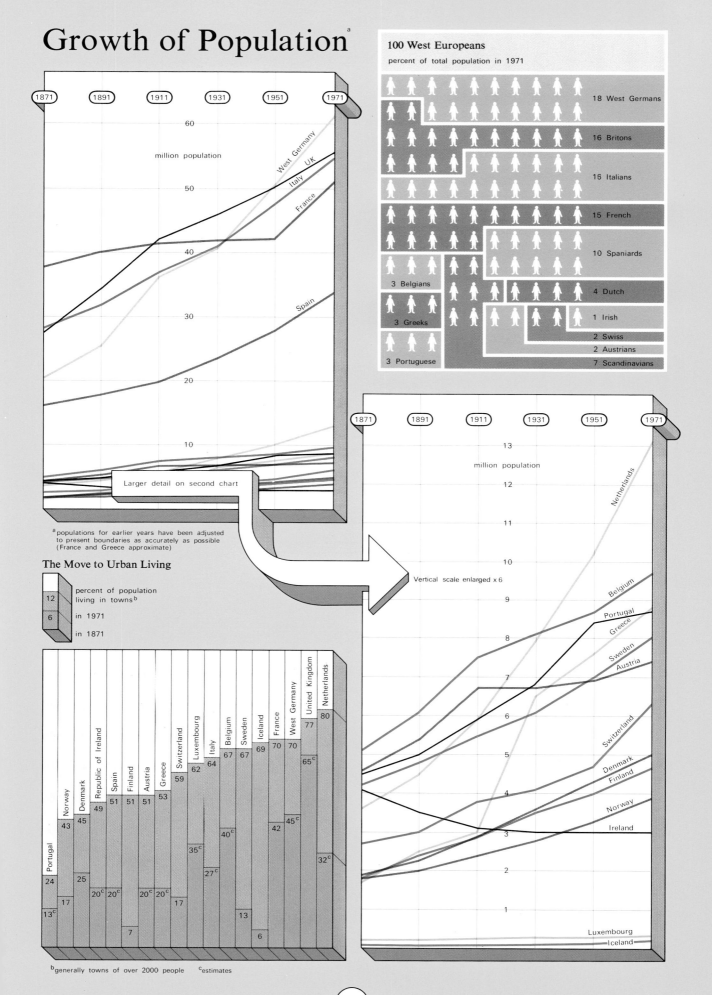

1871 1891 1911 1931 1951 1971

60

million population

50

West Germany
UK
Italy
France

40

Spain

30

20

10

Larger detail on second chart

[a] populations for earlier years have been adjusted to present boundaries as accurately as possible (France and Greece approximate)

The Move to Urban Living

12 — percent of population living in towns[b]

6 — in 1971

in 1871

100 West Europeans

percent of total population in 1971

18 West Germans

16 Britons

16 Italians

15 French

10 Spaniards

3 Belgians

4 Dutch

3 Greeks

1 Irish

2 Swiss

3 Portuguese

2 Austrians

7 Scandinavians

1871 1891 1911 1931 1951 1971

13

million population

12

11

10

Vertical scale enlarged x 6

9

8

7

6

5

4

3

2

1

Netherlands
Belgium
Portugal
Greece
Sweden
Austria
Switzerland
Denmark
Finland
Norway
Ireland

Luxembourg
Iceland

Portugal	Norway	Denmark	Republic of Ireland	Spain	Finland	Austria	Greece	Switzerland	Luxembourg	Italy	Belgium	Sweden	Iceland	France	West Germany	United Kingdom	Netherlands
24	43	45	49	51	51	51	53	59	62	64	67	67	69	70	70	77	80
13[c]	17	25	20[c]	20[c]		20[c]	20[c]	35[c]	27[c]	40[c]		17	13	42	45[c]	65[c]	32[c]
					7								6				

[b] generally towns of over 2000 people   [c] estimates

Where Europeans Live

I: NORTHWEST EUROPE

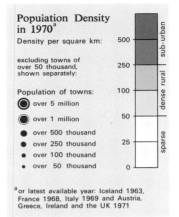

The administrative divisions are shown in detail on pages 14 to 17.

The fact that standard population density maps show only one variable, average population by area, and can only use a limited range of shading steps mean that there are serious drawbacks to their use. In Western European countries, Finland excepted, over a third of the total population is concentrated in towns of over 50 000 and in the UK and the Netherlands the figure exceeds one half. A more genuine population density pattern can, therefore, be achieved by taking out these urban clusters and showing them separately. The effect of doing this can be seen by comparing these pages of *Where Europeans Live* with the *Density of Population* map on page 26. For both, the steps of average density are the same, but isolating the urban element gives a result which is closer to the actual distribution of population in Western Europe. The use of isolines modifies the artificial boundaries between administrative divisions and more closely describes the actual settlement of people on the ground, although it does introduce a degree of subjective interpretation.

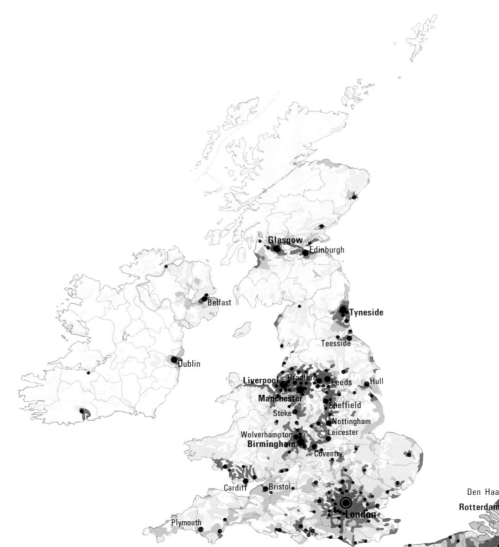

Murmansk

Leningrad

Helsinki

Tallinn

Oslo

Stockholm

Göteborg

Riga

København Malmö

Kiel

Kaunas

Vilnius

Kaliningrad

Minsk

Gdańsk

Hamburg

Gomel'

Szczecin

Bydgoszcz

Berlin

Poznań

Warszawa

Magdeburg

Łódź

29

1 : 7 500 000

0 50 100 150 200 250 300 350 400 450 500 km

© Bartholomew/Warne 1974

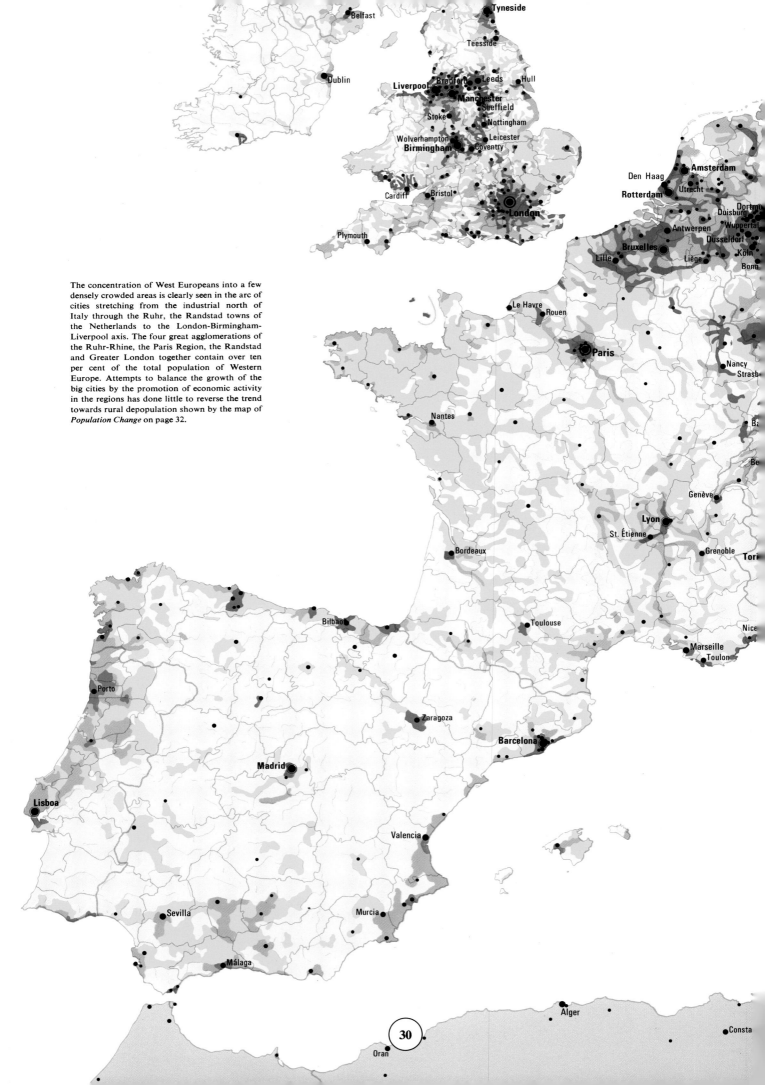

The concentration of West Europeans into a few
densely crowded areas is clearly seen in the arc of
cities stretching from the industrial north of
Italy through the Ruhr, the Randstad towns of
the Netherlands to the London-Birmingham-
Liverpool axis. The four great agglomerations of
the Ruhr-Rhine, the Paris Region, the Randstad
and Greater London together contain over ten
per cent of the total population of Western
Europe. Attempts to balance the growth of the
big cities by the promotion of economic activity
in the regions has done little to reverse the trend
towards rural depopulation shown by the map of
Population Change on page 32.

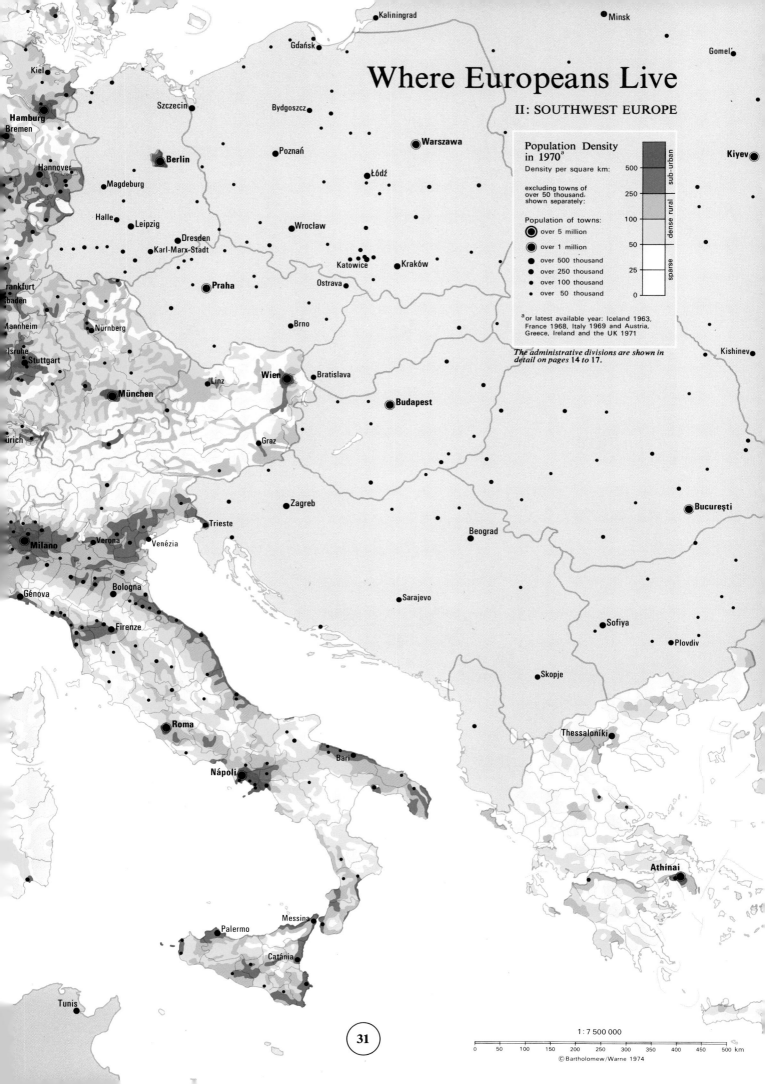

Where Europeans Live

II: SOUTHWEST EUROPE

Population Density
in 1970[a]

Density per square km:

excluding towns of
over 50 thousand,
shown separately:

Population of towns:

- over 5 million
- over 1 million
- over 500 thousand
- over 250 thousand
- over 100 thousand
- over 50 thousand

500	sub-urban
250	dense rural
100	
50	
25	sparse
0	

[a] or latest available year: Iceland 1963,
France 1968, Italy 1969 and Austria,
Greece, Ireland and the UK 1971

*The administrative divisions are shown in
detail on pages 14 to 17.*

Kaliningrad

Minsk

Gdańsk

Gomel'

Kiel

Szczecin

Bydgoszcz

Hamburg
Bremen

Poznań

Warszawa

Kiyev

Berlin

Łódź

Magdeburg

Hannover

Halle   Leipzig

Wrocław

Dresden

Karl-Marx-Stadt

Katowice   Kraków

rankfurt
baden

Praha

Ostrava

Kishinev

Mannheim   Nürnberg

Brno

sruhe

Stuttgart

Wien   Bratislava

Linz

Budapest

München

Graz

ürich

Zagreb

Bucureşti

Trieste

Milano   Verona

Venézia

Beograd

Génova   Bologna

Firenze

Sarajevo

Sofiya

Plovdiv

Roma

Bari

Skopje

Nápoli

Thessaloníki

Athínai

Messina

Palermo

Catánia

Tunis

1 : 7 500 000

0	50	100	150	200	250	300	350	400	450	500 km

© Bartholomew/Warne 1974

Population Change

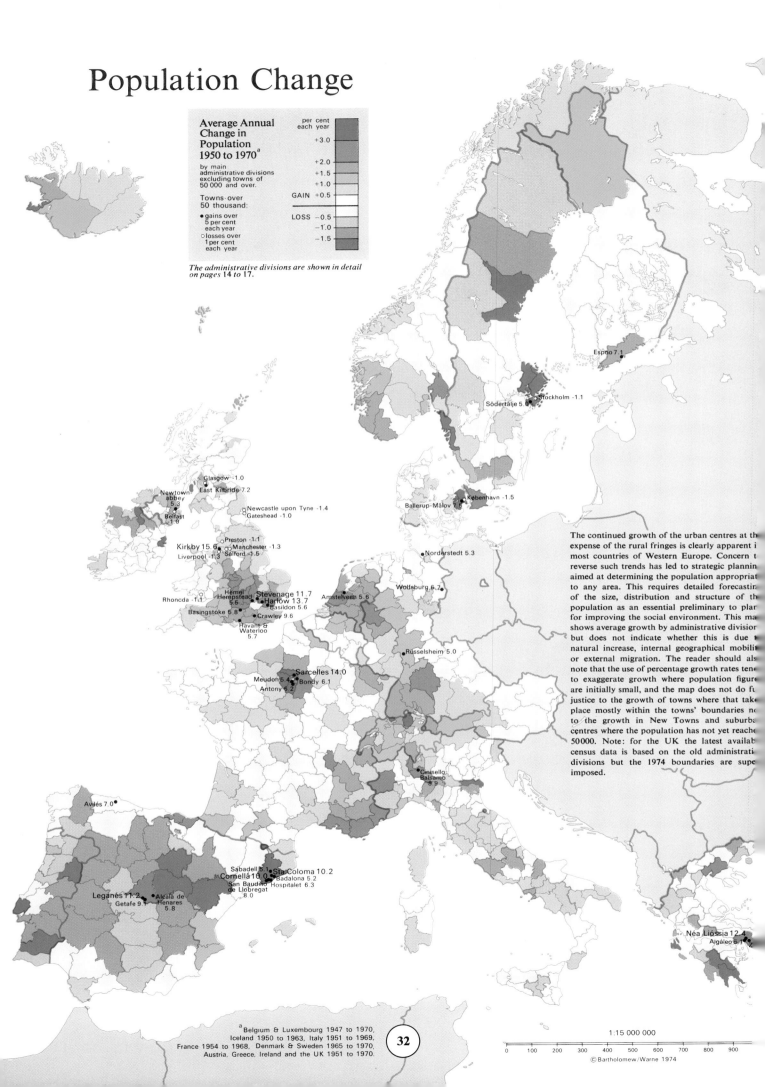

Average Annual Change in Population 1950 to 1970[a]

by main administrative divisions excluding towns of 50 000 and over.

	per cent each year
	+3.0
	+2.0
	+1.5
	+1.0
GAIN	+0.5
LOSS	−0.5
	−1.0
	−1.5

Towns over 50 thousand:

● gains over 5 per cent each year

○ losses over 1 per cent each year

The administrative divisions are shown in detail on pages 14 to 17.

The continued growth of the urban centres at the expense of the rural fringes is clearly apparent in most countries of Western Europe. Concern to reverse such trends has led to strategic planning aimed at determining the population appropriate to any area. This requires detailed forecasting of the size, distribution and structure of the population as an essential preliminary to plan for improving the social environment. This map shows average growth by administrative divisions but does not indicate whether this is due to natural increase, internal geographical mobility or external migration. The reader should also note that the use of percentage growth rates tends to exaggerate growth where population figures are initially small, and the map does not do full justice to the growth of towns where that takes place mostly within the towns' boundaries nor to the growth in New Towns and suburban centres where the population has not yet reached 50000. Note: for the UK the latest available census data is based on the old administrative divisions but the 1974 boundaries are superimposed.

Espoo 7.1

Stockholm -1.1
Södertälje 5.0

Glasgow -1.0
East Kilbride 7.2

Newtown abbey 5.3
Belfast -1.0

Newcastle upon Tyne -1.4
Gateshead -1.0

København -1.5
Ballerup-Målov 7.5

Kirkby 15.6
Preston -1.1
Manchester -1.3
Liverpool -1.3
Salford -1.5

Nordersted 5.3

Wolfsburg 6.7

Hemel Hempstead 5.5
Stevenage 11.7
Harlow 13.7
Basildon 5.6
Amstelveen 5.6
Basingstoke 5.8
Crawley 9.6
Rhoncda -1.1
Havant & Waterloo 5.7

Rüsselsheim 5.0

Sarcelles 14.0
Meudon 5.4
Bondy 6.1
Antony 5.2

Cinisello Balsamo 8.9

Avilés 7.0

Sabadell 5.1
Sta. Coloma 10.2
Cornellá 10.0
Badalona 5.2
San Baudilio Hospitalet 6.3
de Llobregat 8.0
Leganés 11.2
Alcalá de Henares 5.8
Getafe 9.1

Néa Lióssia 12.4
Aigáleo 5.

32

[a] Belgium & Luxembourg 1947 to 1970, Iceland 1950 to 1963, Italy 1951 to 1969, France 1954 to 1968, Denmark & Sweden 1965 to 1970, Austria, Greece, Ireland and the UK 1951 to 1970.

1:15 000 000

0 100 200 300 400 500 600 700 800 900

Population Characteristics

The Components of Population Change – per thousand population

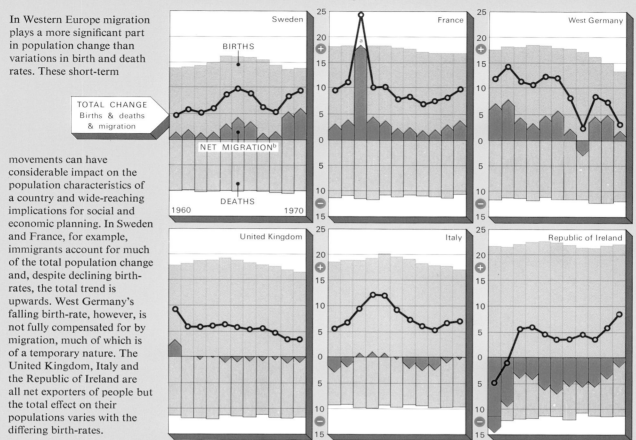

In Western Europe migration plays a more significant part in population change than variations in birth and death rates. These short-term

TOTAL CHANGE
Births & deaths & migration

movements can have considerable impact on the population characteristics of a country and wide-reaching implications for social and economic planning. In Sweden and France, for example, immigrants account for much of the total population change and, despite declining birth-rates, the total trend is upwards. West Germany's falling birth-rate, however, is not fully compensated for by migration, much of which is of a temporary nature. The United Kingdom, Italy and the Republic of Ireland are all net exporters of people but the total effect on their populations varies with the differing birth-rates.

[a] repatriation from Algeria   [b] balance of immigrants and emigrants

Natural Increase

At 18 per 1000, Europe's average birth-rate contrasts markedly with that of the under-developed continents. Africa with 46 per 1000 and Asia with 38 per 1000 have fast-growing populations which keep the world average of 34 per 1000 at a level high enough to cause serious international concern in relation to world resources. This rapid world population increase is unlikely to be checked until these continents follow the European pattern of falling birth-rates.

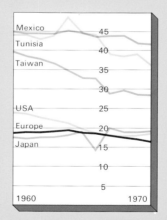

Birth Rates
per thousand in selected countries compared with Europe

The high birth-rates of under-developed countries such as Mexico are in marked contrast to the low levels typical of the urban societies of Western Europe. In a sense, this gap between birth-rates is the gap between the rich and the poor world.

Old and Young Populations in 1970

The age structure of a country is a function of changing birth and death rates, migration patterns, the effects of war and developments in medicine and social welfare. In north-west Europe the result

is an ageing population whereas southern Europe, typified by Portugal, retains the broad-based characteristics of under-developed countries.

Age groups of the total population

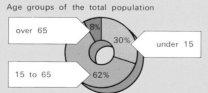

over 65 — 8%
under 15 — 30%
15 to 65 — 62%

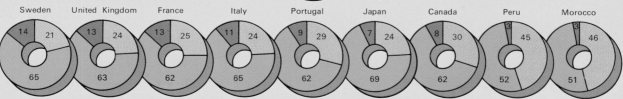

Sweden	United Kingdom	France	Italy	Portugal	Japan	Canada	Peru	Morocco
14 / 21	13 / 24	13 / 25	11 / 24	9 / 29	7 / 24	8 / 30	3 / 45	3 / 46
65	63	62	65	62	69	62	52	51

Migration

Trans-frontier migration as a means of escaping from the poverty and hardship of rural areas, has long been a significant feature of Western Europe. The pattern has been from the fringes to the centre and outwards particularly to North America and more recently Australia. Just after World War II the major movement was the stream of refugees from east to west but, today, the main flows are from southern Europe to the industrial areas of the north and centre. In addition, a variety of national migratory patterns exists such as the colonial links of countries like the United Kingdom and France and the self-contained movements between the Scandinavian nations.

Resulting from these movements, there exist large concentrations of foreign workers in some of the cities of industrial Europe and this has led to problems of social integration particularly where the migrations are short-term in duration.

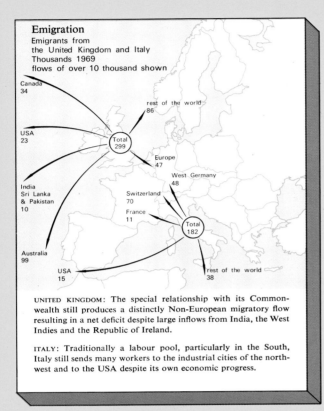

Emigration
Emigrants from
the United Kingdom and Italy
Thousands 1969
flows of over 10 thousand shown

UNITED KINGDOM: The special relationship with its Commonwealth still produces a distinctly Non-European migratory flow resulting in a net deficit despite large inflows from India, the West Indies and the Republic of Ireland.

ITALY: Traditionally a labour pool, particularly in the South, Italy still sends many workers to the industrial cities of the north-west and to the USA despite its own economic progress.

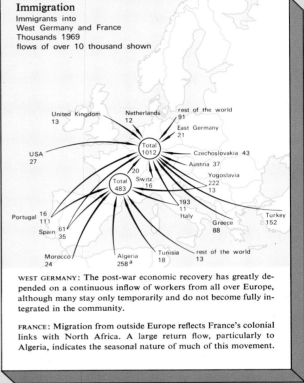

Immigration
Immigrants into
West Germany and France
Thousands 1969
flows of over 10 thousand shown

WEST GERMANY: The post-war economic recovery has greatly depended on a continuous inflow of workers from all over Europe, although many stay only temporarily and do not become fully integrated in the community.

FRANCE: Migration from outside Europe reflects France's colonial links with North Africa. A large return flow, particularly to Algeria, indicates the seasonal nature of much of this movement.

a includes seasonal workers

Europeans on the Move – in thousands

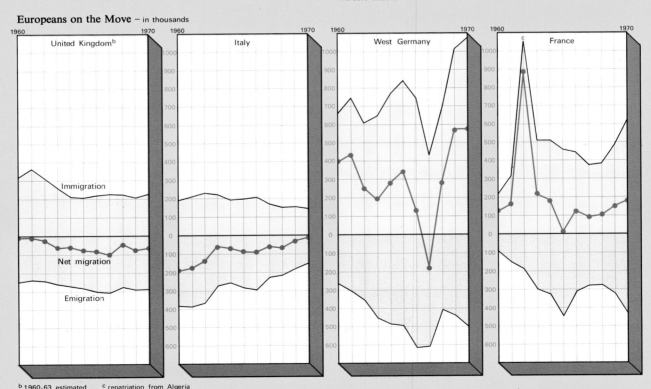

b 1960-63 estimated   c repatriation from Algeria

Transnationals in Europe

countries with over 1 percent foreigners [a]

Nationality per thousand of the host countries' populations

Nationality	Switzerland 1970	Luxembourg 1961	United Kingdom 1971	Sweden 1970	Belgium 1961	West Germany 1970	Republic of Ireland 1961	Iceland 1950	Netherlands 1968	Austria 1968	Denmark 1961
Norwegian				3					3		
Swedish									1		
Finnish				26							
Danish				4					7		
British					1	1	29	1	1	1	1
Irish			13								
West German	18	46	3[b]	3[b]			1	1	4[b]	6	2
Dutch		5			6	2					
Belgian		19								2	
French	8	34			7		1				
Swiss		1									
Austrian	7	1		1					2		
Italian	84	34		2	22	9				1	1
Spanish	16			1	1	2	4			1	
Greek	1				2	6	1				
Yugoslavian	4	1			5	8				1	1
Turkish	2				1	8				1	1
American			2	2	1			2	1	1	1
Other	17	6	36		3	8	7	3	3	7	4
Total percent of foreigners in each country	**15.7**	**14.9**	**5.8**	**5.1**	**4.9**	**4.8**	**3.5**	**2.0**	**1.6**	**1.4**	**1.0**

[a] as defined by each country   [b] including East Germans

Languages in Europe

There are some forty different languages and many hundreds of dialects spoken in Europe. Some, like English and French, are widespread, while others like Romansch in Italy and Switzerland or Lappish in Scandinavia are limited to specific areas. These language differences obviously create problems of communication between Europeans. Indeed, in countries with more than one official language like Belgium, language has tended to polarise cultural and political differences to the detriment of national unity. Elsewhere, preservation of minority languages such as Basque in France and Spain and Welsh in Britain is seen as a symbol of nationalist aspiration. It is not easy to assess the real significance of minority languages as most countries expect their citizens to speak and understand the official national language. In many of the border areas, people often speak several languages or they may use a patois which is hardly recognisable as the country's principal language. The table shows some of the distinctive minority languages of western Europe.

Although language differences create problems for both the tourist and the businessman in Europe, in practice the difficulties are lessening. French, German and English are the common working languages of the EEC and the extent of American interests in Europe since World War II has meant that English is widely used in commercial transactions. The expansion of tourism throughout Europe, the migration of foreign workers into the northern cities, and the contacts resulting from technological co-operation, television and advertising have led to a wide exchange of foreign words and expressions many of which have taken on a truly international meaning. Wider use of new teaching methods is ensuring that the numbers of multi-lingual people continue to rise, while the spread of international symbols, as in road signs, is also making language differences less important than they used to be.

The Main Languages Used in Western Europe

The language families and where they are spoken

GERMANIC	German: *West Germany: Austria: Switzerland: Belgium: France: Luxembourg: Italy*
	English: *United Kingdom: Republic of Ireland*
	Dutch: *Netherlands*
	Swedish: *Sweden: Finland*
	Danish: *Denmark: Sweden: Iceland*
	Flemish: *Belgium: France*
	Norwegian: *Norway*
	Icelandic: *Iceland*
	Faeroese: *Faeroes*
	Frisian: *Netherlands*
	Letzeburgish: *Luxembourg*
ROMANCE	Italian: *Italy: Switzerland: Corse*
	French: *France: Belgium: Switzerland: Italy: Luxembourg*
	Spanish: *Spain: France*
	Portuguese: *Portugal*
	Romansch: *Switzerland: Italy*
GREEK	Greek: *Greece: Italy*
ALBANIAN	Albanian: *Greece: Italy*
FINNO-UGRIAN	Finnish: *Finland: Sweden*
	Lappish: *Finland: Sweden: Norway*
SLAVIC	Macedonian: *Greece*
	Slovene: *Italy: Austria*
	Russian: *Finland*
	Croat: *Austria*
CELTIC	Welsh: *United Kingdom (Wales)*
	Erse: *Republic of Ireland*
	Gaelic: *United Kingdom (Scotland)*
BASQUE	Basque: *Spain: France*

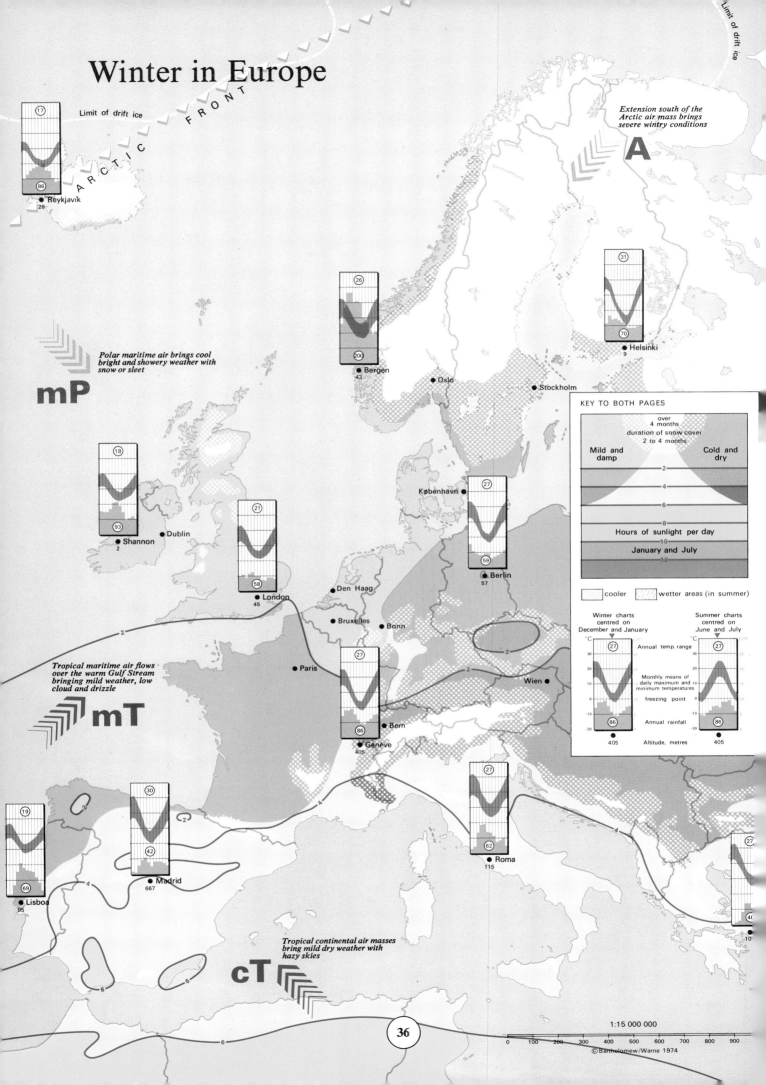

Winter in Europe

© Bartholomew/Warne 1974

KEY TO BOTH PAGES

over 4 months
duration of snow cover
2 to 4 months

Mild and damp — Cold and dry

Hours of sunlight per day

January and July

cooler — wetter areas (in summer)

Winter charts centred on December and January

Summer charts centred on June and July

Annual temp. range

Monthly means of daily maximum and minimum temperatures

freezing point

Annual rainfall

Altitude, metres

Limit of drift ice

ARCTIC FRONT

Extension south of the Arctic air mass brings severe wintry conditions

A

Polar maritime air brings cool bright and showery weather with snow or sleet

mP

Tropical maritime air flows over the warm Gulf Stream bringing mild weather, low cloud and drizzle

mT

Tropical continental air masses bring mild dry weather with hazy skies

cT

Reykjavík

Bergen

Helsinki

Oslo

Stockholm

Shannon

Dublin

København

London

Den Haag

Bruxelles

Bonn

Berlin

Paris

Wien

Bern

Genève

Roma

Lisboa

Madrid

1:15 000 000

0 100 200 300 400 500 600 700 800 900

Summary in Europe

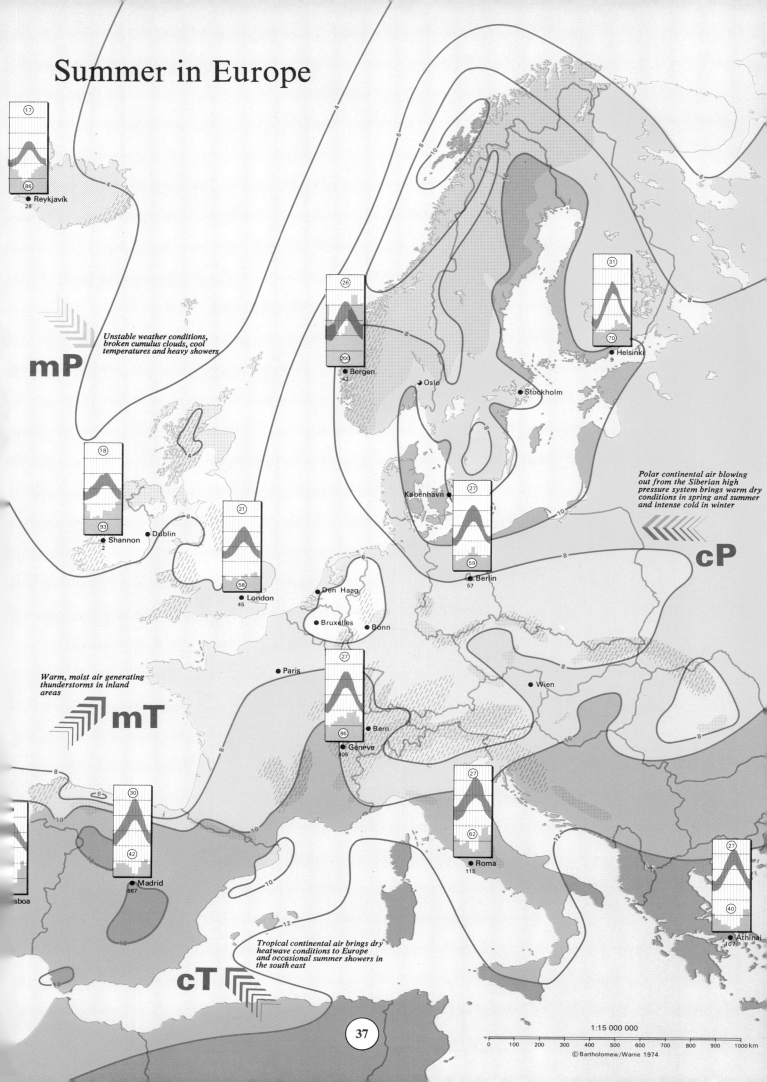

Summer in Europe

mP — Unstable weather conditions, broken cumulus clouds, cool temperatures and heavy showers

Warm, moist air generating thunderstorms in inland areas
mT

cT — Tropical continental air brings dry heatwave conditions to Europe and occasional summer showers in the south east

Polar continental air blowing out from the Siberian high pressure system brings warm dry conditions in spring and summer and intense cold in winter
cP

Reykjavík
28

Bergen
43

Helsinki
9

Oslo

Stockholm

Shannon
2

Dublin

London
45

København

Berlin
57

Den Haag

Bruxelles

Bonn

Paris

Wien

Bern
Genève
405

Madrid
667

Roma
115

Athinai
107

sboa

37

1:15 000 000

0 100 200 300 400 500 600 700 800 900 1000 km

© Bartholomew/Warne 1974

Farming Populations

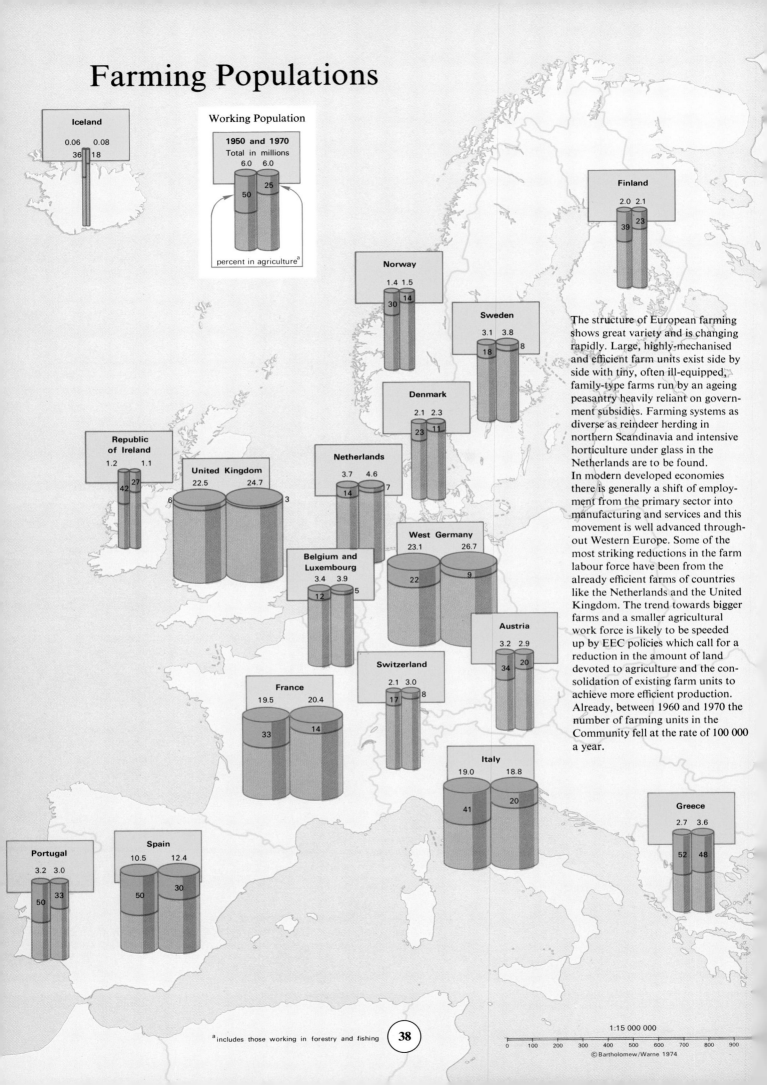

Iceland

0.06   0.08
36   18

Working Population

1950 and 1970
Total in millions
6.0   6.0
50   25

percent in agriculture[a]

Finland

2.0   2.1
39   23

Norway

1.4   1.5
30   14

Sweden

3.1   3.8
18   8

Denmark

2.1   2.3
23   11

Republic of Ireland

1.2   1.1
42   27

United Kingdom

22.5   24.7
6   3

Netherlands

3.7   4.6
14   7

West Germany

23.1   26.7
22   9

Belgium and Luxembourg

3.4   3.9
12   5

Austria

3.2   2.9
34   20

Switzerland

2.1   3.0
17   8

France

19.5   20.4
33   14

Italy

19.0   18.8
41   20

Greece

2.7   3.6
52   48

Portugal

3.2   3.0
50   33

Spain

10.5   12.4
50   30

The structure of European farming
shows great variety and is changing
rapidly. Large, highly-mechanised
and efficient farm units exist side by
side with tiny, often ill-equipped,
family-type farms run by an ageing
peasantry heavily reliant on government subsidies. Farming systems as
diverse as reindeer herding in
northern Scandinavia and intensive
horticulture under glass in the
Netherlands are to be found.
In modern developed economies
there is generally a shift of employment from the primary sector into
manufacturing and services and this
movement is well advanced throughout Western Europe. Some of the
most striking reductions in the farm
labour force have been from the
already efficient farms of countries
like the Netherlands and the United
Kingdom. The trend towards bigger
farms and a smaller agricultural
work force is likely to be speeded
up by EEC policies which call for a
reduction in the amount of land
devoted to agriculture and the con-
solidation of existing farm units to
achieve more efficient production.
Already, between 1960 and 1970 the
number of farming units in the
Community fell at the rate of 100 000
a year.

[a]includes those working in forestry and fishing

1:15 000 000

0   100   200   300   400   500   600   700   800   900

© Bartholomew/Warne 1974

Using the Farm Land

The Size of Farms

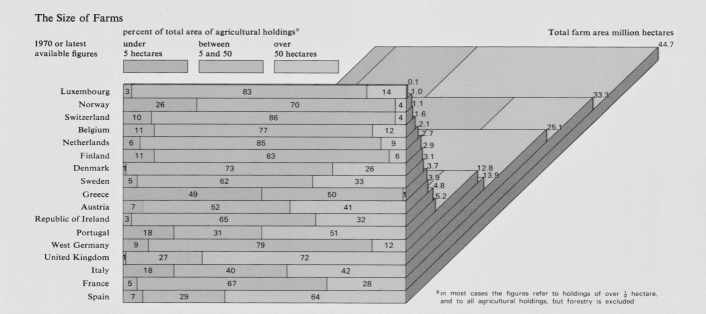

1970 or latest available figures

percent of total area of agricultural holdings[a]

	under 5 hectares	between 5 and 50	over 50 hectares

Total farm area million hectares

Luxembourg	3	83	14	0.1
Norway	26	70	4	1.0
Switzerland	10	86	4	1.1
Belgium	11	77	12	1.6
Netherlands	6	85	9	2.1
Finland	11	83	6	2.7
Denmark	1	73	26	2.9
Sweden	5	62	33	3.1
Greece	49	50	1	3.7
Austria	7	52	41	3.9
Republic of Ireland	3	65	32	4.8
Portugal	18	31	51	5.2
West Germany	9	79	12	12.8
United Kingdom	1	27	72	13.9
Italy	18	40	42	25.1
France	5	67	28	33.3
Spain	7	29	64	44.7

[a] in most cases the figures refer to holdings of over ½ hectare, and to all agricultural holdings, but forestry is excluded

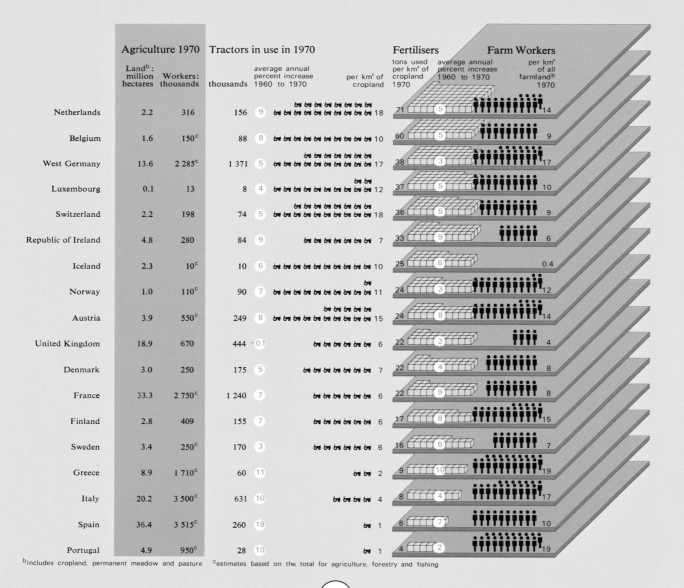

	Agriculture 1970		Tractors in use in 1970			Fertilisers		Farm Workers	
	Land[b]: million hectares	Workers: thousands	thousands	average annual percent increase 1960 to 1970	per km² of cropland	tons used per km² of cropland 1970	average annual percent increase 1960 to 1970	per km² of all farmland[b] 1970	
Netherlands	2.2	316	156	9	18	71	5	14
Belgium	1.6	150[c]	88	8	10	60	5	9
West Germany	13.6	2 285[c]	1 371	5	17	38	3	17
Luxembourg	0.1	13	8	4	12	37	5	10
Switzerland	2.2	198	74	5	18	36	5	9
Republic of Ireland	4.8	280	84	9	7	33	9	6
Iceland	2.3	10[c]	10	6	10	25	6	0.4
Norway	1.0	110[c]	90	7	11	24	3	12
Austria	3.9	550[c]	249	8	15	24	8	14
United Kingdom	18.9	670	444	−0.1	6	22	2	4
Denmark	3.0	250	175	5	7	22	4	8
France	33.3	2 750[c]	1 240	7	6	22	9	8
Finland	2.8	409	155	7	6	17	8	15
Sweden	3.4	250[c]	170	3	6	16	6	7
Greece	8.9	1 710[c]	60	11	2	9	10	19
Italy	20.2	3 500[c]	631	10	4	8	4	17
Spain	36.4	3 515[c]	260	18	1	6	7	10
Portugal	4.9	950[c]	28	10	1	4	2	19

[b] includes cropland, permanent meadow and pasture   [c] estimates based on the total for agriculture, forestry and fishing

Food Production

Since World War II the increasing use of fertilisers, the improvement of seed varieties and better farming techniques generally have led to substantially higher yields of most agricultural products. Despite the decline in the size of the labour force, production from the land has increased and indeed, for some produce, has caused serious problems of over-production.

Although climatic conditions obviously affect crop yields, the degree of farming efficiency is a more significant factor. This is clearly shown by the constant performance of the Dutch farmers whose highly intensive methods, often under glass for some products, achieve much higher yields than those obtained by traditional growing practice further south.

Increases in Productivity

Averages per year

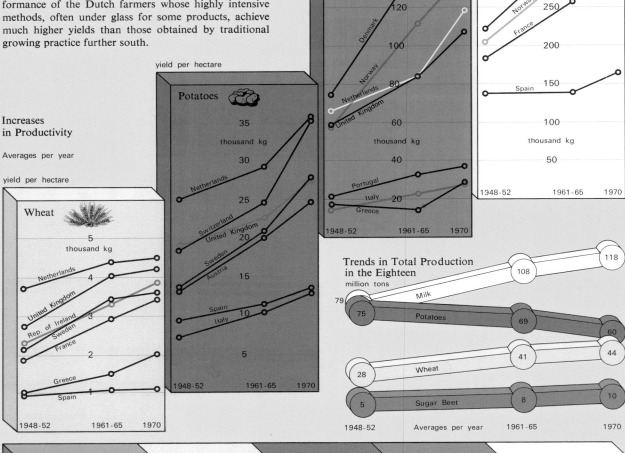

yield per hectare

Wheat

yield per hectare

Potatoes

yield per hectare

Tomatoes

yield per milking cow

Milk

Trends in Total Production in the Eighteen
million tons

Annual Production	Wheat			Potatoes			Sugar Beet			Milk		
thousand tons							unprocessed					
averages: 1950 = 1948–52 1963 = 1961–65	1950	1963	1970	1950	1963	1970	1950	1963	1970	1950	1963	1970
West Germany	2 669	4 607	5 662	24 264	22 230	16 250	823	1 737	2 075	13 498	20 727	21 893
United Kingdom	2 397	3 520	4 236	9 443	6 889	7 482	626	875	984	9 887	11 973	12 675
Italy	7 170	8 857	9 689	2 732	3 850	3 668	598	1 053	1 202	7 897	9 982	10 018
France	7 791	12 495	12 921	13 734	13 297	8 904	1 085	2 034	2 696	15 333	26 039	31 820
Spain	3 625	4 365	4 064	3 346	4 496	4 937	315[a]	514[a]	795[a]	2 229	2 708	4 115
Netherlands	324	606	640	4 679	3 773	5 648	364	542	713	5 437	7 068	8 239
Belgium	525	826	735	2 127	1 673	1 597	330	436	606	3 161	3 831	3 749
Portugal	510	562	556	1 145	1 096	1 285	10[a]	15[a]	9[a]	335	471	604
Greece	894	1 765	1 930	385	466	731	—	48	188	521	1 064	1 265
Sweden	677	909	962	1 814	1 594	1 490	285	247	218	4 609	3 796	2 955
Austria	348	704	810	2 270	3 217	2 704	103	270	324	2 125	3 113	3 358
Switzerland	260	355	348	1 021	1 145	1 090	27	42	58	2 534	3 101	3 230
Denmark	285	535	512	2 170	1 227	1 033	319	290	291	4 915	5 313	4 630
Finland	263	448	409	1 442	1 067	1 136	20	55	60	2 415	3 725	3 310
Norway	58	19	12	1 174	1 059	857	—	—	—	1 552	1 660	1 730
Republic of Ireland	327	343	368	2 903	1 881	1 550	93	134	150	2 265	2 938	3 634
Luxembourg	30	43	28	137	96	68	—	—	—	162	199	217
Iceland	—	—	—	7	11	5	—	—	—	75	118	118
Total Production	28 153	40 959	43 882	74 793	69 067	60 435	4 998	8 292	10 369	78 950	107 826	117 560

[a] including some sugar cane

The Major Producers in Western Europe

1970 production in thousand tons

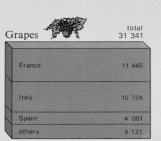

Grapes — total 31 341

France	11 445
Italy	10 724
Spain	4 051
others	5 121

Barley — 35 503

France	8 009
United Kingdom	7 529
Denmark	4 813
West Germany	4 754
Spain	3 069
others	7 329

Wheat — 43 866

France	12 921
Italy	9 689
West Germany	5 662
United Kingdom	4 236
Spain	4 064
others	7 294

Potatoes — 60 370

West Germany	16 250
France	8 904
United Kingdom	7 482
Netherlands	5 648
Spain	4 937
Italy	3 668
others	13 481

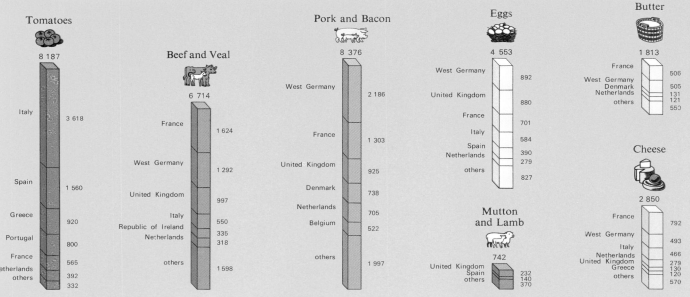

Tomatoes — 8 187

Italy	3 618
Spain	1 560
Greece	920
Portugal	800
France	565
Netherlands	392
others	332

Beef and Veal — 6 714

France	1 624
West Germany	1 292
United Kingdom	997
Italy	550
Republic of Ireland	335
Netherlands	318
others	1 598

Pork and Bacon — 8 376

West Germany	2 186
France	1 303
United Kingdom	925
Denmark	738
Netherlands	705
Belgium	522
others	1 997

Eggs — 4 553

West Germany	892
United Kingdom	880
France	701
Italy	584
Spain	390
Netherlands	279
others	827

Mutton and Lamb — 742

United Kingdom	232
Spain	140
others	370

Butter — 1 813

France	506
West Germany	505
Denmark	131
Netherlands	121
others	550

Cheese — 2 850

France	792
West Germany	493
Italy	466
Netherlands	279
United Kingdom	130
Greece	120
others	570

EEC Farming Policies: Article 39 of the Rome Treaty contains the Common Agricultural Policy (CAP)[a]. Traditionally, Continental agriculture has been protected by high tariff barriers in marked contrast to the cheap food policy followed by the United Kingdom. The farming community's political strength when the Treaty of Rome was signed ensured that a complex system of market support would be fundamental to the CAP. In effect, guaranteed prices set annually by the Council of Ministers are maintained by import levies and intervention agencies that purchase surplus production. The administration of the CAP is the responsibility of the Agricultural Guidance and Guarantee Fund (FEOGA).

The enlargement of the EEC in 1973 emphasised the need for changes in the CAP. The EEC Commission has proposed drastic structural reforms, including persuading 5 million farmers and workers to leave the land by 1980, and the conversion of 5 million hectares of farmland to forest, national parks and other recreational use. This should eventually do much to solve the major farming problems.

[a]see Glossary for details

Self-sufficiency in Food Production in 1970

Percentage of food in each country which is home produced. The surplus over 100 per cent is exported.

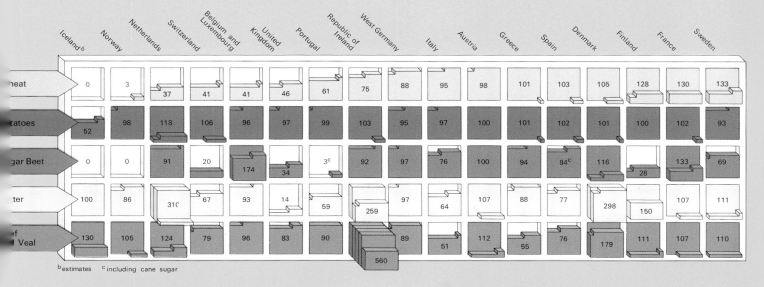

	Iceland[b]	Norway	Netherlands	Switzerland	Belgium and Luxembourg	United Kingdom	Portugal	Republic of Ireland	West Germany	Italy	Austria	Greece	Spain	Denmark	Finland	France	Sweden
Wheat	0	3	37	41	41	46	61		75	88	95	98	101	103	105	128	130	133
Potatoes	52	98	118	106	96	97	99	103	95	97	100	101	102	101	100	102	93
Sugar Beet	0	0	91	20	174	34	3[c]		92	97	76	100	94	84[c]	116	28	133	69
Butter	100	86	310	67	93	14	59		97	259	64	107	88	77	298	150	107	111
Beef and Veal	130	105	124	79	96	83	90	560	89	51	112	55	76	179	111	107	110

[b]estimates [c]including cane sugar

Working the Sea

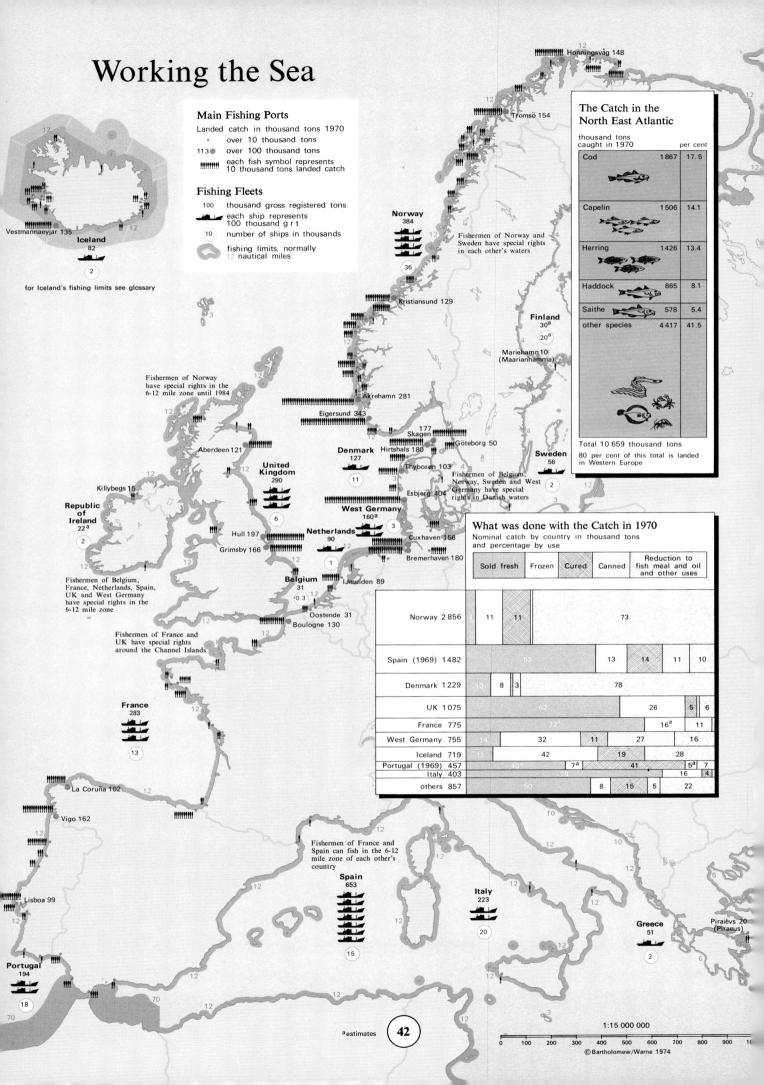

Main Fishing Ports

Landed catch in thousand tons 1970

- ·   over 10 thousand tons
- 113●   over 100 thousand tons
- ⁞⁞⁞⁞⁞   each fish symbol represents 10 thousand tons landed catch

Fishing Fleets

- 100   thousand gross registered tons
- ⛴   each ship represents 100 thousand g r t
- (10)   number of ships in thousands
- ◯   fishing limits, normally 12 nautical miles

for Iceland's fishing limits see glossary

Fishermen of Norway have special rights in the 6-12 mile zone until 1984

Fishermen of Norway and Sweden have special rights in each other's waters

Fishermen of Belgium, Norway, Sweden and West Germany have special rights in Danish waters

Fishermen of Belgium, France, Netherlands, Spain, UK and West Germany have special rights in the 6-12 mile zone

Fishermen of France and UK have special rights around the Channel Islands

Fishermen of France and Spain can fish in the 6-12 mile zone of each other's country

Honningsvåg 148
Tromsö 154
Norway 384 (36)
Kristiansund 129
Åkrehamn 281
Eigersund 343
Finland 30[a]   20[a]
Mariehamn 10 (Maarianhamma)
177 Skagen
Hirtshals 180
Göteborg 50
Denmark 127 (11)
Thyborøn 103
Esbjerg 404
Sweden 56 (2)
West Germany 160[a] (3)
Cuxhaven 156
Bremerhaven 180
Aberdeen 121
United Kingdom 290 (6)
Killybegs 15
Republic of Ireland 22[a] (2)
Hull 197
Grimsby 166
Netherlands 90 (1)
IJmuiden 89
Belgium 31   0.3
Oostende 31
Boulogne 130
France 283 (13)
La Coruña 102
Vigo 162
Lisboa 99
Spain 653 (15)
Italy 223 (20)
Greece 51 (2)
Piraièvs 20 (Piraeus)
Portugal 194 (18)
Vestmannaeyjar 135
Iceland 82 (2)

The Catch in the North East Atlantic

thousand tons caught in 1970

		thousand tons	per cent
Cod		1 867	17.5
Capelin		1 506	14.1
Herring		1 426	13.4
Haddock		865	8.1
Saithe		578	5.4
other species		4 417	41.5

Total 10 659 thousand tons
80 per cent of this total is landed in Western Europe

What was done with the Catch in 1970

Nominal catch by country in thousand tons and percentage by use

	Sold fresh	Frozen	Cured	Canned	Reduction to fish meal and oil and other uses
Norway 2 856	4	11	11		73
Spain (1969) 1 482	52	13	14	11	10
Denmark 1 229	10	8	3		78
UK 1 075	62		26	5	6
France 775	72[a]		16[a]		11
West Germany 755	14	32	11	27	16
Iceland 719	11	42	19		28
Portugal (1969) 457	40[a]	7[a]	41	5[a]	7
Italy 403	79			16	4
others 857	50	8	15	5	22

[a] estimates

42

1:15 000 000
0 100 200 300 400 500 600 700 800 900

© Bartholomew/Warne 1974

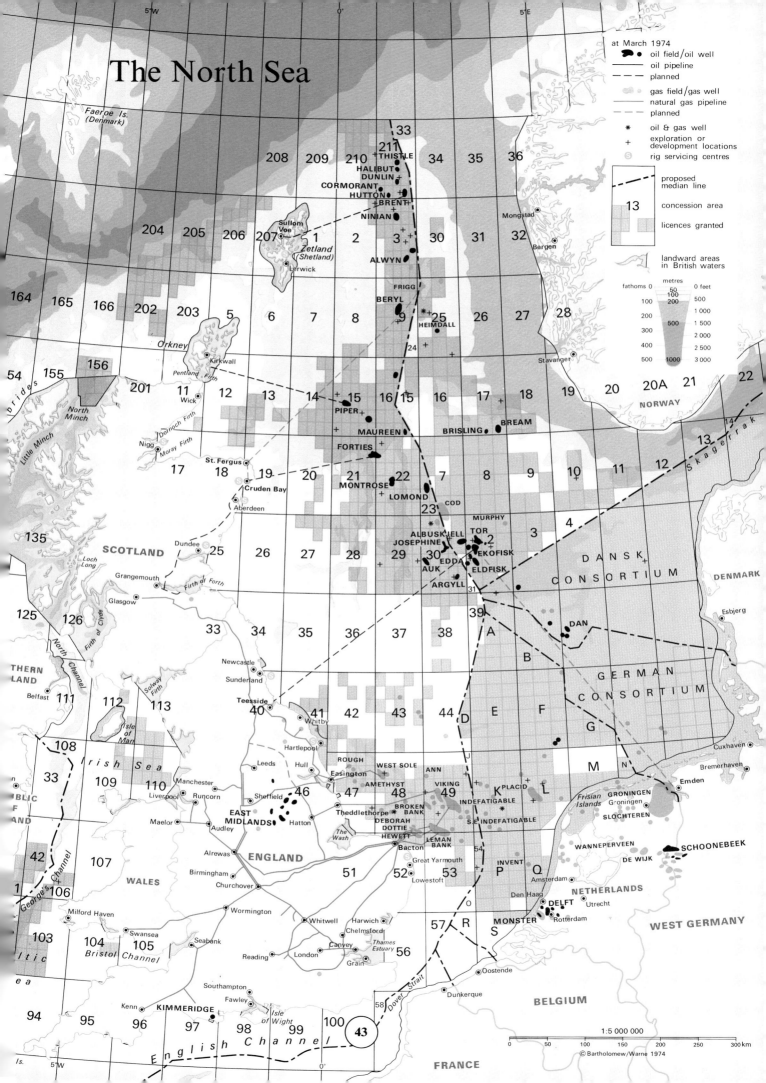

The North Sea

Faeroe Is.
(Denmark)

at March 1974
- oil field/oil well
— oil pipeline
-- planned
- gas field/gas well
— natural gas pipeline
-- planned
* oil & gas well
+ exploration or
development locations
Ⓢ rig servicing centres

-·-· proposed
median line
13 concession area
licences granted

landward areas
in British waters

fathoms 0	metres	0 feet
	50	
	100	
100	200	500
200		1 000
	500	1 500
300		2 000
400		2 500
500	1000	3 000

208 209 210 211 THISTLE 34 35 36
+THISTLE
HALIBUT
DUNLIN
CORMORANT
HUTTON
BRENT
NINIAN

Sullom
Voe Ⓢ
204 205 206 207 1 Zetland 2 3 30 31 32
(Shetland) ALWYN
Lerwick

Mongstad
Bergen

FRIGG
BERYL
164 165 166 202 203 5 6 7 8 9 25 26 27 28
HEIMDALL

Orkney
24

Kirkwall
Stavanger

54 155 156
brides 201 11 12 13 14 15 16 15 16 17 18 19 20 20A 21 22
North Wick PIPER
Minch MAUREEN BRISLING BREAM
NORWAY

Dornoch Firth
Nigg St. Fergus MAUREEN
Moray Firth FORTIES

135 17 18 19 20 21 22 7 8 9 10 11 13 12
MONTROSE LOMOND

Cruden Bay
Aberdeen COD
MURPHY
SCOTLAND Dundee Ⓢ ALBUSKJELL TOR 3 4
JOSEPHINE 2 DANSK
25 26 27 28 29 30 EDDA EKOFISK CONSORTIUM
AUK ELDFISK
Grangemouth Firth of Forth ARGYLL
31
Glasgow DENMARK

125 126 39 Esbjerg
33 34 35 36 37 38 A
North Firth of Clyde DAN
Channel B

THERN DANSK
LAND Newcastle GERMAN
Belfast 111 112 113 Sunderland CONSORTIUM

108 Teesside 40 41 42 43 44 D E F G Cuxhaven
33 109 Whitby J Bremerhaven
Irish Sea 110 Manchester Hartlepool ROUGH WEST SOLE ANN Emden
Leeds Hull Easington AMETHYST VIKING M N
Isle Liverpool Runcorn AMETHYST PLACID Frisian GRONINGEN
of Man Sheffield 46 47 48 INDEFATIGABLE K L Islands G-roningen
EAST Hatton Theddlethorpe BROKEN S.E. INDEFATIGABLE SLOCHTEREN
MIDLANDS BANK
Maelor Audley DEBORAH WANNEPERVEEN
Alrewas DOTTIE 54 DE WIJK SCHOONEBEEK
42 107 HEWETT INVENT
1 106 WALES ENGLAND Bacton P Q
George's Channel Birmingham 51 LEMAN NETHERLANDS
Milford Haven Churchover 52 BANK Amsterdam
Wormington 53 Den Haag DELFT Utrecht
103 104 105 Whitwell Harwich 57 R MONSTER Rotterdam
Swansea Bristol Channel Chelmsford S
Seabank Reading London 56 WEST GERMANY
Kenn KIMMERIDGE Thames Grain Oostende
Southampton Fawley Estuary BELGIUM
94 95 96 97 Isle 99 100 58 Dover Strait
of Wight Ⓐ43 Dunkerque
Is. 5°W English Channel 0° FRANCE

1:5 000 000
0 50 100 150 200 250 300 km
© Bartholomew/Warne 1974

Coal and Iron Ore

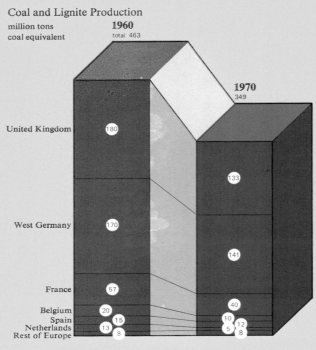

Coal and Lignite Production

million tons
coal equivalent

1960 total 463

1970 349

- United Kingdom 180
- West Germany 170
- France 57
- Belgium 20
- Spain 15
- Netherlands 13
- Rest of Europe 8

1970:
- 133
- 141
- 40
- 10
- 5 / 12
- 8

Although it met 30 per cent of the Eighteen's total energy needs, coal generally lost ground to oil during the 1960s. Across Europe coal mining was run down and the industry depended widely on substantial government support. A reappraisal of coal as a source of power is a likely development in the face of higher world prices for oil and uncertainty about supplies.

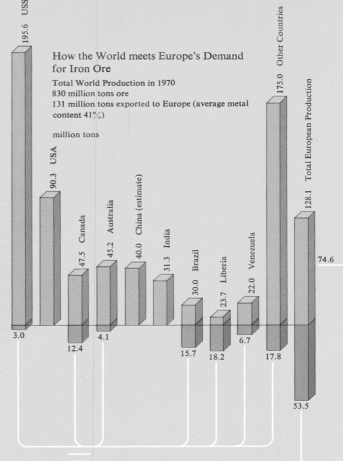

How the World meets Europe's Demand for Iron Ore

Total World Production in 1970
830 million tons ore
131 million tons exported to Europe (average metal content 41%)

million tons

- USSR 195.6 / 3.0
- USA 90.3 / 12.4
- Canada 47.5
- Australia 45.2 / 4.1
- China (estimate) 40.0
- India 31.3
- Brazil 30.0 / 15.7
- Liberia 23.7 / 18.2
- Venezuela 22.0 / 6.7
- Other Countries 175.0 / 17.8
- Total European Production 128.1 / 74.6
- 53.5

Exported to Europe

only main flows of over 100 000 tons tabulated

77.9 / 53.5

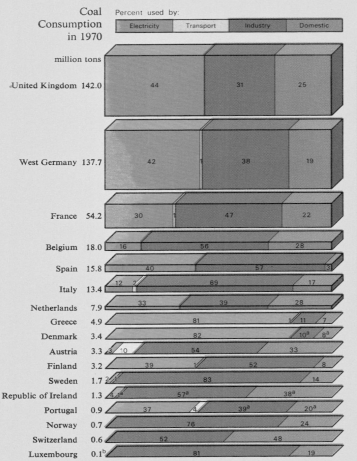

Coal Consumption in 1970

Percent used by: Electricity | Transport | Industry | Domestic

million tons

Country	Electricity	Transport	Industry	Domestic
United Kingdom 142.0	44		31	25
West Germany 137.7	42	1	38	19
France 54.2	30	1	47	22
Belgium 18.0	16		56	28
Spain 15.8	40		57	3
Italy 13.4	12	2	69	17
Netherlands 7.9	33		39	28
Greece 4.9	81		11	7
Denmark 3.4	82		10[a]	8[a]
Austria 3.3	3 / 10		54	33
Finland 3.2	39	1	52	8
Sweden 1.7	2 / 1		83	14
Republic of Ireland 1.3	4[a]	57[a]		38[a]
Portugal 0.9	37	4	39[a]	20[a]
Norway 0.7		76		24
Switzerland 0.6		52		48
Luxembourg 0.1[b]		81		19

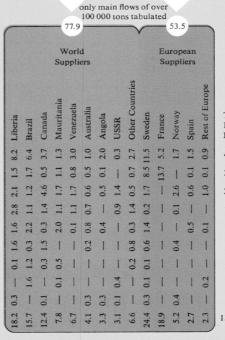

77.9 / 53.5

World Suppliers | European Suppliers

	Liberia	Brazil	Canada	Mauritania	Venezuela	Australia	Angola	USSR	Other Countries	Sweden	France	Norway	Spain	Rest of Europe	Total European Imports	
	1.5	8.2	6.4	3.7	1.3	3.0	1.0	2.0	0.3	2.7	11.5	5.2	1.7	1.5	0.9	49.4 West Germany
	1.5	1.7	0.5	1.1	0.8	0.5	0.1	—	0.7	2.7	8.5	13.7	1.7	0.1	0.1	29.3 Belgium & Luxembourg
	2.1	1.2	4.6	1.7	1.7	0.6	0.5	1.4	0.5	1.7		2.6	0.6	1.0	0.1	20.2 United Kingdom
	2.8	1.1	1.4	1.1	1.1	0.7	—	0.9	1.4	0.2	1.7	—	—	—	—	10.8 Italy
	1.6	2.2	0.3	2.0	0.1	0.8	0.4	—	0.3	1.4	0.2	0.1	0.5	—	—	9.7 France
	1.6	0.3	1.5	—	—	0.2	—	0.8	0.6	1.4	0.4	—	—	—	—	5.4 Netherlands
	0.1	1.2	0.3	0.5	—	—	—	—	0.2	0.1	—	0.1	—	—	0.2	2.4 Spain
	—	1.6	0.1	0.1	0.1	0.3	0.3	0.1	—	0.1	—	0.5	—	—	—	2.4 Austria
	0.3	—	0.1	—	—	0.3	0.3	0.1	0.4	—	0.2	—	0.1	—	—	1.8 Rest of Europe
	18.2	15.7	12.4	7.8	6.7	4.1	3.3	3.1	6.6	24.4	18.9	5.2	2.7	2.3		131.4 Total European Imports

Total European Imports

Europe's Total Consumption of Iron Ore

in 1970   206   million tons

- 77.9 Imported from outside Europe
- 53.5 Imported from within Europe
- 74.6 Domestic Production

Old Industries

The traditional basis for heavy industry in Western Europe has been a coalfield location and most of the major coalfields followed a similar pattern of rapid and unplanned industrial development. For a decade these industrial regions have faced common problems due to the relative decline of coal as a source of power, the use of imported iron ores and the need to enlarge and modernise industrial plant to remain competitive.

Industrial South Wales and the Ruhr illustrate the changes that have been taking place. The Ruhr is a distinctive economic region of Western Germany containing some 9% of its total population and producing nearly 75% of its coal, iron and steel, a large part of its chemicals and, increasingly, a wide range of light industrial products. South Wales with 3% of the United Kingdom's population produces some 10% of its coal and 30% of its iron and steel. Both areas face similar problems of readjustment to changing conditions.

The decline in coal, clearly shown on the previous page, has resulted in a substantial programme of mine closures and concentration on the high-yielding parts of the coalfields. The social consequence of this rationalization has been a massive reduction in the mine labour force in both regions. In the Ruhr during the 1960's the total drop in employment in the coal mining industry was about 200 000, while in South Wales manpower dropped from 85 000 to 36 000 during the same decade. Unemployment has been tackled by encouraging diversification. This has brought manufacturers like Opel to Bochum and Hoover to Merthyr

Tydfil. Redeployment schemes have channelled away many of the younger workers to the fast-growing new industries of the North Ruhr and the South Wales coastal plain.

The social problems created by the restructuring of these heavy industrial regions also include dealing with the depradations which over a century of iron and steel production has made on the environment. Obsolete factory buildings, mining operations, inadequate housing, poor communications and serious river and air pollution have necessitated regional planning schemes to provide a remodelled infrastructure appropriate to the needs of modern society. Typical outcomes have been the planned urban communities at Cwmbran and Llantrisant in South Wales and at Wulfen and Marl-Hüls in the Ruhr, and the determined efforts in both regions to preserve substantial areas as 'green belt' countryside.

In both regions this social engineering has so far met with varying success. The Ruhr has the advantage of having had a central planning agency (Siedlungsverband Ruhrkohlenbezirk) for half a century and a master plan exists to deal comprehensively with land use, communications and pollution to achieve a balanced environment. In South Wales designation as a Special Development Area has brought with it government grants to encourage new industrial investment. A variety of proposals exist for urban renewal, improvement of communications and redeployment of labour, but, despite piecemeal improvements, a coherent programme has yet to appear.

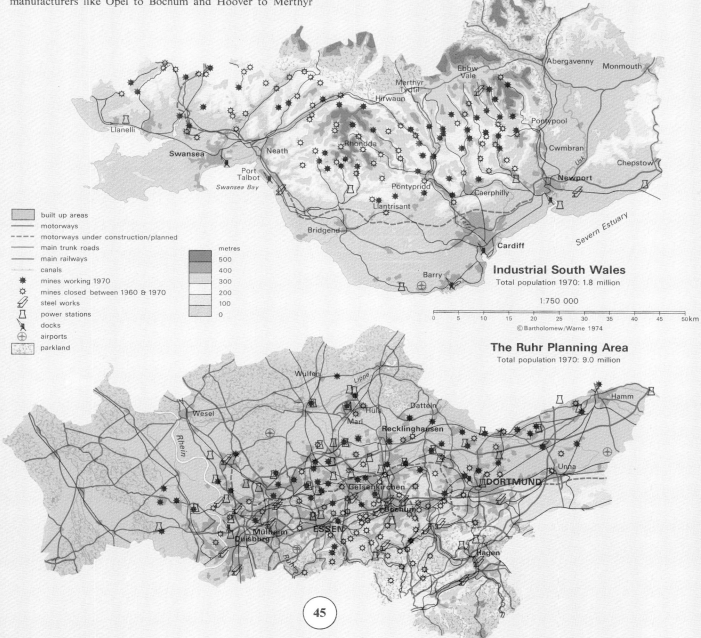

Industrial South Wales
Total population 1970: 1.8 million

1:750 000

0 5 10 15 20 25 30 35 40 45 50km

© Bartholomew/Warne 1974

The Ruhr Planning Area
Total population 1970: 9.0 million

built up areas
motorways
motorways under construction/planned
main trunk roads
main railways
canals
mines working 1970
mines closed between 1960 & 1970
steel works
power stations
docks
airports
parkland

metres
500
400
300
200
100
0

Energy in Europe

The Consumption of Energy in Western Europe 1970

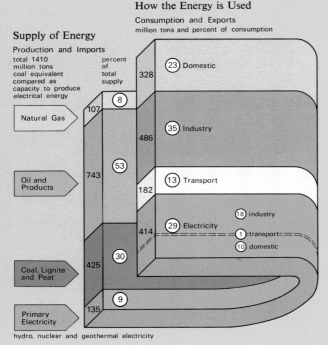

Supply of Energy
Production and Imports
total 1410
million tons
coal equivalent
compared as
capacity to produce
electrical energy

percent
of
total
supply

Natural Gas — 107 — ⑧

Oil and Products — 743 — ㊳

Coal, Lignite and Peat — 425 — ㉚

Primary Electricity — 135 — ⑨

hydro, nuclear and geothermal electricity

How the Energy is Used
Consumption and Exports
million tons and percent of consumption

328 — ㉓ Domestic

486 — ㉟ Industry

182 — ⑬ Transport

414 — ㉙ Electricity
⑱ industry
① transport
⑩ domestic

Western Europe is a major energy-consuming area and uses some 20% of the world's total energy output. Over two-thirds of its energy needs are met by crude oil which has displaced solid fuels as the main primary source of power. The growing demand for oil has been matched by the expansion of ancillary facilities for refining and distribution including nearly 7 000 km of pipeline and the remodelling of many ports to accept today's giant supertankers. In contrast, Western Europe's coal mining industry is contracting. The result of this trend is an increasing adverse energy balance which has made the countries of Western Europe heavily dependent on imported oil. The uncertainties of this situation make the North Sea oil and gas discoveries and the use of alternative sources of energy strategically and economically very important.

Electricity is the major source of generated power in Western Europe and production has more than doubled in most countries in the past ten years. Because it is a secondary source of energy which is pollution-free in use, its future in an environment-conscious society is assured. Moreover, expansion makes sense with the doubts raised by energy policies which place Western Europe in competition with America and Japan for overseas sources of primary energy. Most electrical generation is in thermal stations using coal, petroleum and increasingly natural gas, but, in the longer term, the replacement of these fuels by nuclear power will occur. The future for hydro stations is limited by the availability of suitable sites and most of the best in Europe are now in use.

As energy demands continue to grow in Western Europe the need for a common policy to co-ordinate and rationalize supplies and distribution becomes more pressing. Organizations such as the European Coal and Steel Community and Euratom are only a partial solution to the need and have not so far proved capable of establishing effective common policies in Community countries. The establishment of a Community approach aimed at achieving a balanced use of the energy sources likely to be available, guaranteeing supplies, agreeing pricing provisions and harmonizing technical production and distribution methods would be a significant test of the members readiness to modify national interests for the common good.

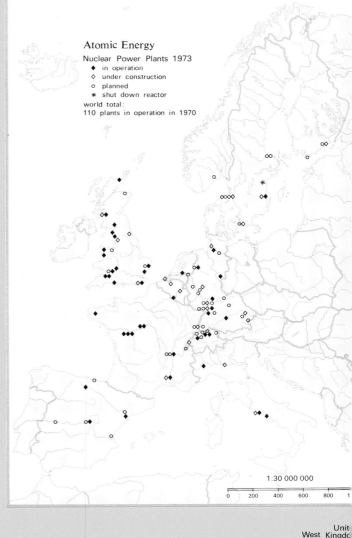

Atomic Energy
Nuclear Power Plants 1973
♦ in operation
◇ under construction
○ planned
✳ shut down reactor
world total:
110 plants in operation in 1970

1:30 000 000

0   200   400   600   800   1

Growth in Electricity Generation over ten years
thousand million KWh generated
in 1960 and 1970

Between 1960 and 1970 the average increase in the use of electricity in Western Europe was 8% each year

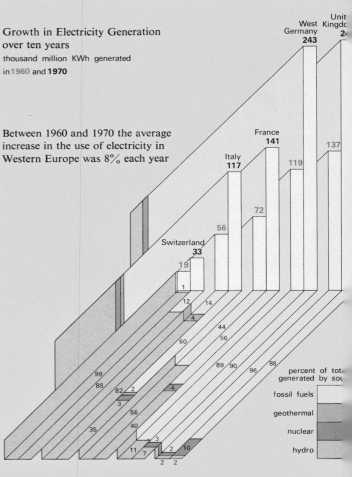

West Germany 243

United Kingdom 2

France 141

Italy 117

119

137

Switzerland 33

72

56

19

1

12 14

4

44

56

60

88

89 90 96 88

99

88   82   2

3   4

56

35   40

3

56

11 7   2 10

2 2

percent of tot
generated by sou

fossil fuels
geothermal
nuclear
hydro

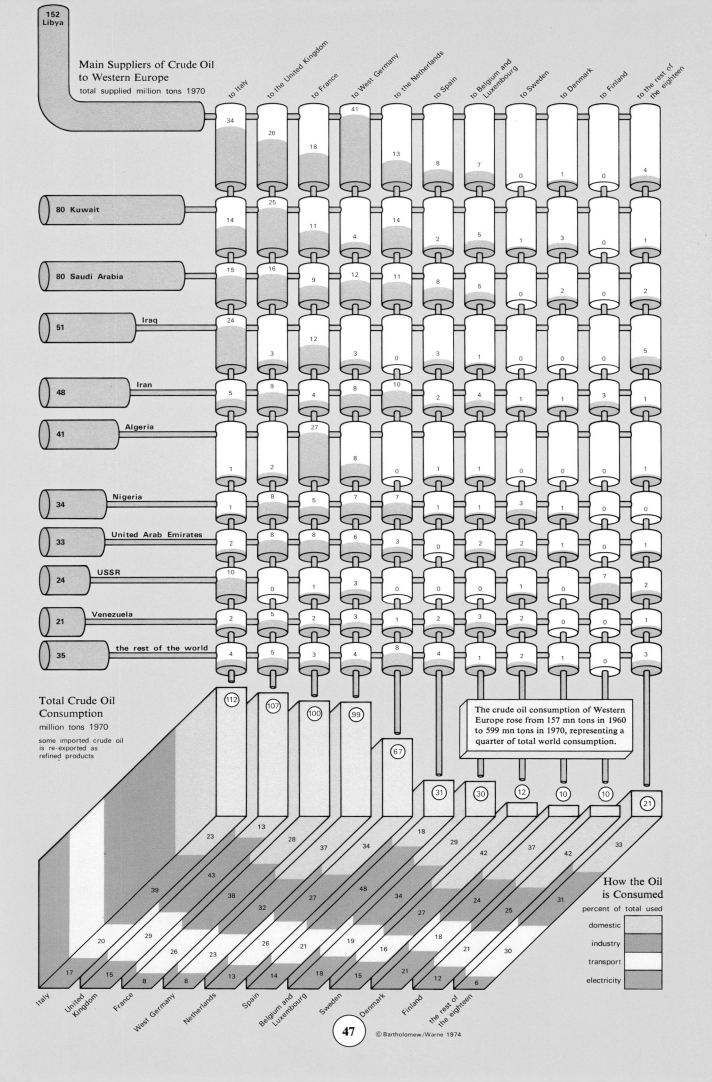

152 Libya

Main Suppliers of Crude Oil to Western Europe

total supplied million tons 1970

	to Italy	to the United Kingdom	to France	to West Germany	to the Netherlands	to Spain	to Belgium and Luxembourg	to Sweden	to Denmark	to Finland	to the rest of the eighteen
152 Libya	34	26	18	41	13	8	7	0	1	0	4
80 Kuwait	14	25	11	4	14	2	5	1	3	0	1
80 Saudi Arabia	15	16	9	12	11	8	5	0	2	0	2
51 Iraq	24	3	12	3	0	3	1	0	0	0	5
48 Iran	5	9	4	8	10	2	4	1	1	3	1
41 Algeria	1	2	27	8	0	1	1	0	0	0	1
34 Nigeria	1	8	5	7	7	1	1	3	1	0	0
33 United Arab Emirates	2	8	8	6	3	0	2	1	1	0	1
24 USSR	10	0	1	3	0	0	0	1	0	7	2
21 Venezuela	2	5	2	3	1	2	3	2	0	0	1
35 the rest of the world	4	5	3	4	8	4	1	2	1	0	3

Total Crude Oil Consumption

million tons 1970

some imported crude oil is re-exported as refined products

| 112 | 107 | 100 | 99 | 67 | 31 | 30 | 12 | 10 | 10 | 21 |

The crude oil consumption of Western Europe rose from 157 mn tons in 1960 to 599 mn tons in 1970, representing a quarter of total world consumption.

How the Oil is Consumed

percent of total used

- domestic
- industry
- transport
- electricity

	Italy	United Kingdom	France	West Germany	Netherlands	Spain	Belgium and Luxembourg	Sweden	Denmark	Finland	the rest of the eighteen
domestic	23	20	29	26	23	13	21	19	16	21	30
industry	39	15	8	8		32	18	15	21	12	6
transport	17				13	26	27	48	34	18	31
electricity			43	38					27	24	25
	112				18	29	42	37	42	33	

47

© Bartholomew/Warne 1974

Industrial Populations

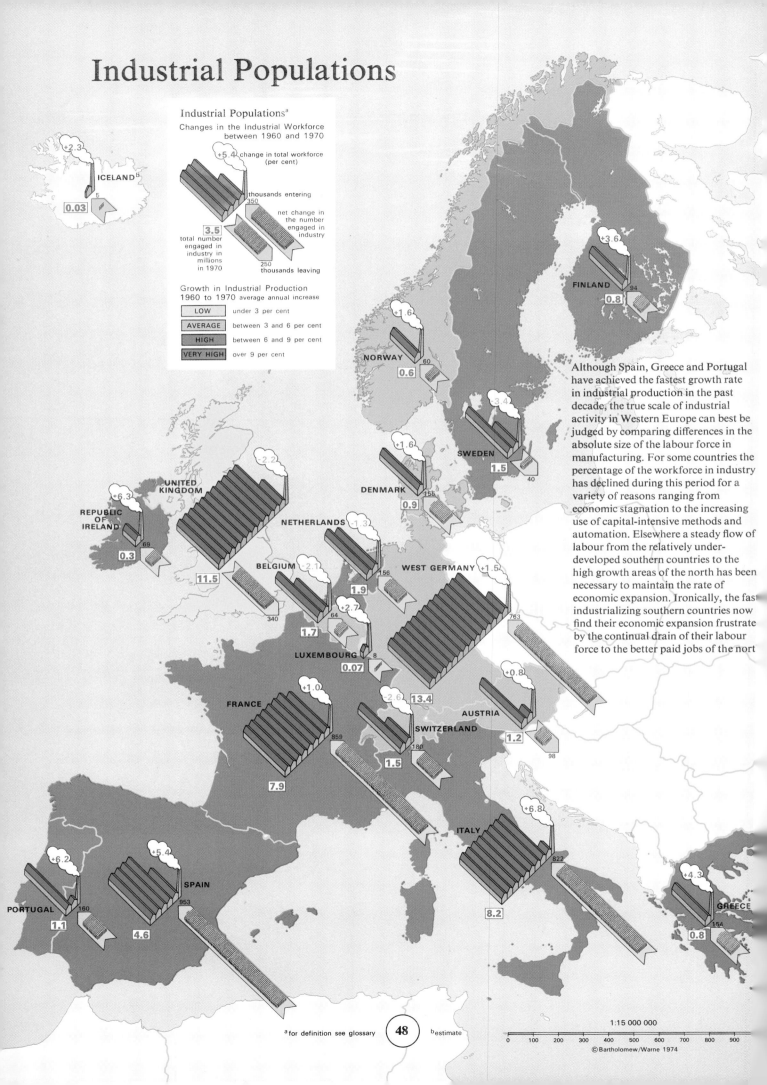

Industrial Populations[a]

Changes in the Industrial Workforce between 1960 and 1970

+5.4 change in total workforce (per cent)

350 thousands entering

3.5 total number engaged in industry in millions in 1970

net change in the number engaged in industry

250 thousands leaving

Growth in Industrial Production
1960 to 1970 average annual increase

LOW	under 3 per cent
AVERAGE	between 3 and 6 per cent
HIGH	between 6 and 9 per cent
VERY HIGH	over 9 per cent

ICELAND[b] +2.3 · 5 · 0.03

FINLAND +3.6 · 94 · 0.8

NORWAY +1.6 · 60 · 0.6

SWEDEN -3.4 · 40 · 1.5

DENMARK +1.6 · 155 · 0.9

UNITED KINGDOM -2.2 · 340 · 11.5

REPUBLIC OF IRELAND +6.3 · 69 · 0.3

NETHERLANDS -1.3 · 156 · 1.9

BELGIUM -2.1 · 64 · 1.7

WEST GERMANY +1.5 · 763 · 13.4

LUXEMBOURG +2.7 · 8 · 0.07

FRANCE +1.0 · 859 · 7.9

SWITZERLAND -2.6 · 180 · 1.5

AUSTRIA +0.8 · 98 · 1.2

ITALY +6.8 · 822 · 8.2

PORTUGAL +6.2 · 160 · 1.1

SPAIN +5.4 · 953 · 4.6

GREECE +4.3 · 154 · 0.8

Although Spain, Greece and Portugal have achieved the fastest growth rate in industrial production in the past decade, the true scale of industrial activity in Western Europe can best be judged by comparing differences in the absolute size of the labour force in manufacturing. For some countries the percentage of the workforce in industry has declined during this period for a variety of reasons ranging from economic stagnation to the increasing use of capital-intensive methods and automation. Elsewhere a steady flow of labour from the relatively under-developed southern countries to the high growth areas of the north has been necessary to maintain the rate of economic expansion. Ironically, the fast industrializing southern countries now find their economic expansion frustrate by the continual drain of their labour force to the better paid jobs of the nort

[a] for definition see glossary

48

[b] estimate

1:15 000 000

0 100 200 300 400 500 600 700 800 900

© Bartholomew/Warne 1974

Manufacturing Industry

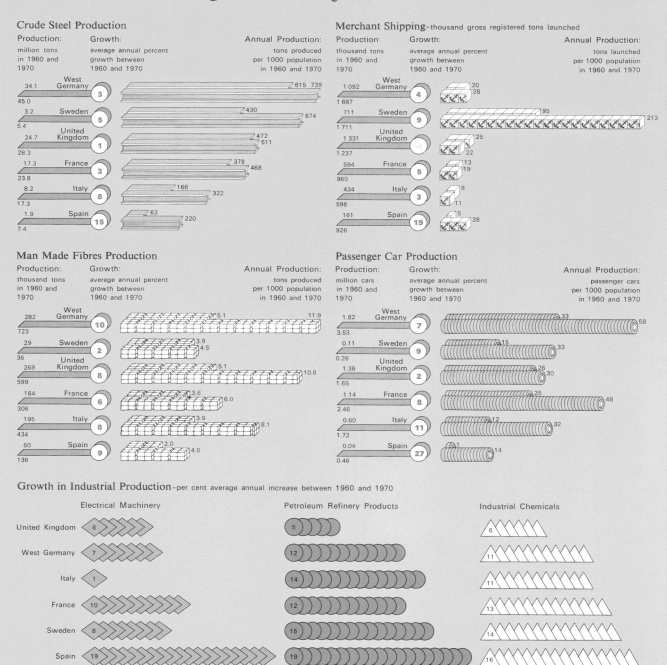

Crude Steel Production

Production:	Growth:	Annual Production:
million tons in 1960 and 1970	average annual percent growth between 1960 and 1970	tons produced per 1000 population in 1960 and 1970

West Germany — 34.1 / 45.0 — **3** — 615 / 739
Sweden — 3.2 / 5.4 — **5** — 430 / 674
United Kingdom — 24.7 / 28.3 — **1** — 472 / 511
France — 17.3 / 23.8 — **3** — 378 / 468
Italy — 8.2 / 17.3 — **8** — 166 / 322
Spain — 1.9 / 7.4 — **15** — 63 / 220

Merchant Shipping - thousand gross registered tons launched

Production:	Growth:	Annual Production:
thousand tons in 1960 and 1970	average annual percent growth between 1960 and 1970	tons launched per 1000 population in 1960 and 1970

West Germany — 1 092 / 1 687 — **4** — 20 / 28
Sweden — 711 / 1 711 — **9** — 95 / 213
United Kingdom — 1 331 / 1 237 — **-1** — 25 / 22
France — 594 / 960 — **5** — 13 / 19
Italy — 434 / 598 — **3** — 9 / 11
Spain — 161 / 926 — **19** — 5 / 28

Man Made Fibres Production

Production:	Growth:	Annual Production:
thousand tons in 1960 and 1970	average annual percent growth between 1960 and 1970	tons produced per 1000 population in 1960 and 1970

West Germany — 282 / 723 — **10** — 5.1 / 11.9
Sweden — 29 / 36 — **2** — 3.9 / 4.5
United Kingdom — 269 / 599 — **8** — 5.1 / 10.8
France — 164 / 306 — **6** — 3.6 / 6.0
Italy — 195 / 434 — **8** — 3.9 / 8.1
Spain — 60 / 136 — **9** — 2.0 / 4.0

Passenger Car Production

Production:	Growth:	Annual Production:
million cars in 1960 and 1970	average annual percent growth between 1960 and 1970	passenger cars per 1000 population in 1960 and 1970

West Germany — 1.82 / 3.53 — **7** — 33 / 58
Sweden — 0.11 / 0.26 — **9** — 15 / 33
United Kingdom — 1.36 / 1.65 — **2** — 26 / 30
France — 1.14 / 2.46 — **8** — 25 / 48
Italy — 0.60 / 1.72 — **11** — 12 / 32
Spain — 0.04 / 0.46 — **27** — 1 / 14

Growth in Industrial Production - per cent average annual increase between 1960 and 1970

	Electrical Machinery	Petroleum Refinery Products	Industrial Chemicals
United Kingdom	6	5	6
West Germany	7	12	11
Italy	1	14	11
France	10	12	13
Sweden	8	15	14
Spain	19	19	16

The Growth Industries and Areas

Much of Western Europe's growth industry is located in the giant agglomerations like London, Paris, the Randstad cities and the Ruhr, which are all significant centres of industrial expansion. Most of this industry depends on imported fuels and raw materials and this has encouraged its location at deep-water terminals able to handle today's giant bulk carriers and possessing wide stretches of estuarine land suitable for large-scale port/industrial complexes. Seaports like Europort at Rotterdam, Dunkerque, Teesside and the new port of Marseille-Fos have monopolized the location decisions of the petroleum, chemical and steel industries.

Planned government investment has directed some fast-growing industries to regional locations. In some cases, this has been part of restructuring schemes such as those which created new industrial patterns in the Ruhr and South Wales, but else-where the result has been completely new industrial investment to help solve regional employment problems. In Italy, for example, the Cassa per il Mezzogiorno, the official intervention agency, has for many years been offering substantial incentives in the form of capital grants to industrial investors in the southern parts of the country, Sicily and Sardinia.

The success of these schemes has been limited, however, and most of the industrial growth in Western Europe has continued to be drawn inevitably to the 'golden triangle', the economic magnet of the enlarged Community stretching from London to Milan to the Ruhr. The concentration of industrial expansion in this part of Europe has aroused great interest in policies to deal with the economic disparities between regions either by direct national or Community intervention.

The Workforce

The bulk of the labour force is employed in manufacturing and service industries and the decline in the primary sector continues. The rapid economic growth of the northern industrial areas has created labour shortages which have been met by increases in the numbers of women working and by the employment of foreign labour. Regional unemployment resulting from these trends can be countered mainly by policies directing the growth industries to areas of available labour.

Free movement of labour within the EEC is one of the fundamental principles set out in the Rome treaty and, since 1968, its citizens have had the right to take paid employment in any member state without fear of discrimination except where mutual recognition of professional qualifications has yet to be agreed. EEC workers receive equal treatment under national laws throughout the Community in taxation, social security, the right to send for their families, to obtain accommodation and to be elected to workers' representative bodies.

Language and cultural obstacles have restricted widespread movements of labour between countries and general business conditions more than legislation determine labour mobility. One major movement of labour has been from outside the EEC with a substantial increase between 1965 and 1970 (see page 34). In 1970, this flow of foreign workers was four times higher than the movement of labour within the Community. Seasonal or "frontier" workers who often form a significant addition to the workforce are not included in the adjoining figures because comparable data is not available for all countries. As examples, however, the Netherlands has some 26 000 "frontier" workers while 135 000 seasonal workers enter France each year. The figures for the United Kingdom exclude Commonwealth and Irish citizens who form 2.7% and 1.8% respectively of the British labour force.

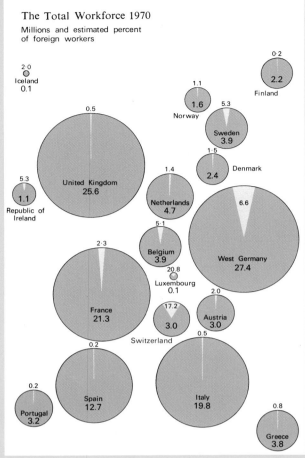

The Total Workforce 1970
Millions and estimated percent of foreign workers

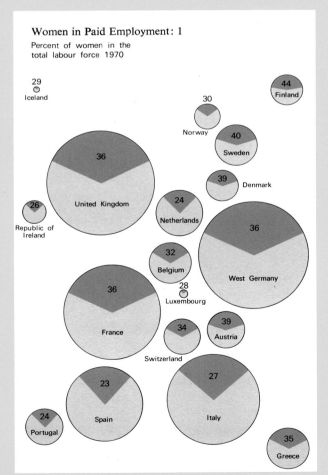

Women in Paid Employment: 1
Percent of women in the total labour force 1970

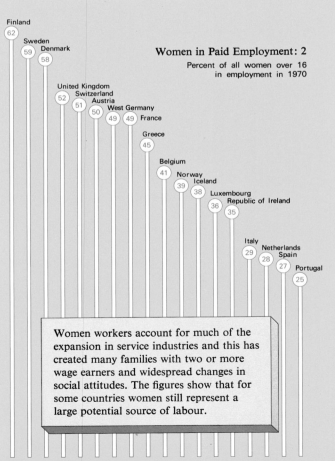

Women in Paid Employment: 2
Percent of all women over 16 in employment in 1970

Women workers account for much of the expansion in service industries and this has created many families with two or more wage earners and widespread changes in social attitudes. The figures show that for some countries women still represent a large potential source of labour.

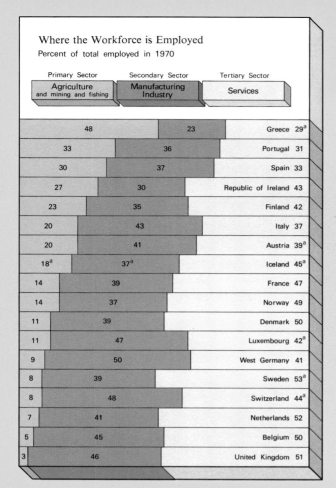

Where the Workforce is Employed
Percent of total employed in 1970

	Primary Sector	Secondary Sector	Tertiary Sector
	Agriculture and mining and fishing	Manufacturing Industry	Services

Primary	Secondary	Country	Tertiary
48	23	Greece	29[a]
33	36	Portugal	31
30	37	Spain	33
27	30	Republic of Ireland	43
23	35	Finland	42
20	43	Italy	37
20	41	Austria	39[a]
18[a]	37[a]	Iceland	45[a]
14	39	France	47
14	37	Norway	49
11	39	Denmark	50
11	47	Luxembourg	42[a]
9	50	West Germany	41
8	39	Sweden	53[a]
8	48	Switzerland	44[a]
7	41	Netherlands	52
5	45	Belgium	50
3	46	United Kingdom	51

The Sizes of the Trade Unions

The 28 million unionized workers in the European section of the International Confederation of Free Trade Unions represent one of the most powerful trade union movements in the world. But although membership figures are very difficult to correlate reliably it appears that less than half the workforce in Western Europe belong to a recognized trade union. Union solidarity is strongest in certain industries such as engineering, building, and public and municipal work, and in most countries these workers form the largest unions. In countries like West Germany and Sweden federations of workers such as the German DGB with 6 million members from 16 different industries form strong, disciplined organizations dedicated to raising the standards of living of the working population and the retired and to the improvement of working conditions. In contrast, the unions of France and Italy are split by religious and

	Estimated membership in millions	Percent of all employees
United Kingdom	11·0	47
West Germany	8·0	36
Italy	7·0	52
France	6·5	40
Sweden	2·4	70
Belgium	1·9	62
Netherlands	1·5	46
Austria	1·5	72
Denmark	1·2	62
Finland	0·9	51
Switzerland	0·8	29
Norway	0·6	49
Portugal	0·4	18
Greece	0·4	27
Republic of Ireland	0·4	48
Luxembourg	0·05	40
Iceland	0·04	72
Spain	not applicable	
Total	44·5	40

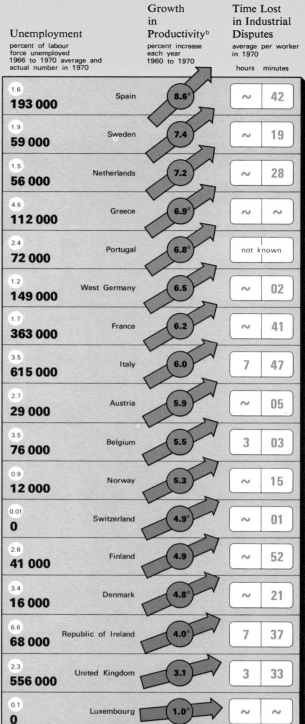

	Unemployment		Growth in Productivity[b]	Time Lost in Industrial Disputes	
	percent of labour force unemployed 1966 to 1970 average and actual number in 1970		percent increase each year 1960 to 1970	average per worker in 1970 hours	minutes
1.6	193 000	Spain	8.6[a]	~	42
1.9	59 000	Sweden	7.4	~	19
1.5	56 000	Netherlands	7.2	~	28
4.6	112 000	Greece	6.9[a]	~	~
2.4	72 000	Portugal	6.8[a]	not known	
1.2	149 000	West Germany	6.5	~	02
1.7	363 000	France	6.2	~	41
3.5	615 000	Italy	6.0	7	47
2.7	29 000	Austria	5.9	~	05
3.5	76 000	Belgium	5.5	3	03
0.9	12 000	Norway	5.3	~	15
0.01	0	Switzerland	4.9[a]	~	01
2.6	41 000	Finland	4.9	~	52
3.4	16 000	Denmark	4.8[a]	~	21
6.6	68 000	Republic of Ireland	4.0[a]	7	37
2.3	556 000	United Kingdom	3.1	3	33
0.1	0	Luxembourg	1.0[a]	~	~

Figures for Iceland not comparable because of limited industrial output.

political rivalry and do not present a united front against employers.

The weakness of European unions is clearly seen in their attitude to the establishment of the EEC. Dutch and German unions pressed vigorously for it while others such as the TUC in Britain and the communists generally were opposed to it. Unity is still a pressing task facing the trade union movement in order effectively to face the challenge presented by the new industrial patterns of the multinational company in Europe and moves in the direction of greater worker participation in the economy.

[a] estimates   [b] output per man-hour in the industrial sector

The E-Route System

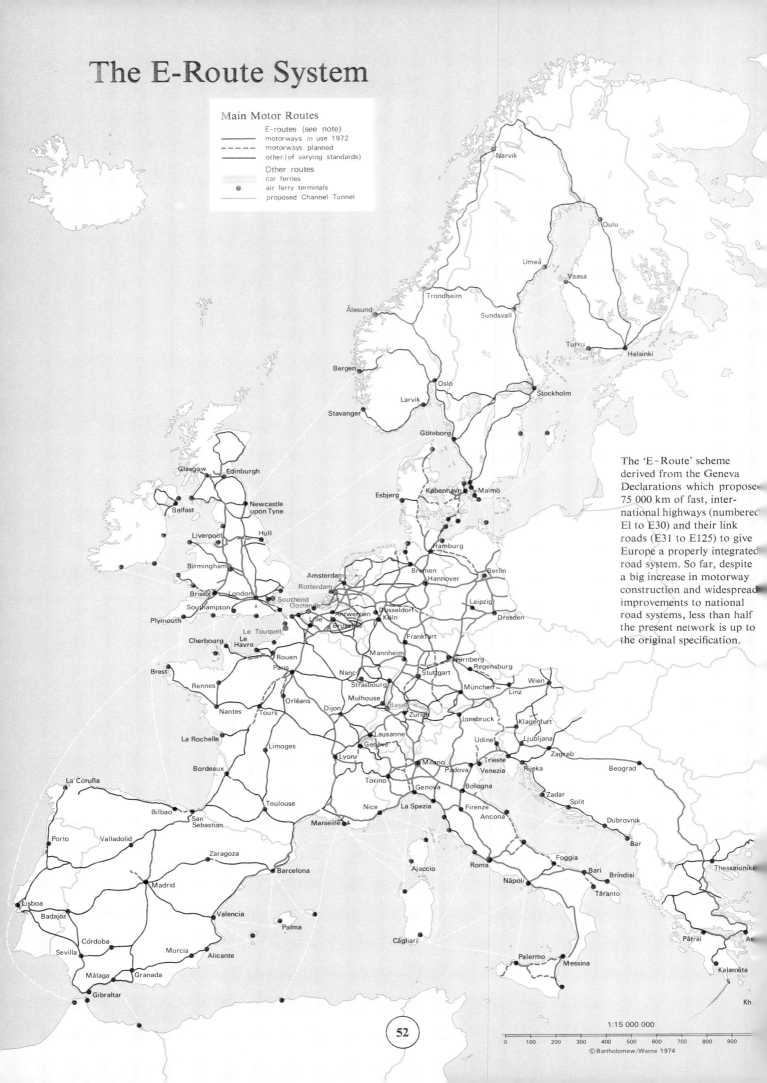

Main Motor Routes

E-routes (see note)
— motorways in use 1972
- - - motorways planned
— other (of varying standards)

Other routes
car ferries
● air ferry terminals
proposed Channel Tunnel

The 'E-Route' scheme derived from the Geneva Declarations which proposed 75 000 km of fast, international highways (numbered E1 to E30) and their link roads (E31 to E125) to give Europe a properly integrated road system. So far, despite a big increase in motorway construction and widespread improvements to national road systems, less than half the present network is up to the original specification.

1:15 000 000

0 100 200 300 400 500 600 700 800 900

© Bartholomew/Warne 1974

52

Road Transport

The number of vehicles on the roads of Western Europe has nearly trebled in the last decade, and nearly half of all families now own motor cars. The figures show contrasts still between countries, but the trend is quite clear. Another element is the rapid expansion in road freight using large container lorries with TIR Customs sealing to allow rapid and flexible transit to all parts of the Continent. The resultant pressure on roads and town centres has forced most countries into an expensive road and motorway building programme which is taking form in an international network of fast, direct highways linking the main industrial and commercial centres.

Average number of People to each Passenger Car in 1970

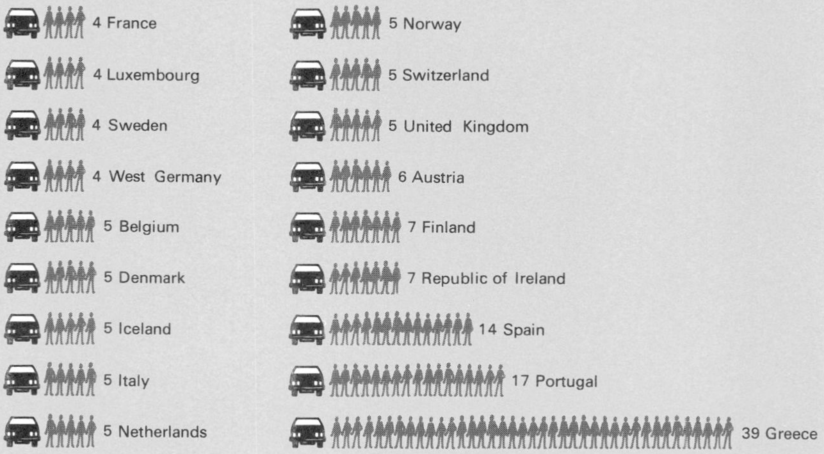

- 4 France
- 4 Luxembourg
- 4 Sweden
- 4 West Germany
- 5 Belgium
- 5 Denmark
- 5 Iceland
- 5 Italy
- 5 Netherlands
- 5 Norway
- 5 Switzerland
- 5 United Kingdom
- 6 Austria
- 7 Finland
- 7 Republic of Ireland
- 14 Spain
- 17 Portugal
- 39 Greece

Vehicles and Road Use

Number of vehicles in use: thousands

	Total 1960	Commercial vehicles[a] 1970	Passenger cars[b] 1970	Total 1970	Average annual growth 1960-70 per cent	Motor-ways 1970 km	Vehicles per km of road
France	7 181	2 672	12 900	15 572	8	1 553	20
West Germany	5 060	1 075	13 941	15 016	12	4 461	36
United Kingdom	6 983	1 748	11 887	13 635	7	1 133	38
Italy	2 631	916	10 209	11 125	16	3 913	39
Spain	450	741	2 378	3 119	21	185	22
Netherlands	680	321	2 500	2 821	15	1 300	29
Sweden	1 324	154	2 288	2 442	6	556	14
Belgium	927	242	2 060	2 302	10	482	24
Switzerland	570	117	1 383	1 500	10	377	25
Denmark	577	251	1 077	1 328	9	184	22
Austria	483	128	1 196	1 324	11	478	14
Norway	337	151	747	898	10	79	12
Finland	258	109	712	821	12	108	11
Portugal	208	79	581	660	12	77	16
Republic of Ireland	219	51	393	444	7	—	5
Greece	80	117	227	344	16	11	10
Luxembourg	46	13	91	104	9	10	21
Iceland	22	6	41	47	8	—	4
The Eighteen	28 036	8 891	64 611	73 502	10	14 907	20

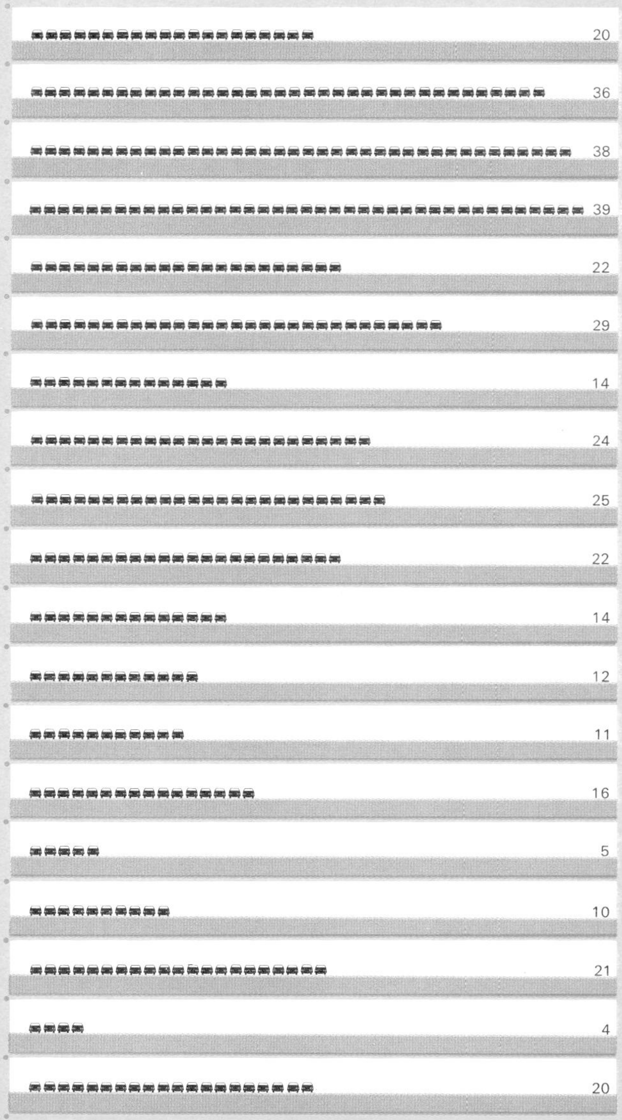

[a] includes buses and coaches   [b] includes taxis

The Railway Network

Main Railways in 1970

— electrified
— diesel and/or steam
— rail ferries
◉ cities with underground railway system
◉ under construction
— proposed Channel Tunnel

Traffic Carried 1970
average per km of rail

1.00	passengers : millions
1.00	freight : million tons

Trans - Europ - Expresses connect major cities in nine European countries by a network of very fast and comfortable trains for which frontier formalities have been reduced to a minimum.

Route	Name of Train
Amsterdam-München	Rembrandt
Amsterdam-Zürich	Edelweiss[a]
Avignon-Milano	Ligure
Basel-Milano	Gottardo
Bremen-Milano	Roland
Bremen-Wien	Prinz Eugen
Bruxelles-Hannover	Diamant
Frankfurt-Amsterdam	van Beethoven
Genève-Barcelona	Catalan-Talgo[a]
Genève-Milano	Lemano
Hamburg-Klagenfurt	Blauer Enzian
Hamburg-Zürich	Helvetia
Hoek v. Holland-Genève	Rheingold
München-Milano	Mediolanum
München-Zürich	Bavaria[a]
Nürnberg-Bruxelles	Saphir
Paris-Amsterdam	L'Etoile du Nord
Paris-Bordeaux	Aquitaine
Paris-Bruxelles	Brabant
Paris-Düsseldorf	Paris-Ruhr
Paris-Frankfurt	Goethe
Paris-Hamburg	Parsifal
Paris-Milano	Le Cisalpin
Paris-Nice	Le Mistral
Paris-Strasbourg	Stanislas
Paris-Toulouse	Le Capitole
Paris-Zürich	L'Arbalète[a]
Zürich-Milano	Ticino

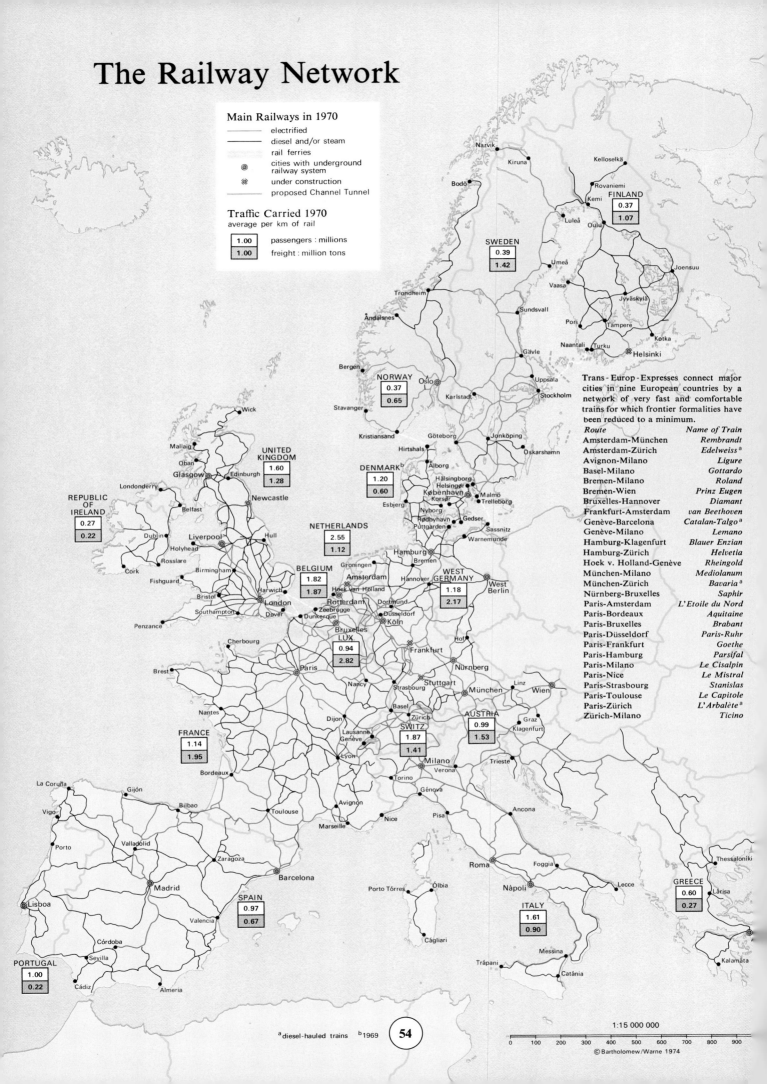

FINLAND 0.37 / 1.07

SWEDEN 0.39 / 1.42

NORWAY 0.37 / 0.65

UNITED KINGDOM 1.60 / 1.28

REPUBLIC OF IRELAND 0.27 / 0.22

DENMARK[b] 1.20 / 0.60

NETHERLANDS 2.55 / 1.12

BELGIUM 1.82 / 1.87

LUX 0.94 / 2.82

WEST GERMANY 1.18 / 2.17

FRANCE 1.14 / 1.95

SWITZ. 1.87 / 1.41

AUSTRIA 0.99 / 1.53

SPAIN 0.97 / 0.67

PORTUGAL 1.00 / 0.22

ITALY 1.61 / 0.90

GREECE 0.60 / 0.27

[a] diesel-hauled trains   [b] 1969

54

1:15 000 000

0   100   200   300   400   500   600   700   800   900

© Bartholomew/Warne 1974

Passenger Rail: Europe has a highly effective railway system despite the difficulties created by physical barriers and national boundaries. Railway transport is particularly competitive in terms of safe, dependable city to city services and for urban commuter traffic. Co-operation between national railway systems has helped to create successful services like the TEE network, and technical improvements like automatic track control and the French high-speed turbo-trains are giving the railways the capacity to compete against the private car and the airlines for inter-city travel. Direct inter-city links with computerised reservation of seats and no-wait connections can be made in high-speed, air-conditioned rolling stock that offers refreshments, secretarial services and, on the Mistral (Paris to Nice), a cinema, book-shop and hair-dressing salon. Despite these facilities railways as a whole are losing business and need large annual subsidies to cover operating deficits caused by soaring costs and falling traffic. Plans to remedy this situation include greater efficiency and EEC regulations that require railways to operate on the same commercial basis as other forms of transport.

Freight Rail: Rail offers special advantages for long-distance bulk freight, and a European-wide service of express container trains, the TEEM system (Trans-Europ-Express-Marchandises), permits fast and safe shipment of goods between twenty countries of Europe, including eastern Europe. As a further example of co-operation, the national railway administrations of twenty-one European countries have set up 'Intercontainer' to develop international container transport in what is virtually a 'European Railway' service. Further thinking along these lines may eventually create a single European railway system although the extent of collaboration so far suggests that this is little more than a long term future prospect.

Eurotunnel: Completion of a rail tunnel under the channel in 1980 will offer dramatic possibilities for new high-speed through services between all the major rail-heads of Europe.

The Changing Use of the Railways
Percent change each year
of rail traffic, average 1960 to 1970

- freight traffic ton km
- passenger traffic passenger km

Country	freight	passenger
Greece	6.6	-1.3
Norway	5.6	-0.8
Switzerland	4.0	1.6
Sweden	4.9	-0.2
Spain[a]	4.7	-0.8
Rep. of Ireland	4.2 / 6.1	-0.5
West Germany	3.2 / 0.2	
Finland	3.1	-1.2
Austria	2.6	
Belgium[a]	2.4 / 2.2	
France	2.1 / 2.5	
Denmark	2.0 / 1.8	
Luxembourg	0.5 / 1.1	
Italy	1.3 / 0.5	
Netherlands	0.4 / 0.3	-1.5
Portugal	-0.2 / 5.1	
United Kingdom	-1.3	

[a] national railways only

The Railway Networks Compared
Km of rail per million population 1970

percent electrified (10)

(2.0) total network thousand km of rail

United Kingdom 343 (17) — 19.0		
Norway 1094 (58) — 4.2	Sweden 1 517 (62) — 12.2	Finland 1 268 (1) — 5.9
Republic of Ireland 744 (0) — 2.2	Netherlands 241 (52) — 3.1	Denmark 587 (3) — 2.9
France 709 (26) — 36.0	Belgium 430 (29) — 4.1; Luxembourg 799 (50) — 0.3	West Germany 543 (27) — 33.1
Spain 402 (23) — 16.6	Switzerland 800 (99) — 5.0	Austria 883 (40) — 6.5
Portugal 398 (12) — 3.6	Italy 369 (46) — 20.1	Greece 292 (0) — 2.6

National Variations in Freight Traffic
based on ton km
Percent of total inland freight handled in 1970

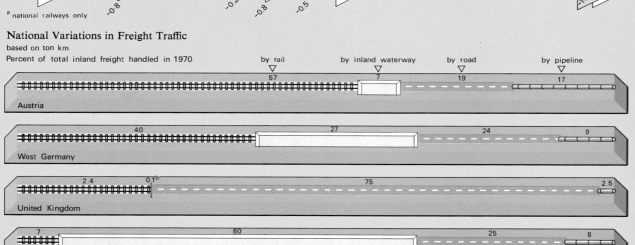

	by rail	by inland waterway	by road	by pipeline
Austria	57	7	19	17
West Germany	40	27	24	9
United Kingdom	2.4 / 0.1[b]		75	2.5
Netherlands	7	60	25	8

[b] coastal shipping is especially important

© Bartholomew/Warne 1974

Airport Traffic

Airport Traffic in 1970[a]
each symbol one million departures
and arrivals

8.0 ● Airport
300

each block 100 thousand tons of
cargo loaded and unloaded

● other airports with scheduled flights

Scheduled air traffic in
Western Europe is heavily
concentrated at a few large
airports. London dominates
with nearly a third of all the
passenger traffic and if Paris,
Frankfurt, Rome, Copenhagen
and Amsterdam are included
almost three-quarters of the
total air traffic is accounted
for. Similarly, air freight,
which is expanding dramatic-
ally, is mostly routed between
the major airports.

2.1 Oslo
22

2.5 Stockholm
41

1.4 Helsinki
17

2.0 Abbotsinch
32 Prestwick

1.1 Belfast
23

1.9 Dublin
40

1.8
46 Manchester

6.2 København
127

3.0 Hamburg
38

5.5 Berlin
37

2.4
14 Hannover

2.0
2 Luton

15.4
372 Heathrow

3.7 Gatwick
31

5.0 Amsterdam
180

3.5
36 Düsseldorf

2.7 Bruxelles
122

1.3 Köln
18

1.1 Jersey
9

12.1 Paris
266

8.8 Frankfurt
345

1.6 Stuttgart
31

1.3 Wien
20

3.4 München
31

4.2 Zürich
103

2.4
31 Genève

3.4
81 Milano

1.4 1.5
16 20 Nice
Marseille

6.8 Roma
129

2.8 Barcelona
36

4.5 Madrid
66

1.8
21
Lisboa

4.7 Palma
16

3.0
31

[a] excludes passengers and cargo in direct transit

1:15 000 000

0 100 200 300 400 500 600 700 800 900

© Bartholomew/Warne 1974

National Airlines

Western Europe has over fifty airlines, most of them nationalized and chiefly operating on international rather than domestic services. In a small, highly urbanized continent such as Europe, internal travel by air is not clearly superior to land transport. Even so, air traffic is booming and Western Europe has a significant share of the world's scheduled air traffic.

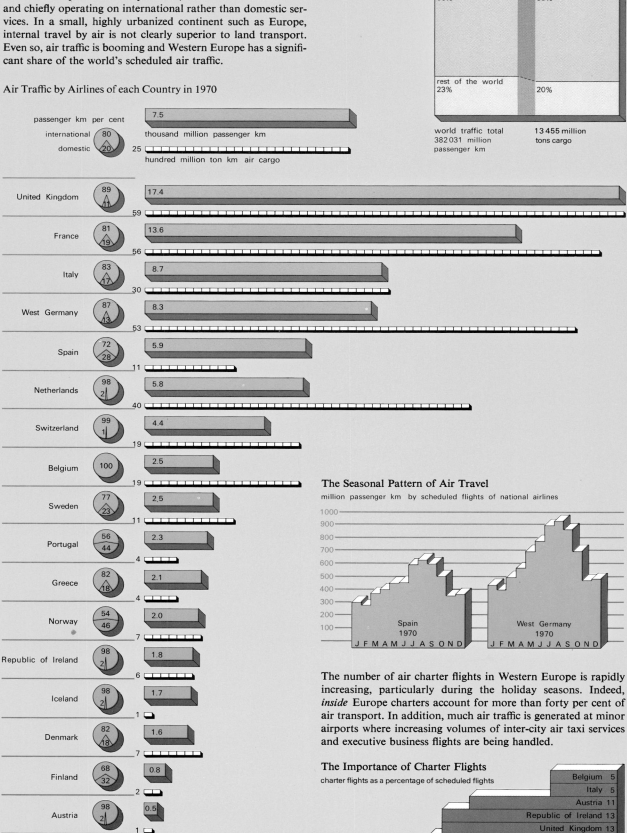

Europe's Share of Scheduled Air Traffic[a] in 1970

[a]excludes USSR

	Passengers by registered airlines	Cargo ton km
Europe	22%	25%
USA	55%	55%
rest of the world	23%	20%

world traffic total 382 031 million passenger km

13 455 million tons cargo

Air Traffic by Airlines of each Country in 1970

passenger km per cent
international 80
domestic 20

7.5 thousand million passenger km

25 hundred million ton km air cargo

United Kingdom 89 / 11 — 17.4 — 59

France 81 / 19 — 13.6 — 56

Italy 83 / 17 — 8.7 — 30

West Germany 87 / 13 — 8.3 — 53

Spain 72 / 28 — 5.9 — 11

Netherlands 98 / 2 — 5.8 — 40

Switzerland 99 / 1 — 4.4 — 19

Belgium 100 — 2.5 — 19

Sweden 77 / 23 — 2.5 — 11

Portugal 56 / 44 — 2.3 — 4

Greece 82 / 18 — 2.1 — 4

Norway 54 / 46 — 2.0 — 7

Republic of Ireland 98 / 2 — 1.8 — 6

Iceland 98 / 2 — 1.7 — 1

Denmark 82 / 18 — 1.6 — 7

Finland 68 / 32 — 0.8 — 2

Austria 98 / 2 — 0.5 — 1

Luxembourg 100 — 0.08 — 0.05

The Seasonal Pattern of Air Travel

million passenger km by scheduled flights of national airlines

Spain 1970
J F M A M J J A S O N D

West Germany 1970
J F M A M J J A S O N D

The number of air charter flights in Western Europe is rapidly increasing, particularly during the holiday seasons. Indeed, *inside* Europe charters account for more than forty per cent of air transport. In addition, much air traffic is generated at minor airports where increasing volumes of inter-city air taxi services and executive business flights are being handled.

The Importance of Charter Flights

charter flights as a percentage of scheduled flights

Belgium	5
Italy	5
Austria	11
Republic of Ireland	13
United Kingdom	13
Netherlands	14
Norway	19
Finland	22

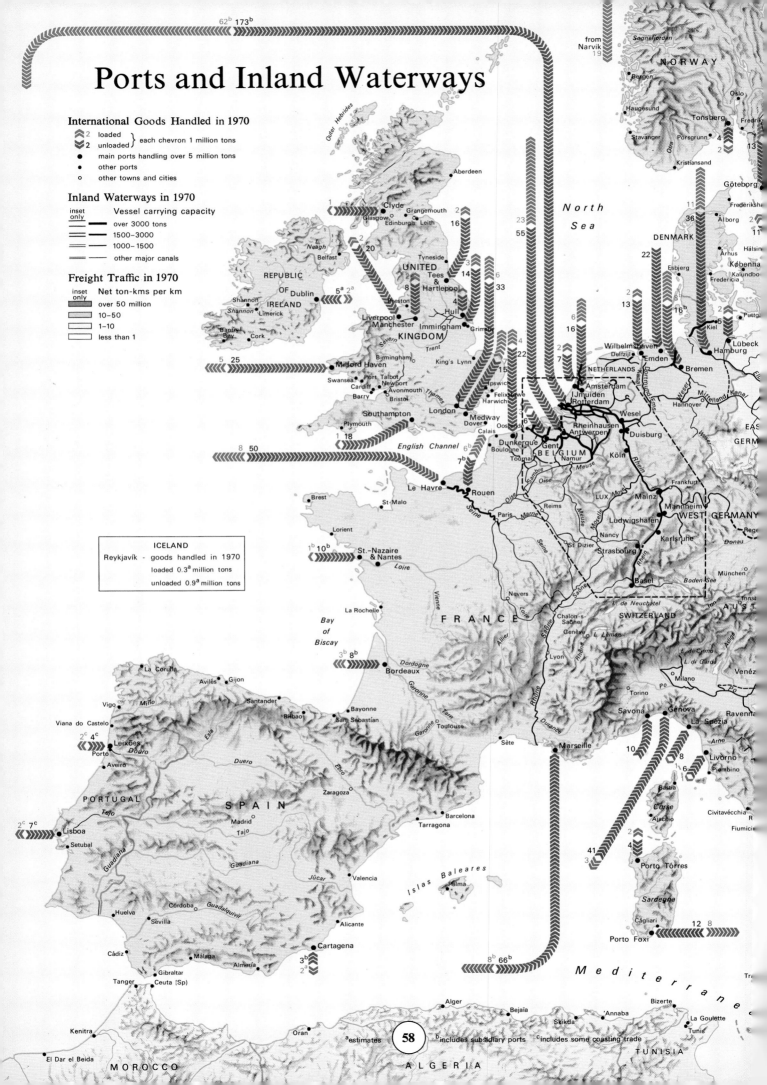

Ports and Inland Waterways

International Goods Handled in 1970

- 2 loaded
- 2 unloaded } each chevron 1 million tons
- ● main ports handling over 5 million tons
- • other ports
- ○ other towns and cities

Inland Waterways in 1970

inset only — Vessel carrying capacity
- over 3000 tons
- 1500–3000
- 1000–1500
- other major canals

Freight Traffic in 1970

inset only — Net ton-kms per km
- over 50 million
- 10–50
- 1–10
- less than 1

ICELAND
Reykjavík – goods handled in 1970
loaded 0.3[a] million tons
unloaded 0.9[a] million tons

[a]estimates   [b]includes subsidiary ports   [c]includes some coasting trade

The World's Merchant Fleet

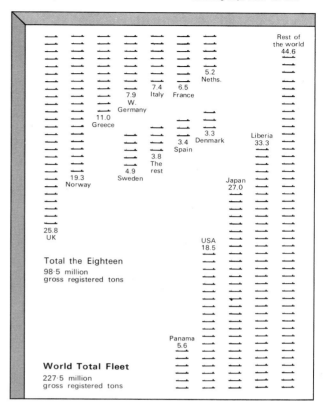

Ships Entered under Each Flag million gross registered tons 1970

→ each ship one million tons   excluding ships under 100 tons

Rest of
the world
44.6

5.2
Neths.

7.4   6.5
Italy   France

7.9
W.
Germany

11.0
Greece

3.3
Liberia
3.4   Denmark   33.3
Spain

3.8
The
19.3   rest
Norway

4.9   Japan
Sweden   27.0

25.8
UK

USA
18.5

Total the Eighteen
98·5 million
gross registered tons

Panama
5.6

World Total Fleet
227·5 million
gross registered tons

The importance of maritime trade to Western Europe can be gauged by the size of its merchant fleet. The heavy dependence on imported food and raw materials, particularly petroleum, has encouraged the growth of large national merchant fleets.

While some traditional maritime fleets have not changed much in the past twenty-five years, phenomenal growth has been registered by the flags of convenience. Liberia and Panama are good examples but so too is Greece, which, although ranked third in the Western Europe fleet, has twice as much tonnage again under other maritime flags.

Increasing international trade and the dramatic increase in the size and manoeuvrability of ships has created navigational problems in the congested shipping lanes around Europe. The convergence of sea-borne traffic on the English Channel poses special problems which have only partially been solved by the creation of separate sea-lanes.

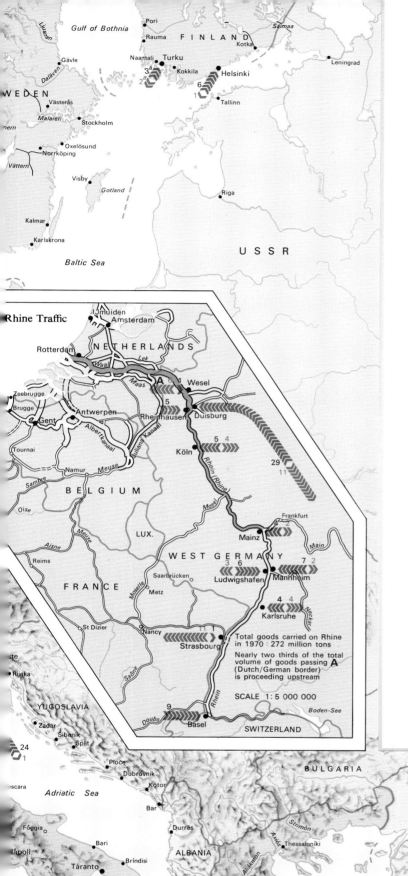

Rhine Traffic

Total goods carried on Rhine in 1970 : 272 million tons

Nearly two thirds of the total volume of goods passing **A** (Dutch/German border) is proceeding upstream

SCALE 1:5 000 000

1:10 000 000

0   100   200   300   400   500   600km

© Bartholomew/Warne 1974

59

National Prosperity

National income per head is the best measure of material living standards although as an indicator it remains a crude one. Expressed as income per head to eliminate differences due to a country's size, it conceals major variations in individual incomes both nationally and regionally. In all countries of Western Europe there exist marked regional differences in income between the metropolitan areas and the rural fringes. It conceals significant differences in the nature of working conditions, it does not take into account the effective purchasing power of income and it gives no indication of important variations in the quality of life available to people. This quality can be seriously affected by unrestrained industrial growth causing destruction of the living environment and there are obviously distinctive individual interpretations on whether the social costs of increased material prosperity are always fully justified.

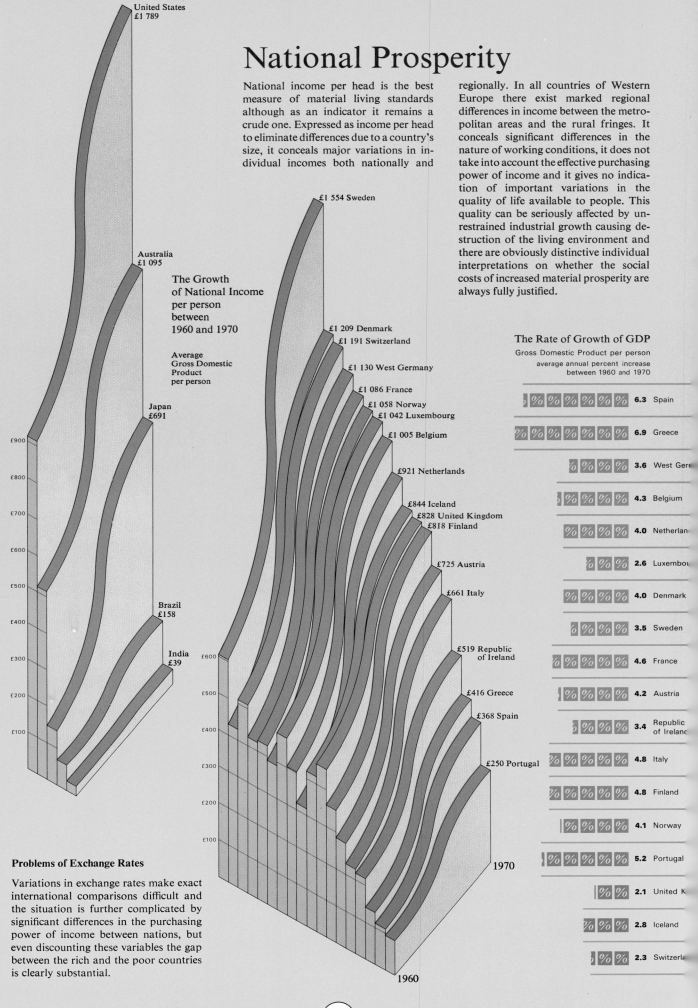

The Growth of National Income per person between 1960 and 1970

Average Gross Domestic Product per person

United States £1 789
Australia £1 095
Japan £691
Brazil £158
India £39

£1 554 Sweden
£1 209 Denmark
£1 191 Switzerland
£1 130 West Germany
£1 086 France
£1 058 Norway
£1 042 Luxembourg
£1 005 Belgium
£921 Netherlands
£844 Iceland
£828 United Kingdom
£818 Finland
£725 Austria
£661 Italy
£519 Republic of Ireland
£416 Greece
£368 Spain
£250 Portugal

1970
1960

The Rate of Growth of GDP

Gross Domestic Product per person average annual percent increase between 1960 and 1970

6.3	Spain
6.9	Greece
3.6	West Germany
4.3	Belgium
4.0	Netherlands
2.6	Luxembourg
4.0	Denmark
3.5	Sweden
4.6	France
4.2	Austria
3.4	Republic of Ireland
4.8	Italy
4.8	Finland
4.1	Norway
5.2	Portugal
2.1	United Kingdom
2.8	Iceland
2.3	Switzerland

Problems of Exchange Rates

Variations in exchange rates make exact international comparisons difficult and the situation is further complicated by significant differences in the purchasing power of income between nations, but even discounting these variables the gap between the rich and the poor countries is clearly substantial.

Wages and Prices

The actual material prosperity of the inhabitants of a country is determined not only by the nation's total economic performance but also by how wealth is distributed and the variable consequences of changing living costs. Inflation or a high cost of living can mean that the income scale is considerable and average figures are, in fact, hiding a surprising amount of poverty. This has tended to be countered by linking wage increases positively to the cost of living. This can, however, create additional problems for the economy where rises in wages outpace the growth in productivity.

The table below shows how the real purchasing power of wages in our eighteen countries has kept ahead of price increases. It is evident that the effective improvement in living standards varies considerably, but, in general, increases in real income have risen faster in the Eighteen than in any other region of the world except Japan. It should, however, be remembered that the growth rate of the poorer countries is enhanced by their lower starting positions.

Growing national prosperity has encouraged the trend to a shorter working week, longer holidays and increased leisure demands.

The Rise in Wages and the Effect of the Cost of Living

the average annual percent increase in earnings 1960 to 1970
reduced by the effect of annual rise in retail prices
equals the real annual gain for wage earners

Country	Real gain	Price effect	Earnings increase	Hours 1960	Hours 1970	TOTAL holidays
Spain	7.0[a]	7.0[a]	14.0[a]	43½	44	18
Greece	6.3	2.2	8.5	44	44½	12
West Germany	5.6	2.9	8.5	45½	44	13
Belgium	5.0	3.1	8.1	41½	38	12
Netherlands	4.9	4.4	9.3	49	44	7
Luxembourg	4.5	2.6	7.1	45	44	10
Denmark	4.4	6.2	10.6	40	36½	11
Sweden	4.4	4.2	8.6	38½	35	11
France	4.2	4.2	8.4	45½	45	11
Austria	4.2	3.8	8.0	43½	37½	12
Republic of Ireland	4.0	4.9	8.9	45½	42½	7
Italy	3.8	4.2	8.0	44½	43	18
Finland	3.7	5.1	8.8	44½	38½	13
Norway	3.3	4.7	8.0	39½	35½	10
Portugal	2.9[b]	4.9[b]	7.8[b]	43	44½	12
United Kingdom	2.3	4.1	6.4	47½	45	9
Iceland	2.2[c]	11.1[c]	13.3[c]	na	53	15
Switzerland	1.7	3.5	5.2	46	44½	8

Average Weekly Hours Worked in manufacturing 1960 and 1970

[a]1963 to 1970 [b]1961 to 1970 [c]1960 to 1966 [d]regional holiday

Consumer Expenditure

Percent of Total Consumer Spending

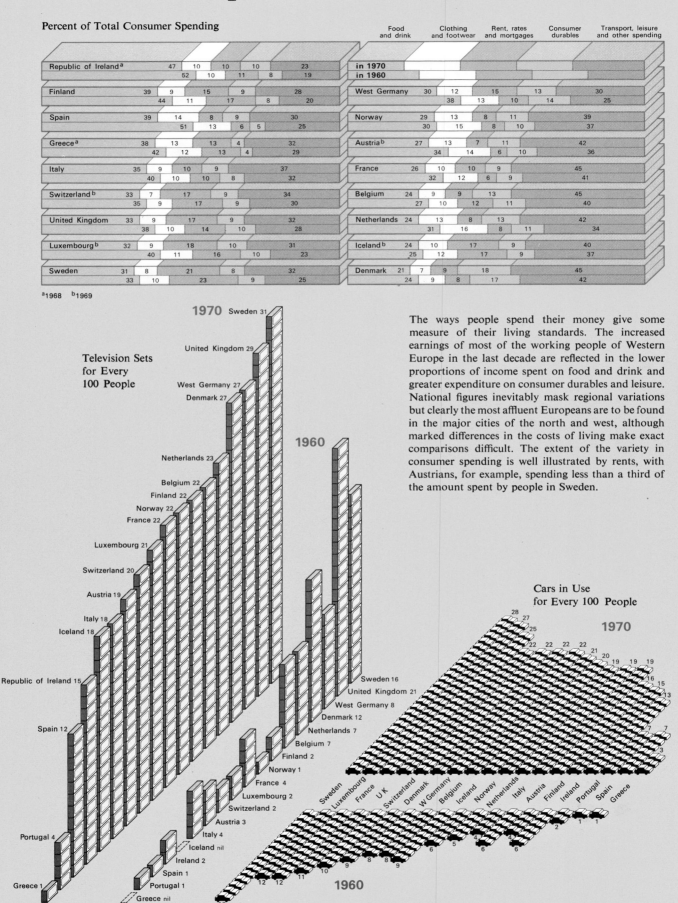

	Food and drink	Clothing and footwear	Rent, rates and mortgages	Consumer durables	Transport, leisure and other spending
Republic of Ireland[a] (1970)	47	10	10	10	23
Republic of Ireland (1960)	52	10	11	8	19
Finland (1970)	39	9	15	9	28
Finland (1960)	44	11	17	8	20
Spain (1970)	39	14	8	9	30
Spain (1960)	51	13	6	5	25
Greece[a] (1970)	38	13	13	4	32
Greece (1960)	42	12	13	4	29
Italy (1970)	35	9	10	9	37
Italy (1960)	40	10	10	8	32
Switzerland[b] (1970)	33	7	17	9	34
Switzerland (1960)	35	9	17	9	30
United Kingdom (1970)	33	9	17	9	32
United Kingdom (1960)	38	10	14	10	28
Luxembourg[b] (1970)	32	9	18	10	31
Luxembourg (1960)	40	11	16	10	23
Sweden (1970)	31	8	21	8	32
Sweden (1960)	33	10	23	9	25
West Germany (1970)	30	12	15	13	30
West Germany (1960)	38	13	10	14	25
Norway (1970)	29	13	8	11	39
Norway (1960)	30	15	8	10	37
Austria[b] (1970)	27	13	7	11	42
Austria (1960)	34	14	6	10	36
France (1970)	26	10	10	9	45
France (1960)	32	12	6	9	41
Belgium (1970)	24	9	13	9	45
Belgium (1960)	27	10	12	11	40
Netherlands (1970)	24	13	8	13	42
Netherlands (1960)	31	16	8	11	34
Iceland[b] (1970)	24	10	17	9	40
Iceland (1960)	25	12	17	9	37
Denmark (1970)	21	7	9	18	45
Denmark (1960)	24	9	8	17	42

[a]1968 [b]1969

Television Sets for Every 100 People

1970

Sweden 31
United Kingdom 29
West Germany 27
Denmark 27
Netherlands 23
Belgium 22
Finland 22
Norway 22
France 22
Luxembourg 21
Switzerland 20
Austria 19
Italy 18
Iceland 18
Republic of Ireland 15
Spain 12
Portugal 4
Greece 1

1960

Sweden 16
United Kingdom 21
West Germany 8
Denmark 12
Netherlands 7
Belgium 7
Finland 2
Norway 1
France 4
Luxembourg 2
Switzerland 2
Austria 3
Italy 4
Iceland nil
Ireland 2
Spain 1
Portugal 1
Greece nil

The ways people spend their money give some measure of their living standards. The increased earnings of most of the working people of Western Europe in the last decade are reflected in the lower proportions of income spent on food and drink and greater expenditure on consumer durables and leisure. National figures inevitably mask regional variations but clearly the most affluent Europeans are to be found in the major cities of the north and west, although marked differences in the costs of living make exact comparisons difficult. The extent of the variety in consumer spending is well illustrated by rents, with Austrians, for example, spending less than a third of the amount spent by people in Sweden.

Cars in Use for Every 100 People

1970: Sweden, Luxembourg, France, U K, Switzerland, Denmark, W Germany, Belgium, Iceland, Norway, Netherlands, Italy, Austria, Finland, Ireland, Portugal, Spain, Greece

28 27 25 22 22 22 21 20 19 19 19 16 15 13 7 7 3

1960: 16 12 12 11 10 9 8 8 6 5 4 4 2 1 1

Housing

The quality of housing is not simply a question of national wealth and personal income. The standard of the total housing stock and its annual replenishment can be affected by many variables such as the characteristics of population growth, the physical and social mobility of the people, custom, the general availability of building land, the problems of providing water and services in remote scattered communities, national differences in housing regulations and planning legislation, and the extent to which governments actively encourage house building and ownership. Clearly, however, the possession of a fixed bath or shower is still very much a luxury in over half the countries of Western Europe.

The Housing Record

Country	Number of Households 1970 or latest census (millions)	Owner Occupied (percent)	People per Room (average occupation)	Total Housing Stock in 1970 — percent without: piped water	flush toilet	fixed bath or shower	Dwellings Built average each year 1966 to 1970 (thousands)	per thousand population
West Germany	21.3	29	0.9	2	17	36	535	9.2
United Kingdom	18.1	50	0.6	1	2	16	396	7.2
France	15.7	45	0.9	7	47	51	550	11.0
Italy	14.8	46	1.1	28	10	71	303	5.7
Spain	8.4	60	1.0	52	34	76	260	7.9
Netherlands	3.5	26	0.8	10	32	73	122	9.6
Belgium	3.2	50	0.6	23	52	76	52	5.4
Sweden	2.9	36	0.8	5	15	27	103	13.0
Austria	2.5	48	0.9	15	30	45	50	6.8
Portugal	2.3	45	1.1	68	58	71	35	3.7
Greece	2.2	n a	1.5	29	85	89	105	12.0
Switzerland	1.9	34	0.7	4	1	31	66[a]	10.5[a]
Denmark	1.7	44	0.8	3	9	37	45	9.3
Finland	1.4	61	1.3	53	65	85[b]	40	8.6
Norway	1.2	53	0.8	6	42	55	35	9.2
Rep. of Ireland	0.7	60	0.9	43	46	67	12	4.2
Luxembourg	0.1	55	0.6	1	18	54	1.8[a]	5.3[a]
Iceland	0.05	71	0.9	1	13	30	1.6	8.1

[a] 1970 only   [b] excludes dwellings with sauna facilities   © Bartholomew/Warne 1974

Life and Health

Twenty Years' Progress I. Longer Lives

The average life expectation of people born in

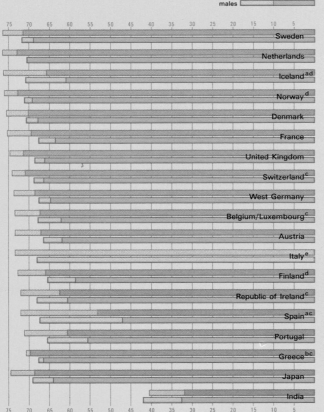

	1970	1950
females		
males		

Sweden
Netherlands
Iceland[ad]
Norway[d]
Denmark
France
United Kingdom
Switzerland[c]
West Germany
Belgium/Luxembourg[c]
Austria
Italy[e]
Finland[d]
Republic of Ireland[c]
Spain[ac]
Portugal
Greece[bc]
Japan
India

[a]1940 not 1950 [b]1955–59 [c]1960 not 1970 [d]1965 not 1970 [e]only 1970 figures available

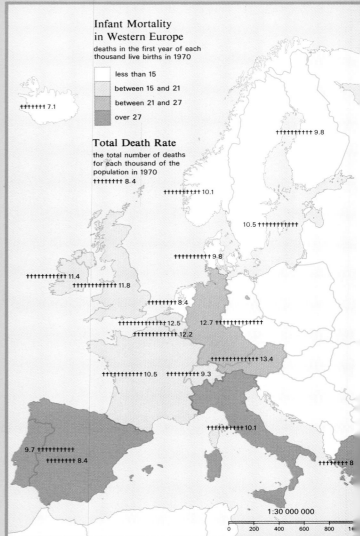

Infant Mortality
in Western Europe
deaths in the first year of each
thousand live births in 1970

- less than 15
- between 15 and 21
- between 21 and 27
- over 27

Total Death Rate
the total number of deaths
for each thousand of the
population in 1970

††††††† 7.1
†††††††††† 9.8
††††††† 8.4
††††††††† 10.1
10.5 †††††††††††
†††††††††† 9.8
†††††††††††† 11.4
†††††††††††† 11.8
†††††††† 8.4
†††††††††††††† 12.5
12.7 †††††††††††††
†††††††††††† 12.2
††††††††††††††† 13.4
†††††††††††† 10.5
†††††††††† 9.3
†††††††††† 10.1
9.7 ††††††††††
††††††† 8.4
†††††† 8

1:30 000 000

0   200   400   600   800   1

Twenty Years' Progress II. The Shift to More Care

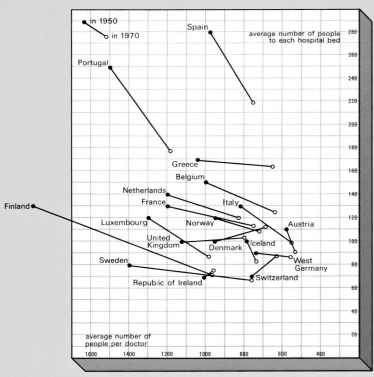

● in 1950
○ in 1970

Spain

Portugal

average number of people
to each hospital bed

Greece
Belgium
Netherlands
France
Italy
Luxembourg
Norway
Austria
United Kingdom
Denmark
Iceland
Sweden
West Germany
Republic of Ireland
Switzerland
Finland

average number of
people per doctor

1600   1400   1200   1000   800   600   400

280
260
240
220
200
180
160
140
120
100
80
60
40
20

National Health Services

Despite the universal improvement of health and medical services throughout Western Europe there are still wide differences between countries. Certainly the survival rate of the Swedish new-born and the longevity of its citizens compared with say Portugal would appear to reflect the substantial difference in expenditure on health between the two countries.

Such generalizations naturally hide regional differences in the medical care provided. In most countries the availability of specialist doctors and hospital facilities tends to be concentrated in the capital and major cities. In France, for example, only twelve per cent of all doctors practice in rural areas although these contain over thirty per cent of the total population. Yet by world standards the worst in Europe is incomparably better than in the developing nations. In Nigeria, as an instance, the life expectancy is half that prevailing in Western Europe and the extent of medical care can be judged by a ratio of physicians to people reaching one in twenty-four thousand.

Marked variations are also apparent in the extent to which medical services are used. Thus the very high accident rate in France and the high rate of suicides in Austria must make considerably greater demands on medical services than in other European countries. Similarly, doctors specialising in heart diseases could expect to find over twice the work in the United Kingdom as in Greece. In fact, the geographical variations in the incidence of diseases pose many questions not least being why heart disease, cancer, strokes and respiratory disease rates should be significantly higher in Austria, the United Kingdom and West Germany than in Iceland, the Netherlands and Spain.

© Bartholomew/Warne 1974

Health and Death

Spending on Health in 1970

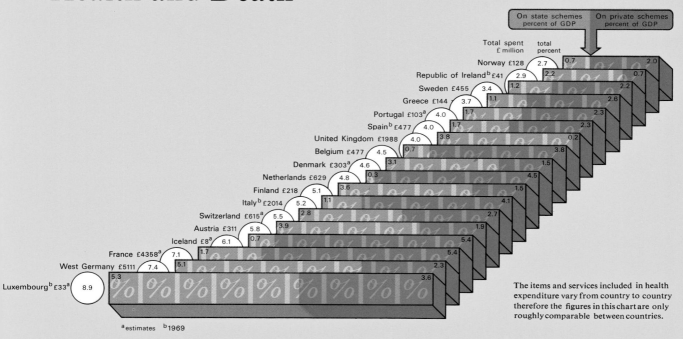

Country	Total spent £ million	total percent	On state schemes percent of GDP	On private schemes percent of GDP
Norway	£128	2.7	0.7	2.0
Republic of Ireland[b]	£41	2.9	2.2	0.7
Sweden	£455	3.4	1.2	2.2
Greece	£144	3.7	1.1	2.6
Portugal	£103[a]	4.0	1.7	2.3
Spain[b]	£477	4.0	1.7	2.3
United Kingdom	£1988	4.0	3.8	0.2
Belgium	£477	4.5	0.7	3.8
Denmark	£303[a]	4.6	3.1	1.5
Netherlands	£629	4.8	0.3	4.5
Finland	£218	5.1	3.6	1.5
Italy[b]	£2014	5.2	1.1	4.1
Switzerland	£615[a]	5.5	2.8	2.7
Austria	£311	5.8	3.9	1.9
Iceland	£8[a]	6.1	0.7	5.4
France	£4358[a]	7.1	1.7	5.4
West Germany	£5111	7.4	5.1	2.3
Luxembourg[b]	£33[a]	8.9	5.3	3.6

[a] estimates   [b] 1969

The items and services included in health expenditure vary from country to country therefore the figures in this chart are only roughly comparable between countries.

Causes of Death

Deaths per 100 thousand population in 1970

Country	Deaths in 1970 (thousands)	motor accidents	other accidents	heart diseases	strokes; cerebrovascular diseases	respiratory diseases; flu, pneumonia, bronchitis, etc.	cancer; malignant cell growth	suicide	other causes	total crude death rate[c]
Austria	99	34	45	363	199	98	262	24	312	1337
West Germany	744	31	32	335	186	86	243	21	334	1268
Belgium	120	27	39	329	170	71	240	15	358	1249
Luxembourg	4.2	39	40	324	117	44	247	14	398	1223
United Kingdom	655	14	22	385	166	160	237	8	191	1183
Republic of Ireland	34	16	27	362	156	161	188	2	232	1144
France	535	23	51	207	146	42	206	15	364	1054
Sweden	83	17	26	384	109	74	203	22	210	1045
Norway	39	15	36	327	159	88	188	8	192	1013
Italy	533	23	22	298	136	90	174	5	262	1010
Denmark	48	26	25	337	102	55	221	21	193	980
Finland	46	23	36	348	137	72	166	23	173	978
Portugal	93	20	25	147	179	110	113	8	365	967
Switzerland	58	26	35	260	97	58	194	19	243	932
Greece	74	12	27	161	117	74	131	3	317	842
Netherlands	110	24	25	256	97	55	195	8	181	841
Spain	277	13	24	185	109	73	131	5	299	839
Iceland	1.5	15	47	228	94	61	131	13	125	714

[c] see Glossary

Education

Education is variously interpreted throughout Western Europe. From pre-school to adult education wide differences exist in curriculum content, school routine, the place of private schools, the provision of further education, the training of teachers and even the length of compulsory full-time education. Moves towards greater co-operation between countries require extensive modifications to teaching methods, text books, examination systems, university standards and professional training. The closest yet to a truly European education is provided by the International Schools in Brussels, Luxembourg and Geneva and some of the schools set up to meet the educational needs of the mobile multi-national communities in the capitals and major business centres of Europe.

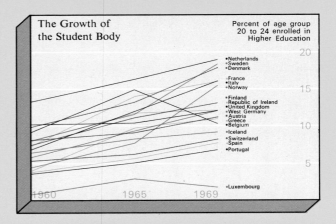

The Growth of the Student Body

Percent of age group 20 to 24 enrolled in Higher Education

- Netherlands
- Sweden
- Denmark
- France
- Italy
- Norway
- Finland
- Republic of Ireland
- United Kingdom
- West Germany
- Austria
- Greece
- Belgium
- Iceland
- Switzerland
- Spain
- Portugal
- Luxembourg

1960   1965   1969

Student Population

compulsory education   regional variation

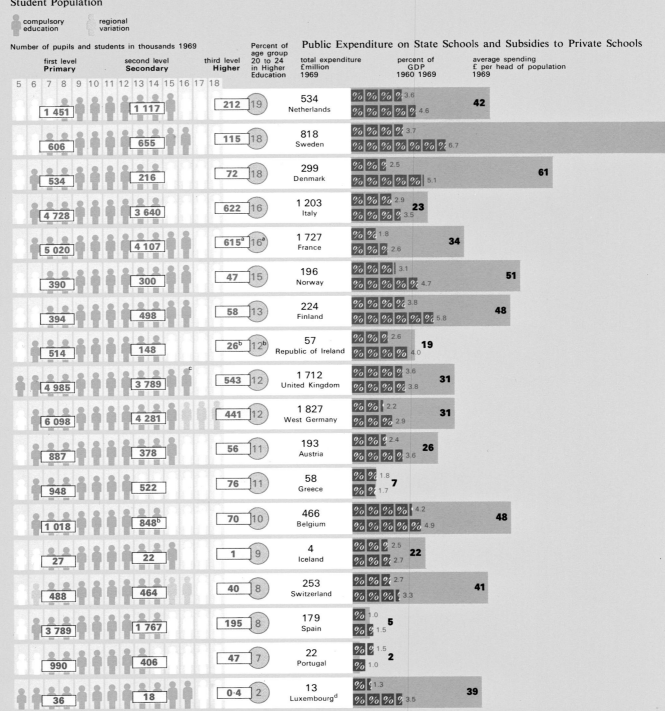

Number of pupils and students in thousands 1969				Percent of age group 20 to 24 in Higher Education	Public Expenditure on State Schools and Subsidies to Private Schools		
first level **Primary**		second level **Secondary**	third level **Higher**		total expenditure £million 1969	percent of GDP 1960 1969	average spending £ per head of population 1969
1 451		1 117	212	19	534 Netherlands	3.6 / 4.6	42
606		655	115	18	818 Sweden	3.7 / 6.7	1.
534		216	72	18	299 Denmark	2.5 / 5.1	61
4 728		3 640	622	16	1 203 Italy	2.9 / 3.5	23
5 020		4 107	615[a]	16[a]	1 727 France	1.8 / 2.6	34
390		300	47	15	196 Norway	3.1 / 4.7	51
394		498	58	13	224 Finland	3.8 / 5.8	48
514		148	26[b]	12[b]	57 Republic of Ireland	2.6 / 4.0	19
4 985		3 789	543	12	1 712 United Kingdom	3.6 / 3.8	31
6 098		4 281	441	12	1 827 West Germany	2.2 / 2.9	31
887		378	56	11	193 Austria	2.4 / 3.6	26
948		522	76	11	58 Greece	1.8 / 1.7	7
1 018		848[b]	70	10	466 Belgium	4.2 / 4.9	48
27		22	1	9	4 Iceland	2.5 / 2.7	22
488		464	40	8	253 Switzerland	2.7 / 3.3	41
3 789		1 767	195	8	179 Spain	1.0 / 1.5	5
990		406	47	7	22 Portugal	1.5 / 1.0	2
36		18	0·4	2	13 Luxembourg[d]	1.3 / 3.5	39

[a] public universities only   [b] 1968   [c] 1972   [d] education is compulsory from the age of 4

Universities

number of students in thousands in 1970
- under 2000
- 2000 to 5000
- 5000 to 10 000
- 10 000 to 20 000
- over 20 000
- universities founded between 1960 and 1970
- technical universities/polytechnics (unnamed)

The definition of a university varies from country to country and most university towns also have other degree awarding institutes of higher education.

The increased flow of students resulting from national policies encouraging higher education for all is being partially met by the foundation of many new universities. A range of other advanced institutions called technical universities and polytechnics also exists to provide a broader, vocational education and it is difficult to distinguish clearly many of these from universities proper. In the universities the proportion of women to men students, although increasing, still rarely exceeds three in ten.

[a] reconstructed foundation

67

1:15 000 000

0 100 200 300 400 500 600 700 800 900 1000 km

© Bartholomew/Warne 1974

The Tourist Business

Tourism is big business in Europe. Most of the countries of Western Europe, with the notable exceptions of West Germany and Sweden, receive a net inflow of money from tourism. For some such as Austria, Ireland and Spain, tourist expenditure forms a significant part of their gross national product.

Increasing affluence and leisure time has made it possible to consider holidays abroad, but the main factor has been the new mobility made possible by widespread ownership of motor cars and the massive expansion of chartered air touring in the hands of package tour operators.

The main boom in tourism has been in the Mediterranean countries which are usually able to provide hot sun and blue skies over their beaches in the peak holiday months of July and August. In winter, too, they compete with the traditional skiing centres of the north by offering cheap off-season escapes to warmer conditions.

The map opposite brings out the significant southerly component of tourist movements in Europe. Countries such as France, Switzerland and Austria benefit from being *en route* to the major tourist sunspots along the Mediterranean coast. Increasing use of air charter and motorail will, however, reduce the value of this transit trade.

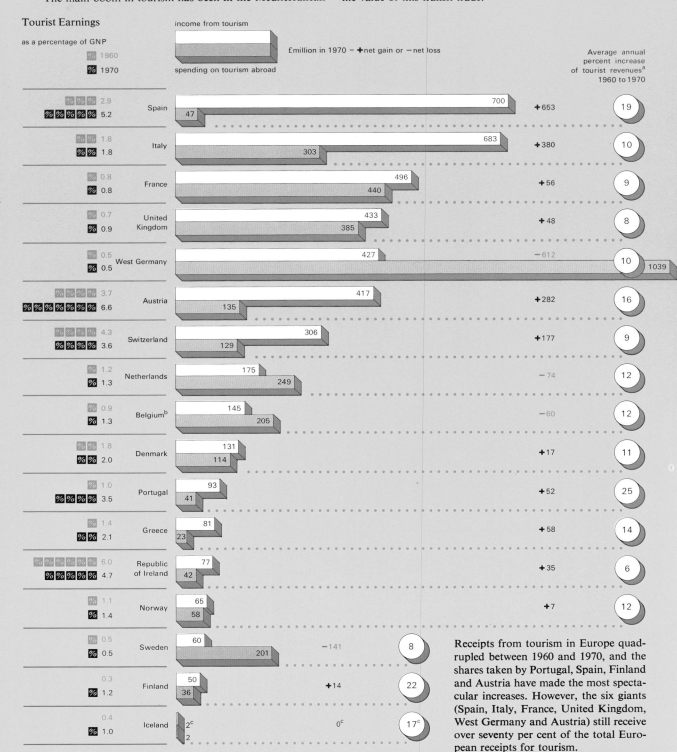

Tourist Earnings

as a percentage of GNP

% 1960
% 1970

income from tourism

spending on tourism abroad

£million in 1970 = +net gain or −net loss

Average annual percent increase of tourist revenues[a] 1960 to 1970

Country	1960	1970	income from tourism	spending abroad	net	avg annual % increase
Spain	2.9	5.2	700	47	+653	19
Italy	1.8	1.8	683	303	+380	10
France	0.8	0.8	496	440	+56	9
United Kingdom	0.7	0.9	433	385	+48	8
West Germany	0.5	0.5	427	1039	−612	10
Austria	3.7	6.6	417	135	+282	16
Switzerland	4.3	3.6	306	129	+177	9
Netherlands	1.2	1.3	175	249	−74	12
Belgium[b]	0.9	1.3	145	205	−60	12
Denmark	1.8	2.0	131	114	+17	11
Portugal	1.0	3.5	93	41	+52	25
Greece	1.4	2.1	81	23	+58	14
Republic of Ireland	6.0	4.7	77	42	+35	6
Norway	1.1	1.4	65	58	+7	12
Sweden	0.5	0.5	60	201	−141	8
Finland	0.3	1.2	50	36	+14	22
Iceland	0.4	1.0	2[c]	2	0[c]	17[c]

Receipts from tourism in Europe quadrupled between 1960 and 1970, and the shares taken by Portugal, Spain, Finland and Austria have made the most spectacular increases. However, the six giants (Spain, Italy, France, United Kingdom, West Germany and Austria) still receive over seventy per cent of the total European receipts for tourism.

[a]in terms of European Communities unit of account, "Eur"
[b]Luxembourg is included with Belgium   [c]estimated

© Bartholomew/Warne 1974

International Travel

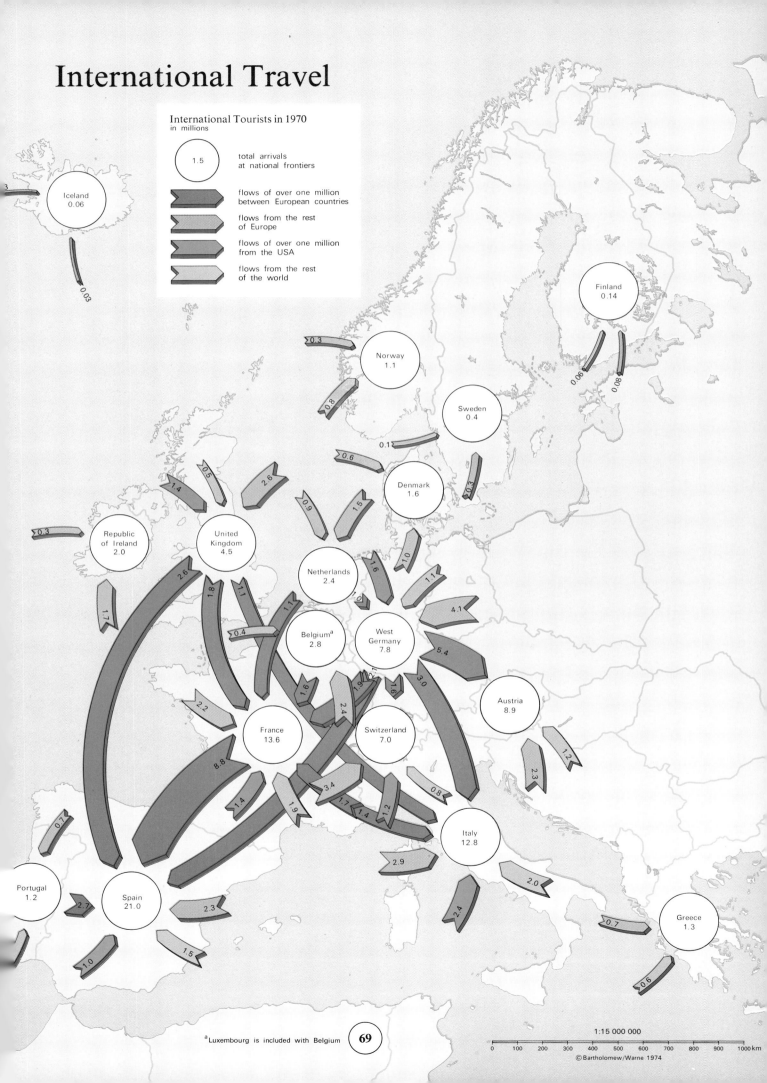

International Tourists in 1970
in millions

1.5 — total arrivals at national frontiers

flows of over one million between European countries

flows from the rest of Europe

flows of over one million from the USA

flows from the rest of the world

Iceland 0.06

Finland 0.14

Norway 1.1

Sweden 0.4

Denmark 1.6

Republic of Ireland 2.0

United Kingdom 4.5

Netherlands 2.4

Belgium[a] 2.8

West Germany 7.8

Austria 8.9

France 13.6

Switzerland 7.0

Italy 12.8

Portugal 1.2

Spain 21.0

Greece 1.3

[a] Luxembourg is included with Belgium

69

1:15 000 000

0 100 200 300 400 500 600 700 800 900 1000 km

© Bartholomew/Warne 1974

Competition for Land

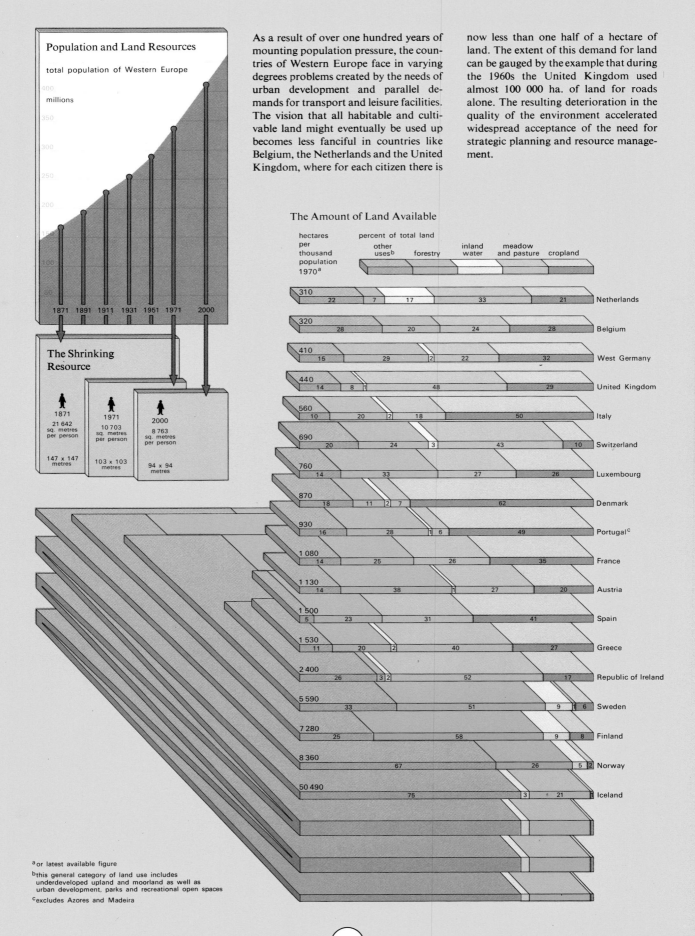

Population and Land Resources

total population of Western Europe

400 millions

350

300

250

200

150

100

50

1871 1891 1911 1931 1951 1971 2000

The Shrinking Resource

1871
21 642
sq. metres
per person

147 x 147
metres

1971
10 703
sq. metres
per person

103 x 103
metres

2000
8 763
sq. metres
per person

94 x 94
metres

As a result of over one hundred years of mounting population pressure, the countries of Western Europe face in varying degrees problems created by the needs of urban development and parallel demands for transport and leisure facilities. The vision that all habitable and cultivable land might eventually be used up becomes less fanciful in countries like Belgium, the Netherlands and the United Kingdom, where for each citizen there is now less than one half of a hectare of land. The extent of this demand for land can be gauged by the example that during the 1960s the United Kingdom used almost 100 000 ha. of land for roads alone. The resulting deterioration in the quality of the environment accelerated widespread acceptance of the need for strategic planning and resource management.

The Amount of Land Available

hectares per thousand population 1970[a]

percent of total land

	other uses[b]	forestry	inland water	meadow and pasture	cropland	
310	22	7	17	33	21	Netherlands
320	28	20		24	28	Belgium
410	15	29	2	22	32	West Germany
440	14	8	1	48	29	United Kingdom
560	10	20	2	18	50	Italy
690	20	24	3	43	10	Switzerland
760	14	33		27	26	Luxembourg
870	18	11	2 7	62		Denmark
930	16	28	1 6	49		Portugal[c]
1 080	14	25		26	35	France
1 130	14	38	1	27	20	Austria
1 500	5	23		31	41	Spain
1 530	11	20	2	40	27	Greece
2 400	26	3 2		52	17	Republic of Ireland
5 590	33		51	9 1	6	Sweden
7 280	25		58	9	8	Finland
8 360	67			26	5 2	Norway
50 490	75		3	21	1	Iceland

[a] or latest available figure

[b] this general category of land use includes underdeveloped upland and moorland as well as urban development, parks and recreational open spaces

[c] excludes Azores and Madeira

Europe's Countryside

National Parks 1971

▦ national parks, state reserves and protected areas

▢ other areas of outstanding natural beauty

Note that extensive areas of great natural beauty are not 'protected' and are not therefore designated as National Parks.

Urban and Other Land: Land is a fixed resource, except where special opportunities exist for reclamation from the sea as in the Netherlands, and most of Western Europe's fertile and accessible land is already in use for farming and forestry. What is left is either economically useless for reasons of slope, climate, soil or remoteness or has been converted to urban uses. In Austria, Finland, Iceland, Ireland, Norway, Sweden and Switzerland the proportion of undeveloped land is high, but for the other countries much of what is neither farmed nor forested is given over to urban needs.

Changing Land Use: The diagram shows that the countries with the greatest population pressures are using their available farmland to satisfy growing urban needs. Only in Finland, France, Greece, Ireland, Norway, Portugal, Spain and Switzerland is land being found to increase the area used for farming and forestry.

Concern over the wise use of the natural environment has been intensified by the increasing pace of urban requirements for space and the acceptance of the relationship between environmental capacity and population growth. One outcome of this has been moves to designate substantial areas of land in most of the eighteen countries as 'protected environment' in the form of national parks, nature reserves and areas of outstanding natural beauty or of scientific or historic value. Conservation planning, at present, is entirely piecemeal.

1:30 000 000

0 200 400 600 800 1000 km

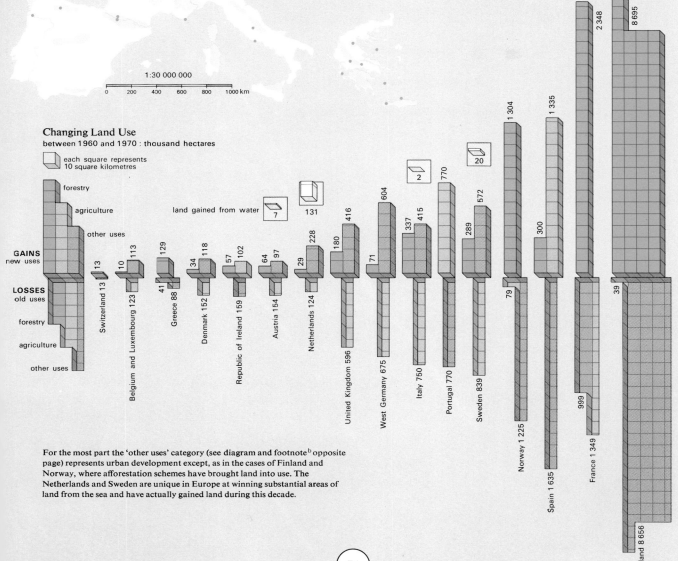

Changing Land Use
between 1960 and 1970 : thousand hectares

▱ each square represents 10 square kilometres

forestry
agriculture
other uses

land gained from water

GAINS new uses

LOSSES old uses

forestry
agriculture
other uses

For the most part the 'other uses' category (see diagram and footnote[b] opposite page) represents urban development except, as in the cases of Finland and Norway, where afforestation schemes have brought land into use. The Netherlands and Sweden are unique in Europe at winning substantial areas of land from the sea and have actually gained land during this decade.

Regional Planning

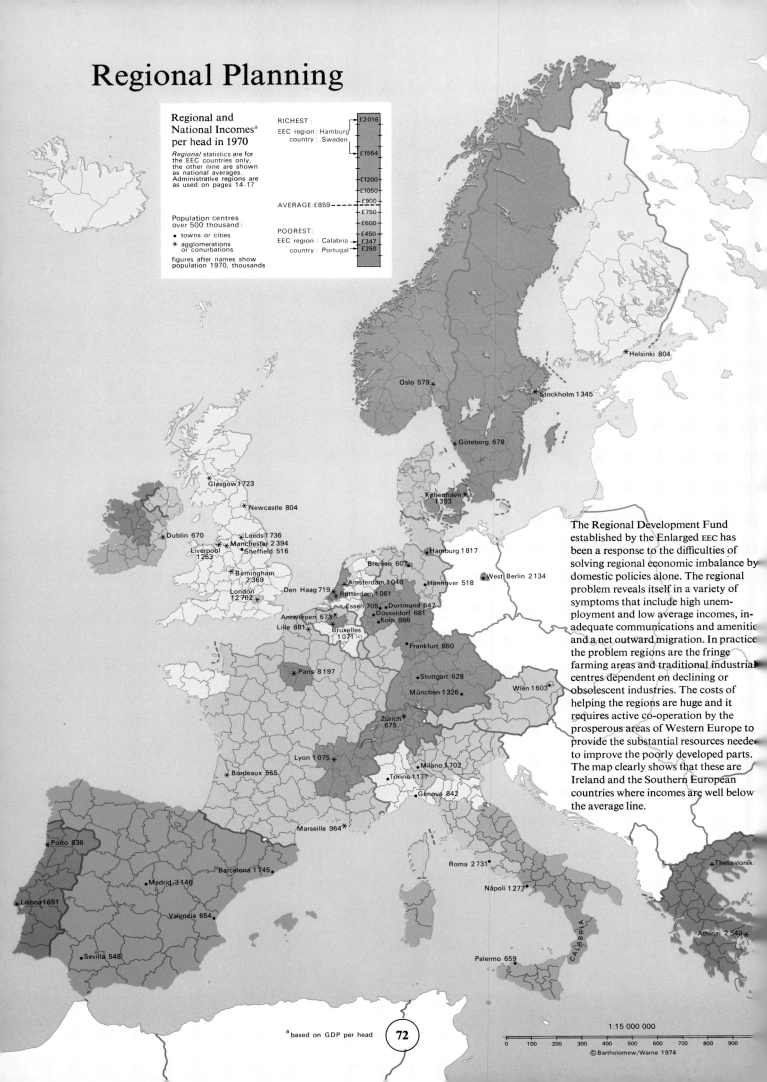

Regional and National Incomes[a] per head in 1970

Regional statistics are for the EEC countries only, the other nine are shown as national averages. Administrative regions are as used on pages 14-17

Population centres over 500 thousand :

- • towns or cities
- ✳ agglomerations or conurbations

figures after names show population 1970, thousands

RICHEST :
EEC region : Hamburg
country : Sweden

£2016
£1554
£1200
£1050
£900
AVERAGE:£859
£750
£600
£450
£347
£250

POOREST :
EEC region : Calabria
country : Portugal

The Regional Development Fund established by the Enlarged EEC has been a response to the difficulties of solving regional economic imbalance by domestic policies alone. The regional problem reveals itself in a variety of symptoms that include high unemployment and low average incomes, inadequate communications and amenities and a net outward migration. In practice the problem regions are the fringe farming areas and traditional industrial centres dependent on declining or obsolescent industries. The costs of helping the regions are huge and it requires active co-operation by the prosperous areas of Western Europe to provide the substantial resources needed to improve the poorly developed parts. The map clearly shows that these are Ireland and the Southern European countries where incomes are well below the average line.

Helsinki 804

Oslo 579
Stockholm 1345

Göteborg 678

Glasgow 1723

Newcastle 804

København 1383

Dublin 670
Leeds 1736
Manchester 2394
Liverpool 1263
Sheffield 516

Hamburg 1817

Bremen 607
West Berlin 2134

Birmingham 2369

Amsterdam 1040
Hannover 518

Den Haag 719
Rotterdam 1061

London 12762

Essen 705
Dortmund 647
Düsseldorf 681
Köln 866

Antwerpen 673
Lille 881
Bruxelles 1071

Frankfurt 660

Paris 8197

Stuttgart 628
München 1326
Wien 1603

Zürich 675

Lyon 1075

Milano 1702
Torino 1177

Bordeaux 555

Génova 842

Marseille 964

Porto 836

Thessaloník

Barcelona 1745
Roma 2731

Madrid 3146
Nápoli 1277

Lisboa 1651
Valencia 654

CALABRIA

Athinai 2540

Sevilla 548

Palermo 659

[a] based on GDP per head

72

1:15 000 000

0 100 200 300 400 500 600 700 800 900

© Bartholomew/Warne 1974

Business in Europe

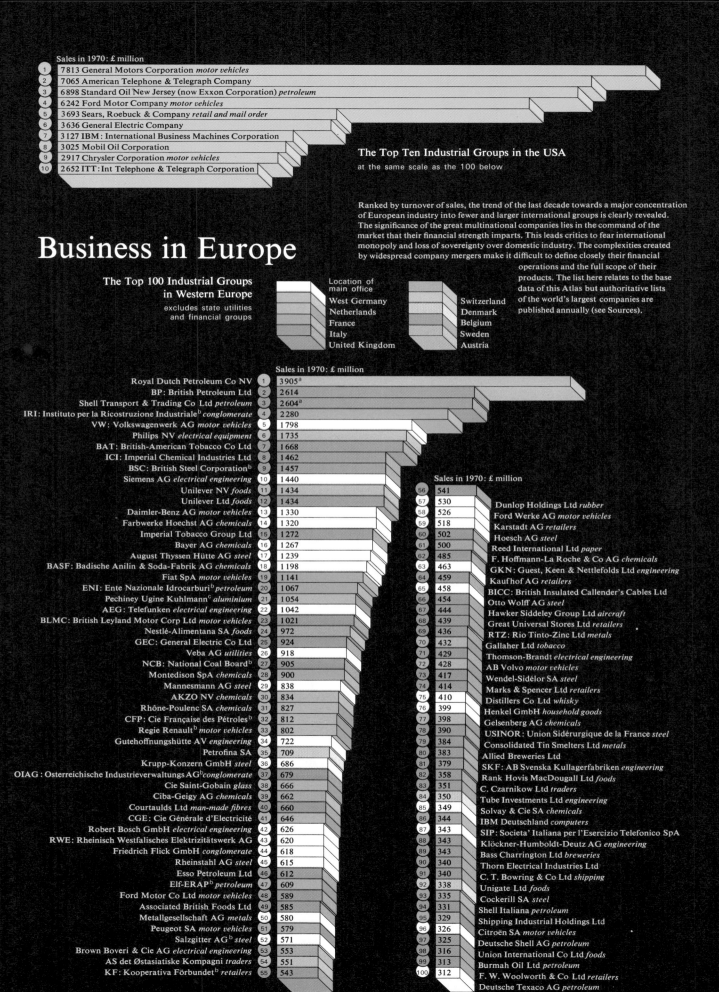

The Top Ten Industrial Groups in the USA
at the same scale as the 100 below

Sales in 1970: £ million

#		Sales
1	7813 General Motors Corporation *motor vehicles*	
2	7065 American Telephone & Telegraph Company	
3	6898 Standard Oil New Jersey (now Exxon Corporation) *petroleum*	
4	6242 Ford Motor Company *motor vehicles*	
5	3693 Sears, Roebuck & Company *retail and mail order*	
6	3636 General Electric Company	
7	3127 IBM: International Business Machines Corporation	
8	3025 Mobil Oil Corporation	
9	2917 Chrysler Corporation *motor vehicles*	
10	2652 ITT: Int Telephone & Telegraph Corporation	

Ranked by turnover of sales, the trend of the last decade towards a major concentration of European industry into fewer and larger international groups is clearly revealed. The significance of the great multinational companies lies in the command of the market that their financial strength imparts. This leads critics to fear international monopoly and loss of sovereignty over domestic industry. The complexities created by widespread company mergers make it difficult to define closely their financial operations and the full scope of their products. The list here relates to the base data of this Atlas but authoritative lists of the world's largest companies are published annually (see Sources).

The Top 100 Industrial Groups in Western Europe
excludes state utilities and financial groups

Location of main office
- West Germany
- Netherlands
- France
- Italy
- United Kingdom
- Switzerland
- Denmark
- Belgium
- Sweden
- Austria

Sales in 1970: £ million

#	Company	Sales
1	Royal Dutch Petroleum Co NV	3905[a]
2	BP: British Petroleum Ltd	2614
3	Shell Transport & Trading Co Ltd *petroleum*	2604[a]
4	IRI: Instituto per la Ricostruzione Industriale[b] *conglomerate*	2280
5	VW: Volkswagenwerk AG *motor vehicles*	1798
6	Philips NV *electrical equipment*	1735
7	BAT: British-American Tobacco Co Ltd	1668
8	ICI: Imperial Chemical Industries Ltd	1462
9	BSC: British Steel Corporation[b]	1457
10	Siemens AG *electrical engineering*	1440
11	Unilever NV *foods*	1434
12	Unilever Ltd *foods*	1434
13	Daimler-Benz AG *motor vehicles*	1330
14	Farbwerke Hoechst AG *chemicals*	1320
15	Imperial Tobacco Group Ltd	1272
16	Bayer AG *chemicals*	1267
17	August Thyssen Hütte AG *steel*	1239
18	BASF: Badische Anilin & Soda-Fabrik AG *chemicals*	1198
19	Fiat SpA *motor vehicles*	1141
20	ENI: Ente Nazionale Idrocarburi[b] *petroleum*	1067
21	Pechiney Ugine Kuhlmann[c] *aluminium*	1054
22	AEG: Telefunken *electrical engineering*	1042
23	BLMC: British Leyland Motor Corp Ltd *motor vehicles*	1021
24	Nestlé-Alimentana SA *foods*	972
25	GEC: General Electric Co Ltd	924
26	Veba AG *utilities*	918
27	NCB: National Coal Board[b]	905
28	Montedison SpA *chemicals*	900
29	Mannesmann AG *steel*	838
30	AKZO NV *chemicals*	834
31	Rhône-Poulenc SA *chemicals*	827
32	CFP: Cie Française des Pétroles[b]	812
33	Regie Renault[b] *motor vehicles*	802
34	Gutehoffnungshütte AV *engineering*	722
35	Petrofina SA	709
36	Krupp-Konzern GmbH *steel*	686
37	OIAG: Osterreichische Industrieverwaltungs AG[b]*conglomerate*	679
38	Cie Saint-Gobain *glass*	666
39	Ciba-Geigy AG *chemicals*	662
40	Courtaulds Ltd *man-made fibres*	660
41	CGE: Cie Générale d'Electricité	646
42	Robert Bosch GmbH *electrical engineering*	626
43	RWE: Rheinisch Westfalisches Elektrizitätswerk AG	620
44	Friedrich Flick GmbH *conglomerate*	618
45	Rheinstahl AG *steel*	615
46	Esso Petroleum Ltd	612
47	Elf-ERAP[b] *petroleum*	609
48	Ford Motor Co Ltd *motor vehicles*	589
49	Associated British Foods Ltd	585
50	Metallgesellschaft AG *metals*	580
51	Peugeot SA *motor vehicles*	579
52	Salzgitter AG[b] *steel*	571
53	Brown Boveri & Cie AG *electrical engineering*	553
54	AS det Østasiatiske Kompagni *traders*	551
55	KF: Kooperativa Förbundet[b] *retailers*	543
56	Dunlop Holdings Ltd *rubber*	541
57	Ford Werke AG *motor vehicles*	530
58	Karstadt AG *retailers*	526
59	Hoesch AG *steel*	518
60	Reed International Ltd *paper*	502
61	F. Hoffmann-La Roche & Co AG *chemicals*	500
62	GKN: Guest, Keen & Nettlefolds Ltd *engineering*	485
63	Kaufhof AG *retailers*	463
64	BICC: British Insulated Callender's Cables Ltd	459
65	Otto Wolff AG *steel*	458
66	Hawker Siddeley Group Ltd *aircraft*	454
67	Great Universal Stores Ltd *retailers*	444
68	RTZ: Rio Tinto-Zinc Ltd *metals*	439
69	Gallaher Ltd *tobacco*	436
70	Thomson-Brandt *electrical engineering*	432
71	AB Volvo *motor vehicles*	429
72	Wendel-Sidélor SA *steel*	428
73	Marks & Spencer Ltd *retailers*	417
74	Distillers Co Ltd *whisky*	414
75	Henkel GmbH *household goods*	410
76	Gelsenberg AG *chemicals*	399
77	USINOR: Union Sidérurgique de la France *steel*	398
78	Consolidated Tin Smelters Ltd *metals*	390
79	Allied Breweries Ltd	384
80	SKF: AB Svenska Kullagerfabriken *engineering*	383
81	Rank Hovis MacDougall Ltd *foods*	379
82	C. Czarnikow Ltd *traders*	358
83	Tube Investments Ltd *engineering*	351
84	Solvay & Cie SA *chemicals*	350
85	IBM Deutschland *computers*	349
86	SIP: Societa' Italiana per l'Esercizio Telefonico SpA	344
87	Klöckner-Humboldt-Deutz AG *engineering*	343
88	Bass Charrington Ltd *breweries*	343
89	Thorn Electrical Industries Ltd	343
90	C. T. Bowring & Co Ltd *shipping*	340
91	Unigate Ltd *foods*	340
92	Cockerill SA *steel*	338
93	Shell Italiana *petroleum*	335
94	Shipping Industrial Holdings Ltd	331
95	Citroën SA *motor vehicles*	329
96	Deutsche Shell AG *petroleum*	326
97	Union International Co Ltd *foods*	325
98	Burmah Oil Ltd *petroleum*	316
99	F. W. Woolworth & Co Ltd *retailers*	313
100	Deutsche Texaco AG *petroleum*	312

Investment and Money

	GROSS FIXED CAPITAL INVESTMENT		DIRECT INVESTMENT 1970		MONEY SUPPLY 1970		SECURITY ISSUES £million 1970		
Percent of Gross Domestic Product (1)		Total in 1970 £million (2)	Inward £million and per cent of ② (3)	Outward (4)	Total £million (5)	£ per person (6)	Domestic market shares (7)	market bonds (8)	International market bonds (9)
23.7 in 1960	Switzerland	£2 390ᵃ	...ᵇ	...	£4 354	£692	£242	£362	—
29.0ᵃ in 1970			...ᵇ	...	53% of GDP				
26.6	Greece	£1 112	£133ᵃ	£4ᵃ	£758	£86	...	...	—
27.8			12.0%	0.4%	19% of GDP				
28.5	Norway	£1 246	£11	£13	£1 004	£258	£37	£179	£38
26.9			0.9%	1.1%	21% of GDP				
24.9	Austria	£1 583	£39	£28	£1 126	£152	£109	£91	—
26.5			2.5%	1.8%	19% of GDP				
24.0	West Germany	£20 615	£125	£286	£11 692	£192	£409	£1 745	£50
26.4			0.6%	1.4%	15% of GDP				
20.4	France	£15 694	£259	£155	£17 565	£344	£652	£783	£106
25.9			1.7%	1.0%	29% of GDP				
27.3	Finland	£1 117	£7	£22	£342	£73	£133	£49	£20
25.8			0.7%	1.9%	8% of GDP				
23.8	Netherlands	£3 389	£223	£213	£2 987	£228	£25	£272	£101
25.7			6.6%	6.3%	23% of GDP				
21.9	Luxembourg	£111	*included with Belgium*		£257	£756	...	...	—
25.7					60% of GDP				
29.4	Iceland	£49	£2.1ᵃ	£0.2ᵃ	£22	£107	...	...	—
24.4			4.2%	0.4%	11% of GDP				
19.1	Belgium	£2 414	£132	£65	£3 487	£361	£190	£785	—
22.6			5.2%	2.6%	33% of GDP				
19.4	Denmark	£1 432	£43	£12	£1 549	£313	£115	£369	£38
22.0			3.0%	0.8%	24% of GDP				
14.0	Republic of Ireland	£356	£17ᵃ	£2ᵃ	£295	£100	...	...	£18
22.0			4.7%	0.7%	18% of GDP				
21.2	Sweden	£2 971	£45	£81	£1 430	£177	£43	£631	£27
21.7			1.5%	2.7%	10% of GDP				
19.4	Spain	£2 869	£92	£18	£4 404	£130	£394	£265	£12
21.3			3.2%	0.6%	33% of GDP				
22.1	Italy	£8 201	£252	£45	£20 887	£389	£740	£1 883	£151
21.2			3.1%	0.6%	54% of GDP				
16.2	United Kingdom	£9 223	£339ᶜ	£508ᵈ	£9 635	£174	£77	£612	£97
18.5			3.7%	5.5%	19% of GDP				
17.4	Portugal	£451	£9ᵉ	£3ᵉ	£1 342	£151	£67	£11	—
17.8			1.9%	0.6%	53% of GDP				

(1) & (2) **Gross Fixed Capital Investment** includes both public and private sector investment in industrial and residential building and the infrastructure as well as in plant and machinery and transport equipment. It also includes any expenditure incurred in improving the availability of natural resources such as afforestation and agricultural investment in livestock.

ᵃ estimates
ᵇ mainly monetary flows
ᶜ excludes oil and insurance
ᵈ excludes oil
ᵉ Escudo area

... nil or negligible
— not available

(3) & (4) **Direct Investment Flows** exclude portfolio investments in securities. Flows into a country from abroad are not valued on the same basis as flows going out from a country, therefore per cent figure estimated.

(5) & (6) **Money Supply** is defined here as notes and coins in circulation and demand deposits with the national banking sector. Other forms of credit are not counted.

(7) & (8) These **Shares and Bonds** are the issues made on national markets.

(9) **The International Bond Market**: These are issues placed on the market of two or more countries. Some £25 million were also issued in European Monetary Units and £22 million in EUR (European Unit of Account) in 1970. The world market at that time totalled £1 467 mn — Western Europe issued £658 mn (45 per cent); USA £335 mn and Japan £45 mn.

National Accounts

A country's total transactions with the rest of the world

RECEIPTS / PAYMENTS	from EXPORTS / for IMPORTS	from INVESTMENTS / to INVESTORS	from TOURISM[a] / for TOURISM[a]	from TRANSPORT / for TRANSPORT	other receipts / other payments	average 1966 to 1970 total / total 1970	£ per head / = number of weeks purchase of imports
£17 384	82 West Germany	3	3	5	7	£3 780 mn	£63
£16 040	73	4	7	7	9	£5 671 mn = 24 weeks	
£3 504	80 Sweden	2	2	12	4	£334 mn	£42
£3 571	78[b]	1	6	10[b]	5	£317 mn = 6 weeks	
£1 201	80 Finland	1	5	9	5	£126 mn	£27
£1 299	81[b]	4	3	7[b]	5	£200 mn = 9 weeks	
£5 326	76 Belgium & Luxembourg	7	3	5	9	£997 mn	£100
£4 957	75	7	4	5	9	£1 186 mn = 13 weeks	
£6 135	75 Netherlands	7	3	8	7	£1 072 mn	£84
£6 303	78	6	4	5	7	£1 347 mn = 13 weeks	
£1 895	73 Denmark	2	7	12	6	£202 mn	£42
£2 104	81	2	5	9	3	£201 mn = 6 weeks	
£10 144	73 France[c]	6	5	7	9	£2 155 mn	£43
£9 879	74	4	5	8	9	£2 067 mn = 13 weeks	
£650	70 Republic of Ireland	9	12	7	2	£231 mn	£79
£770	83[b]	5	5	6[b]	1	£290 mn = 22 weeks	
£7 882	69 Italy	1 9	8		13	£2 106 mn	£40
£7 600	73	1 4	9		13	£2 230 mn = 19 weeks	
£3 337	68 Switzerland	10	9	4	9	£1 701 mn	£277
£3 170	87	1 4	4		4	£2 138 mn = 41 weeks	
£1 785	67 Austria	3	23	2	5	£612 mn	£83
£1 803	79	4	7	3	7	£730 mn = 26 weeks	
£12 563	63 United Kingdom	11	3	14	9	£1 094 mn	£20
£11 767	67	7	3	15	8	£1 178 mn = 7 weeks	
£702	62 Portugal[d]	3	14	9	12	£534 mn	£60
£879	80	3	5	6	6	£627 mn = 49 weeks	
£100	61 Iceland	1 2	21		15	£17 mn	£86
£97	62	4 3	20		11	£22 mn = 18 weeks	
£2 005	52 Norway	3 3	37		5	£277 mn	£73
£2 072	73	4 3	16		4	£339 mn = 11 weeks	
£507	50 Greece	1 16	22		11	£122 mn	£14
£823	86			3 3 2	6	£129 mn = 8 weeks	
£2 059	50 Spain	1 34	8		7	£532 mn	£16
£2 300	78	4 3	8		7	£757 mn = 20 weeks	

(1) The total value of trade seldom balances from year to year because of variations in the nature of transactions between countries. It is made up from:

(2) Visible Trade: The Exports and Imports of goods which are said to be either in surplus or deficit depending on the balance of visible trade. Most West European countries (except notably West Germany) normally run at a deficit and offset the difference by invisible earnings:

(3) Invisible Exports include payments for interest, dividends and profits earned on overseas Investments —

(4) Receipts from tourism, although only some West European countries derive a profit from this trade (see page 69) —

(5) International Transport income from shipping and civil aviation services for both freight and passengers and the associated insurance facilities and

(6) Other receipts from banking, insurance and government transactions.

(7) & (8) International Reserves are used to finance payments abroad in the event of an imbalance in international trade transactions in goods and services. Reserves include holdings of gold, foreign currencies, the reserve position with the International Monetary Fund and the quota of Special Drawing Rights (SDR's).

[a] not necessarily the same figure as that used on page 69 because of slight differences of source and definition
[b] estimates
[c] includes Monaco and Overseas Departments and Territories
[d] Escudo area

© Bartholomew/Warne 1974

World Trade

THE AMERICAS

Country	GDP £ million	Per cent of GDP Exported
USA £405 242		4%
Canada £33 207		21%
Brazil £15 547		7%
Mexico £13 957		4%
Argentina £10 187		7%
Venezuela £4 328		26%
Colombia £3 603		9%
Chile £2 788		19%
Puerto Rico £2 276		33%
Peru £2 267		19%
Cuba £1 830		30%
20 other countries £7 441		23%

GDP and World Trade in 1970

Gross Domestic Products
£ million

GDP is the value of all production and services in a country, but comparisons cannot be exact because of differences in base data and exchange rates. Centrally planned economies use Gross Material Product as a base which does not include many services such as insurance, community services and defence. Many countries have some of their population partly or wholly outside the money economy.

KEY

GDP £ million	Per cent of GDP Exported
Developed Countries	
Less Developed Countries	
Centrally Planned Economies	

WESTERN EUROPE

Country	GDP £ million	Per cent of GDP Exported
West Germany £78 210		18%
France £61 118		12%
United Kingdom £49 700		16%
Italy £38 602		14%
Sweden £13 700		21%
Spain £13 476		7%
Netherlands £13 064		38%
Belgium & Luxembourg £11 123		43%
Switzerland £8 242		26%
Denmark £6 500		21%
Austria £5 992		20%
Yugoslavia £5 500[a]		13%
Norway £4 737		22%
Finland £4 325		22%
Greece £4 008		7%
Portugal £2 530		16%
Republic of Ireland £1 621		26%
Iceland £203		30%
Malta £94		17%

AFRICA

Country	GDP	Per cent of GDP Exported
South Africa £7 215		13%
Egypt £2 977		11%
Nigeria £2 417[a]		21%
Algeria £1 812		23%
Libya £1 552		64%
Morocco £1 397		15%
Ghana £1 050		17%
39 other countries £11 466		23%

MIDDLE EAST

Country	GDP	Per cent of GDP Exported
Turkey £5 053		5%
Iran £4 687		21%
Israel £2 226		15%
Saudi Arabia £1 970		50%
Iraq £1 417[a]		32%
Kuwait £1 263		55%
6 other countries £2 083		17%

World Shares of Land, People, Wealth and Trade

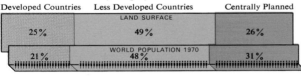

Developed Countries	Less Developed Countries	Centrally Planned
25%	LAND SURFACE 49%	26%
21%	WORLD POPULATION 1970 48%	31%

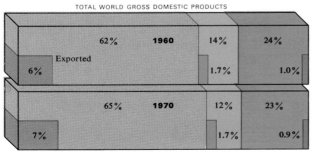

TOTAL WORLD GROSS DOMESTIC PRODUCTS

62% **1960**	14%	24%	
Exported 6%	1.7%	1.0%	
65% **1970**	12%	23%	
7%	1.7%	0.9%	

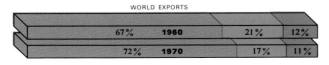

WORLD EXPORTS

67% **1960**	21%	12%
72% **1970**	17%	11%

Trade between Developed and Less Developed Countries in 1970[b]

Main Categories of Trade[b]
Total £ million

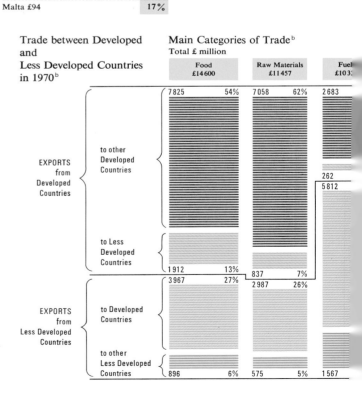

	Food £14 600		Raw Materials £11 457		Fuel £103...
EXPORTS from Developed Countries — to other Developed Countries	7 825	54%	7 058	62%	2 683
					262
EXPORTS from Developed Countries — to Less Developed Countries	1 912	13%	837	7%	5 812
EXPORTS from Less Developed Countries — to Developed Countries	3 967	27%	2 987	26%	
EXPORTS from Less Developed Countries — to other Less Developed Countries	896	6%	575	5%	1 567

[a]estimates   [b]centrally planned economies are not included here as commodity data is not complete

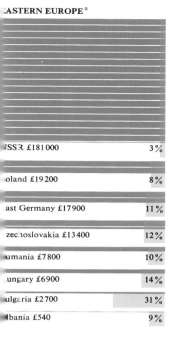

EASTERN EUROPE[a]

USSR £181000		3%
Poland £19200		8%
East Germany £17900		11%
Czechoslovakia £13400		12%
Rumania £7800		10%
Hungary £6900		14%
Bulgaria £2700		31%
Albania £540		9%

OCEANIA

Australia £15250		13%
New Zealand £2579		20%
Fiji £96		30%

ASIA

Japan £82342		10%
China £53000 [a c]		2%
India £22500 [a]		4%
Indonesia £4911		10%
Pakistan £4332		4%
Philippines £3941		11%
South Korea £3450		10%
Thailand £2723		10%
Bangladesh £2387 [a]		4%
Taiwan £2278		26%
South Vietnam £2053		0%
North Korea £1900 [a c]		2%
Malaysia £1576		45%
Hong Kong £1230		85%
Burma £1005		4%
Sri Lanka £905		16%
North Vietnam £900 [a c]		2%
7 other countries £2600		29%

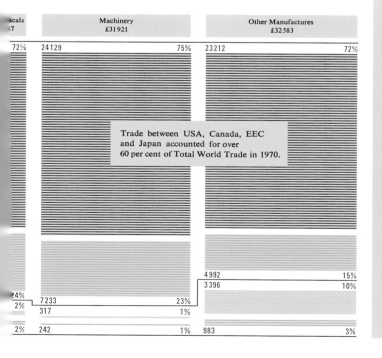

		Machinery £31921		Other Manufactures £32583	
72%	24129		75%	23212	72%

Trade between USA, Canada, EEC and Japan accounted for over 60 per cent of Total World Trade in 1970.

			4992	15%
			3396	10%
24%	7233	23%		
2%	317	1%		
2%	242	1%	983	3%

Barriers to Trade

The Construction and Demolition of Tariffs

In practice, foreign trade patterns partly reflect the impact of various barriers to trade erected by nation states. These barriers usually take the form of tariffs and import controls which produce revenue and protect the home industries of the countries imposing them but also invite retaliation by trading partners. The gradual elimination of such barriers has been a main objective of the General Agreement on Tariffs and Trade (GATT) and, as far as trade between members is concerned, of regional trading blocs like EEC and EFTA.

1959   1962   1968   1972

EEC Tariffs on industrial goods: **1959:** *National tariffs are in operation, different rates for various categories in trade. Tariffs between members are planned to dissolve in 15 years.* **1962:** *Five ten per cent cuts have taken place in differences in internal tariffs and a 30 per cent cut in differences in external tariffs.* **1968:** *Well ahead of schedule, an internal customs union and a common external tariff (CCT) are established.* **1972:** *Further cuts have been made in the CCT reducing it by about one third.*

1973   1975   1977

The New Entrants: **1973:** *The variety of national tariffs are planned to harmonize with those of the EEC of Six.* **1975:** *Over half the differences in tariffs will have been abolished.* **1977:** *The new members of the enlarged EEC will have duty-free access for their goods and services to a market of over 250 million people and will enjoy preferential trading advantages over world competitors in the protected trading area behind the CCT. The phased replacement of national tariffs by the CCT will increase import duties in some cases such as on trade between the UK and Commonwealth countries that previously enjoyed special preference arrangements.*

Free Trade

The emphasis on international free trade since the nineteenth century combined with the industrial and technological pre-eminence of Western Europe, USA and, more recently, Japan, Canada, Australia, New Zealand and South Africa, has led these developed economies to specialize in manufactured goods with the less developed nations producing mainly basic raw materials.

To reduce this economic dependence on the more advanced economies many less developed countries have attempted to quicken their economic growth through industrialization. This has led to the imposition of tariffs and other import controls to protect infant domestic industries and attempts to increase trade within trading blocs offering preferential association.

The widespread changes in the geographical pattern and commodity composition of world trade stemming from economic forces are further complicated by the use of trade sanctions as a political weapon.

[c] exports for China, North Korea and North Vietnam exclude internal trade between them

Exports and Imports

In 1970 total exports of the 18 West European countries were worth over £56 thousand million while imports exceeded £61 thousand million — over 40 per cent of world trade.

Since 1960 the industrialized countries of Western Europe have taken a large share of the general expansion in world trade with the fastest annual rates of growth (Japan excepted) occurring between EEC members (12.7 per cent) and between EFTA members (11.2 per cent).

Shown below, the domination of intra-European trade is apparent for all countries except the UK, and the stimulus for much of this economic integration has clearly been the creation of preferential trading arrangements inside the EEC and EFTA. In a continent of trading nations West Germany towers above the rest, and like the Belgium-Luxembourg Economic Union (BLEU), it exported more than it imported in 1970. However, the deficit in the commodity trade of the other European countries is largely offset by invisible earnings from banking, overseas investment, insurance and tourism (see page 74).

The Value of International Trade

The Dependence of Europe's Trading Nations
on Trading Partners in Europe

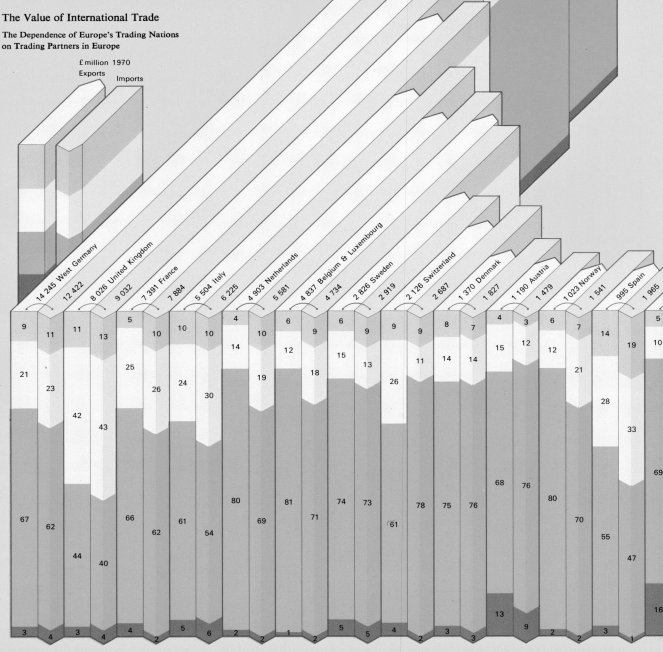

£ million 1970
Exports   Imports

14 245 West Germany
12 422
8 026 United Kingdom
9 032
7 391 France
7 884
5 504 Italy
6 225
4 903 Netherlands
5 581
4 837 Belgium & Luxembourg
4 734
2 826 Sweden
2 919
2 126 Switzerland
2 687
1 370 Denmark
1 827
1 190 Austria
1 479
1 023 Norway
1 541
995 Spain
1 965

Productivity and Exports: per worker

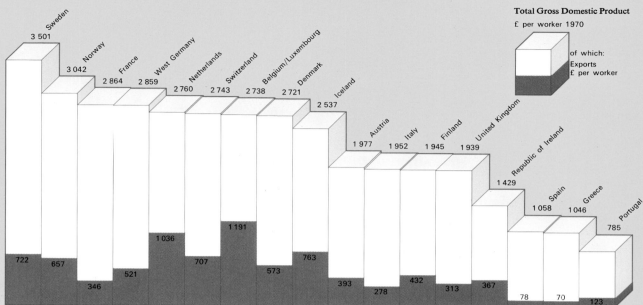

Total Gross Domestic Product
£ per worker 1970

of which:
Exports
£ per worker

Sweden	Norway	France	West Germany	Netherlands	Switzerland	Belgium/Luxembourg	Denmark	Iceland	Austria	Italy	Finland	United Kingdom	Republic of Ireland	Spain	Greece	Portugal
3 501	3 042	2 864	2 859	2 760	2 743	2 738	2 721	2 537	1 977	1 952	1 945	1 939	1 429	1 058	1 046	785
722	657	346	521	707	1 191	573	763	393	278	432	313	367	78	70	123	

The striking export performance of the Belgium-Luxembourg Economic Union reflects the fast economic growth of the EEC during the 1960s and large-scale foreign investment in manufacturing industries like motor vehicles and chemicals. This decade of economic integration, tariff reductions on industrial goods and substantial foreign investment particularly from North America has generated rapid export growth in Western Europe creating even greater dependence on international trade.

Such dependence on foreign trade means that any downturn in the economies of trading partners has inevitable repercussions on the domestic economy. Indeed the apparent trade and monetary stability of the EEC during the 1960s has since been undermined by the uncertainties surrounding the terms of trade between the world manufacturers and the suppliers of primary products, particularly fuels. Profound changes in the geographical and commodity pattern of international trade make predictions about the future for free world trade very unreliable. *More recent trade figures are given in the Statistical Profile on pages 108 to 115.*

Europe's Growing Dependence on Trade

Per cent of Gross Domestic Product which was exported

in 1960

in 1970

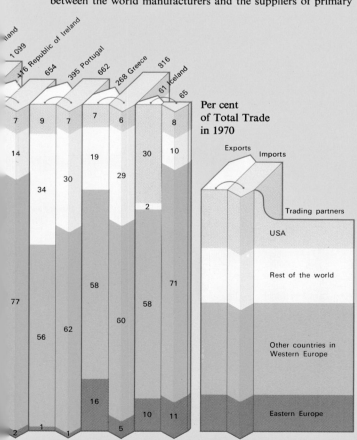

Per cent of Total Trade in 1970

Exports   Imports

Trading partners

USA

Rest of the world

Other countries in Western Europe

Eastern Europe

1:30 000 000
0   200   400   600   800   1000 km

Europe in World Trade

The Pattern of World Trade
Recorded exports £million 1970

The exports of one country or group of countries become the imports of another, although because of variations in timing and recording, trade totals on these two pages do not always match exactly.

The dominance of intra trade reflects not only the trend towards preferential trading blocs like the EEC but also the shift in the pattern of international trade towards more sophisticated products. This has tended to increase trading in manufactures between the developed nations of the world at a time when there has been a relative decrease in trade between the old colonial powers and their former overseas territories.

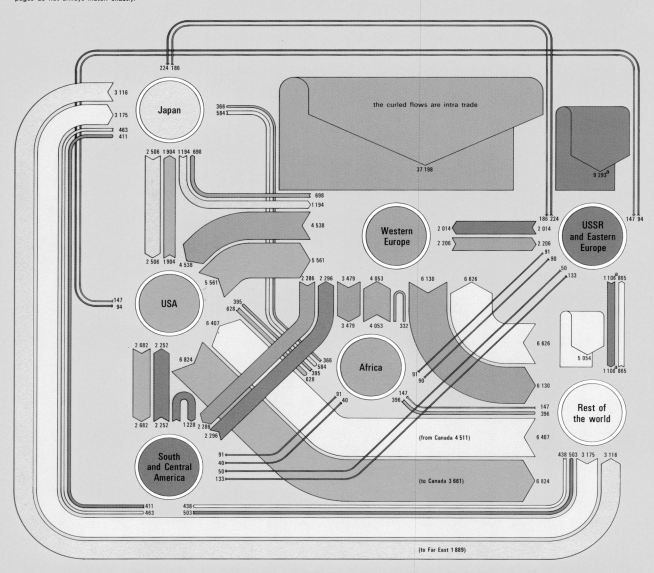

the curled flows are intra trade

Japan
Western Europe
USSR and Eastern Europe
USA
Africa
Rest of the world
South and Central America

(from Canada 4 511)
(to Canada 3 661)
(to Far East 1 889)

The continually expanding demand for goods and services generated by Western Europe's 335 million people has accounted for its pre-eminence in world trade.

The substantial expansion in world trade in the past decade has had its problems. The trade flows show that growth has not been uniform and exports from developed countries have grown at a faster rate than those from developing countries or centrally planned economies. The terms of trade have worked against developing countries, which were heavily reliant on the export of primary products, although recently commodity scarcity and the energy crisis have increased inflationary pressures on the industrial economies of Western Europe and Japan. This is particularly true of oil supplies where heavy dependence on a limited number of world suppliers has made the developed nations extremely vulnerable to trade sanctions. The immense gap which still exists between the rich and the poor nations of the world and the realization that the resources of the world are limited suggest a need for a co-ordinated appraisal of the world's assets so that they may be put to the most effective use for the well-being of all.

The Growth of World Trade

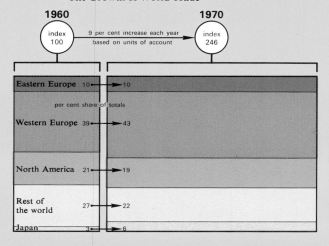

1960 index 100 → 9 per cent increase each year based on units of account → **1970** index 246

per cent share of totals

	1960	1970
Eastern Europe	10	10
Western Europe	39	43
North America	21	19
Rest of the world	27	22
Japan	3	6

ᵃestimates   © Bartholomew/Warne 1974

Europe's Commodity Trade

Imports and Exports to and from Western Europe

£million 1970

see key below

The widths of the blocks show the amount of Europe's trade with the world. The sub-divisions (within blocks) show the percentage breakdown of each commodity group. Numerals in italic amplify subdivision percentages.

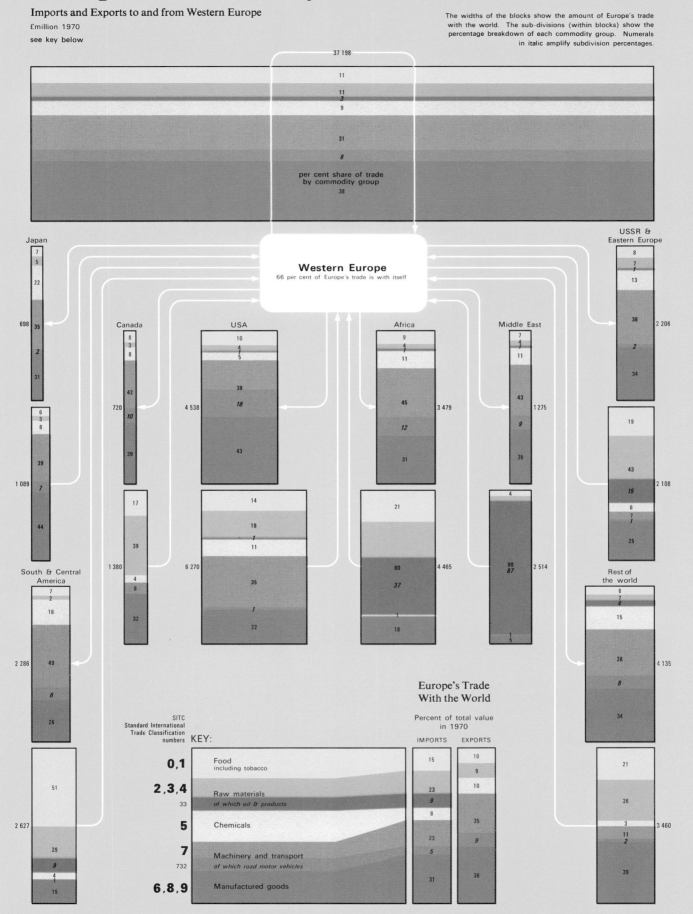

per cent share of trade by commodity group

Western Europe
66 per cent of Europe's trade is with itself

Europe's Trade With the World

Percent of total value in 1970

SITC
Standard International Trade Classification numbers

KEY:

0,1	Food including tobacco
2,3,4	Raw materials
33	of which oil & products
5	Chemicals
7	Machinery and transport
732	of which road motor vehicles
6,8,9	Manufactured goods

Europe Overseas

The last four hundred years witnessed the spread of European influence and domination to all continents. At the time of greatest influence most of the world was subject to European methods of government and law, and developed by European capital and European technology. These empires have withered as nations have gained independence but frequently links of culture, language and trade have endured keeping nations together. Today old colonial patterns are being recast and refashioned in the form of trading agreements and associations between EEC members and their former overseas territories. The result has been the creation of a huge trading empire in which the developing nations retain preferential rights of access to what is the world's largest market for primary products, and, in addition, receive financial and technical aid.

ASSOCIATION OF THE OVERSEAS COUNTRIES AND TERRITORIES:
Part 4 of the Rome Treaty grants associate status to dependent territories of member states in order to promote their economic and social development.

THE YAOUNDE CONVENTION:
The two Yaoundé agreements of 1963 and 1969 govern the association of former territories of member states who have subsequently won political independence but prefer to retain trading links with the Community. Most of the products of these associated overseas territories enter the Common Market free of duty and they also get the benefit of aid from the European Development Fund.

1. Zaïre: 22 860 000
2. Malagasy Republic: 6 777 000
3. Cameroun: 5 840 000
4. Upper Volta: 5 610 000
5. Mali: 5 260 000
6. Ivory Coast: 4 530 000
7. Niger: 4 210 000
8. Senegal: 4 022 000
9. Rwanda: 3 900 000
10. Chad: 3 800 000
11. Burundi: 3 400 000
12. Somalia: 2 940 000
13. Dahomey: 2 870 000
14. Togo: 2 090 000
15. Central African Republic: 1 637 000
16. Congo: 940 000
17. Mauritius: 836 000
18. Gabon: 500 000

THE ARUSHA CONVENTION:
This agreement came into effect on January 1 1971 and provides for substantial liberalization of trade between the Community and Kenya, Tanzania and Uganda although specifically excluding financial and technical aid.

19. Tanzania: 13 634 000
20. Kenya: 11 694 000
21. Uganda: 10 127 000

OTHER EEC AGREEMENTS:
Various trading agreements have been concluded particularly with Mediterranean countries which are designed to gradually eliminate tariff barriers and lead eventually to full association and Community membership. Special Relations Agreements exist between the EEC and EFTA countries to create a free trade in industrial products and, since 1969, Community countries have been committed to a common trade policy towards third countries.

22. Greece (Association 1961) 8 850 000
23. Turkey (Association 1963) 35 010 000
24. Malta (Association 1970) 326 000
25. Cyprus (Association 1973) 640 000
26. Morocco (Partial Association 1969) 15 830 000
27. Tunisia (Partial Association 1969) 5 380 000
28. Algeria (Association in negotiation 1973) 15 270 000

The Times Projection (Bartholomew)

Overseas Territories of Western Europe
the dates of their effective possession
and their population in 1970 or latest available date

UNITED KINGDOM

49	1615 Bermuda: 67 000
50	1632–1713 Leeward Islands: 157 000
51	1659 St Helena: 5 000
52	1662 Belize[a]: 130 000
53	1670 Cayman Islands: 10 700
54	1678 Turks and Caicos: 6 100
55	1704 Gibraltar: 56 000
56	1763–1803 Windward Islands: 361 000
57	1790 Pitcairn: 82
58	1794 Seychelles: 52 000
59	1815 Ascension Island: 1 300
60	1815 Tristan da Cunha: 300
61	1833 Falkland Islands & Dependencies: 2 500
62	1841 Hong Kong: 3 948 000
63	1887 New Hebrides[b]: 84 000
64	1888 Brunei: 137 000
65	1891 Rhodesia[c]: 5 270 000
66	1892 Gilbert & Ellice Islands: 56 000
67	1893 British Solomon Islands: 163 000
68	1965 British Indian Territory: 2 000

NETHERLANDS

| 69 | 1616 Surinam: 406 000 |
| 70 | 1815 Antilles: 225 000 |

SPAIN

| 71 | 1884 Spanish Sahara: 70 000 |

FRANCE

OVERSEAS DEPARTMENTS

72	1635 Martinique: 338 000
73	1640 Guyane: 51 000
74	1645 Réunion: 455 000
75	1816 Guadeloupe: 330 000

OVERSEAS TERRITORIES

76	1635 St Pierre and Miquelon: 5 200
77	1842 French Polynesia: 119 000
78	1842 Wallis and Futuna: 9 000
79	1853 New Caledonia: 110 000
80	1886 Comoro Archipelago: 275 000
81	1887 New Hebrides[b]: 84 000
82	1888 Afars and Issas: 125 000

PORTUGAL

83	1440 Portuguese Guinea: 487 000
84	1466 Cape Verde: 272 000
85	1480 São Tomé E Príncipe: 74 000
86	1483 Angola: 5 673 000
87	1505 Moçambique: 8 233 000
88	1557 Macao: 310 000
89	1859 Timor: 611 000

DENMARK

| 90 | 1380 Faeroes: 39 000 |
| 91 | 1721 Greenland: 46 000 |

EC ASSOCIATE STATUS:
Association has been offered to the developing Commonwealth countries but the final terms have still to be negotiated.

29	Nigeria: 66 174 000	39	Lesotho: 970 000
30	Tanzania: 13 634 000	40	Mauritius: 836 000
31	Kenya: 11 694 000	41	Guyana: 763 000
32	Uganda: 10 127 000	42	Botswana: 668 000
33	Ghana: 8 858 000	43	Fiji: 533 000
34	Malawi: 4 530 000	44	Swaziland: 421 000
35	Zambia: 4 300 000	45	The Gambia: 375 000
36	Sierra Leone: 2 630 000	46	Barbados: 244 000
37	Jamaica: 1 920 000	47	Western Samoa: 143 000
38	Trinidad & Tobago: 1 070 000	48	Tonga: 90 000

[a] independent 1974   [b] joint French/British rule   [c] unilateral declaration of independence 1965

© Bartholomew/Warne 1974

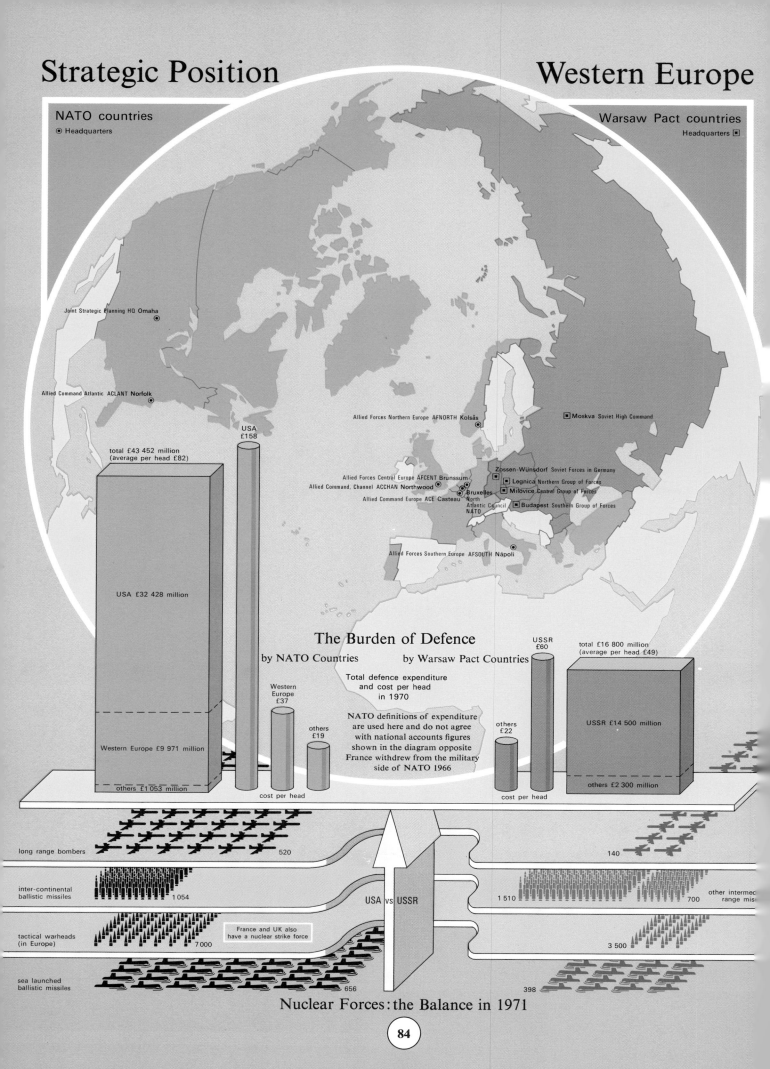

NATO countries
⊙ Headquarters

Warsaw Pact countries
Headquarters ▣

Joint Strategic Planning HQ Omaha ⊙

Allied Command Atlantic ACLANT Norfolk ⊙

Allied Forces Northern Europe AFNORTH Kolsås ⊙

▣ Moskva Soviet High Command

USA
£158

total £43 452 million
(average per head £82)

Allied Forces Central Europe AFCENT Brunssum ⊙
Allied Command, Channel ACCHAN Northwood ⊙

Zossen-Wünsdorf Soviet Forces in Germany
▣ Legnica Northern Group of Forces
▣ Milovice Central Group of Forces

Bruxelles
North
Atlantic Council
NATO

▣ Budapest Southern Group of Forces

Allied Command Europe ACE Casteau ⊙

USA £32 428 million

Allied Forces Southern Europe AFSOUTH Nápoli ⊙

The Burden of Defence

by NATO Countries   by Warsaw Pact Countries

USSR
£60

total £16 800 million
(average per head £49)

Total defence expenditure
and cost per head
in 1970

Western
Europe
£37

NATO definitions of expenditure
are used here and do not agree
with national accounts figures
shown in the diagram opposite
France withdrew from the military
side of NATO 1966

others
£19

USSR £14 500 million

others
£22

Western Europe £9 971 million

others £1 053 million

cost per head

cost per head

others £2 300 million

long range bombers   520

140

inter-continental
ballistic missiles   1 054

1 510   700   other intermed
range mis

USA vs USSR

tactical warheads
(in Europe)   7 000

France and UK also
have a nuclear strike force

3 500

sea launched
ballistic missiles   656

398

Nuclear Forces: the Balance in 1971

NATO

Warsaw Pact

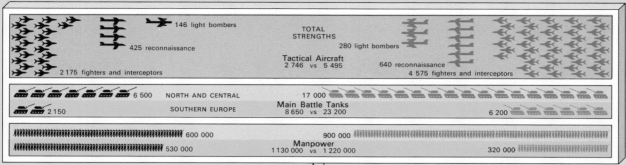

TOTAL STRENGTHS

146 light bombers
425 reconnaissance
2 175 fighters and interceptors

280 light bombers
640 reconnaissance
4 575 fighters and interceptors

Tactical Aircraft
2 746 vs 5 495

6 500 NORTH AND CENTRAL 17 000
2 150 SOUTHERN EUROPE 6 200

Main Battle Tanks
8 650 vs 23 200

600 000 900 000
530 000 320 000

Manpower
1 130 000 vs 1 220 000

The North Atlantic Treaty Organization became effective on 4 April 1949 to counter the threat of Soviet expansionist policies in Europe following World War II. Under the Treaty the fifteen member nations retain full independence of action.

The Warsaw Pact was formally established on 14 May 1955 primarily to create a large military force under unified Soviet command. Because bilateral treaties of mutual assistance exist, the defence of Eastern Europe is not totally dependent on the Warsaw alliance.

The manpower and equipment strengths of the opposing alliances in Europe vary considerably. Technological advance on the battlefield has reduced the significance of conventional weapons lists and the best measure of military might is now likely to be in terms of missile totals of ATGWs and SAMs. In this respect, significance attaches to the continued increase in Soviet defence and defence related spending, which rose by an average of 5 per cent per year during the period 1965–70 when defence spending by the NATO allies actually fell by almost 1 per cent per year.

Clearly, for mobilization and reinforcement the advantages lie with the Warsaw Pact which can quickly move its forces overland and could only be matched by NATO in the event of a slow buildup to crisis. The lack of equipment standardization amongst NATO forces is also a problem and the absence of any effective central co-ordination weakens its logistic capability, although this is offset by the superiority of many of its weapons, its elaborate early warning systems and its greater strategic strike force. Finally, there are imponderable considerations such as differences in the morale and reliability of the troops which it is not possible to quantify. Certainly there is little depth in the NATO central and northern areas and the withdrawal of the French and reductions in the numbers of American forces stationed in Europe have swung the numerical advantage decidedly to the Soviet Bloc. This disparity in force levels gives some urgency to NATO planning which continues to be based on deterrence and defence as a basis for negotiation and co-operation within Europe. Moreover, in order to demonstrate the solidarity of NATO and to improve and extend the European defence effort it is essential that member states agree over cost sharing and the commitment of troops and weapons.

National Defence: Counting the Costs

Serving the Armed Forces 1970

Defence Expenditure 1970

Conscription: compulsory service in months	Servicemen per thousand population	Total number serving in armed forces		Total defence expenditure £million	Defence spending as a percentage of Gross Domestic Product	Defence spending average per head
7½–15	12	93 000[a]	Sweden	478	3.5	£59
none	7	372 000	United Kingdom	2 408	4.9	£43
12	11	564 000	France	2 070	3.4	£41
12–15	12	48 000	Norway	158	3.3	£41
15	8	499 000	West Germany	2 249	2.9	£37
16–21	9	111 000	Netherlands	453	3.5	£35
9	10	48 000	Denmark	162	2.5	£33
12–15	10	95 000	Belgium	270	2.5	£28
4	1	3 000[a]	Switzerland	170	2.0	£27
15–24	7	388 000	Italy	1 391	3.6	£26
23–30	18	160 000[a]	Greece	201	5.2	£23
none	6	1 000[a]	Iceland	5	2.3	£23
18–48	23	204 000[a]	Portugal	185	7.2	£21
8–11	9	41 000	Finland	65	1.5	£14
none	1	400[a]	Luxembourg	3	0.8	£10
6	8	60 000	Austria	66	1.1	£9
18	5	167 000	Spain	250	1.9	£7
none	3	8 000	Republic of Ireland	18	1.4	£6

The eighteen
total expenditure £10 602 million
average per head £32

Europe and Overseas Aid

The 1960s were designated as the first Development Decade by the UN with the intention that by 1970 developed countries would be achieving an aid flow of one per cent of their GDPs to less developed countries. Economic aid from the USSR has been advanced to many countries: chiefly India, United Arab Republic, Iraq, Afghanistan, Indonesia, Argentina, Ethiopia, Guinea and Cuba. This aid is in the form of repayable loans.

Official Aid to Developing Countries average annual flow 1968 to 1970

The Givers:

The main suppliers[a]: average per person and per cent of Gross Domestic Product and totals given in £ million

TOTAL FROM DEVELOPED ECONOMIES
£3003 million

A	£6.90 0.61%	Australia: £85
B	£6.70 0.35%	USA: £1362
C	£5.80 0.40%	Canada: £122
D	£3.30 0.48%	Japan: £337
		other countries: £12

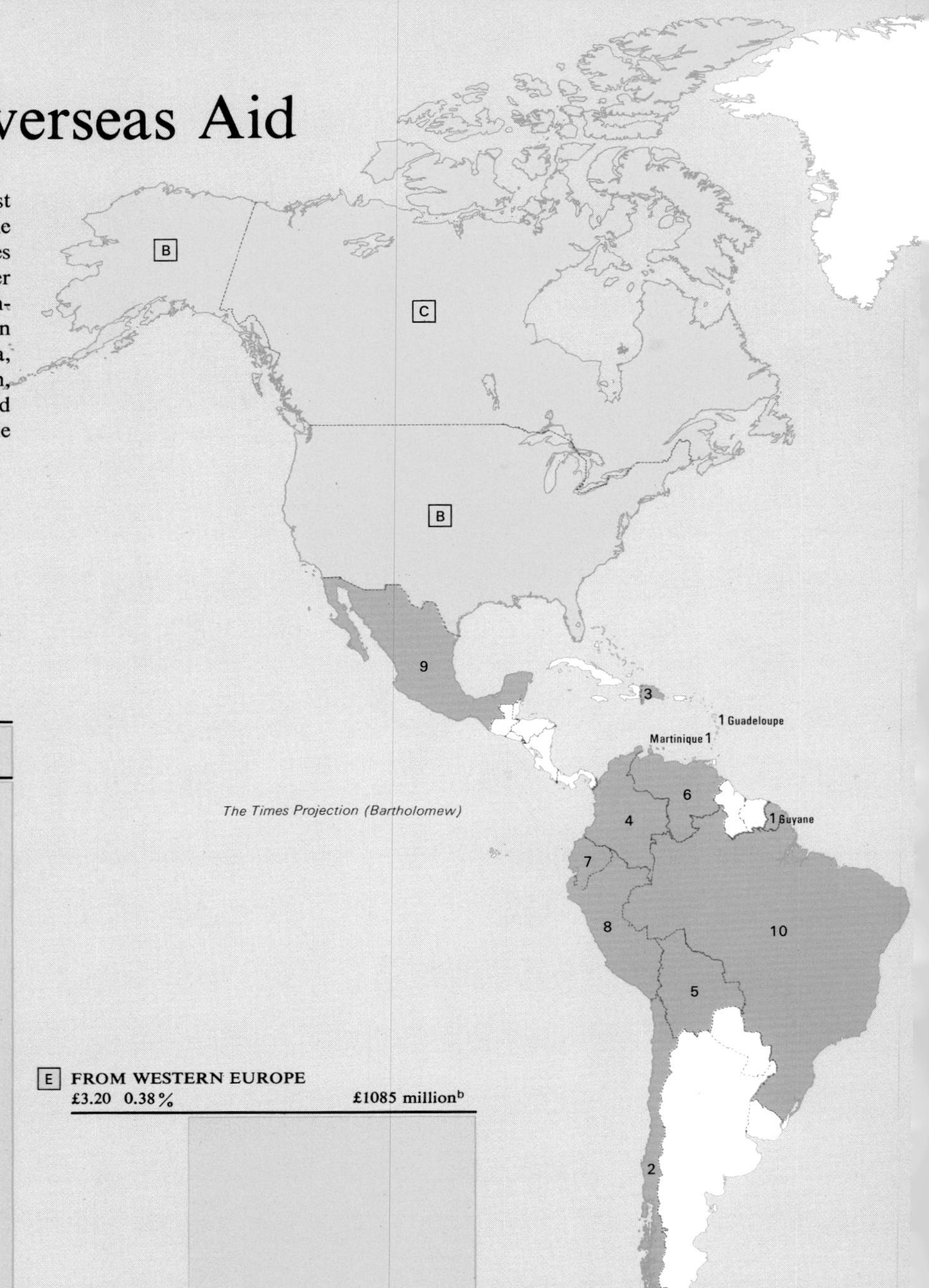

E FROM WESTERN EUROPE
£3.20 0.38%   **£1085 million[b]**

£7.70 0.67%	France: £385
£5.40 0.34%	Sweden: £43
£5.20 0.52%	Belgium: £50
£5.20 0.58%	Netherlands: £67
£4.40 0.49%	Denmark: £22
£4.10 0.38%	Norway: £16
£3.60 0.33%	West Germany: £220
£3.10 0.37%	United Kingdom: £172
£2.70 1.05%	Portugal: £24
£1.50 0.20%	Austria: £11
£1.50 0.12%	Switzerland: £9
£1.20 0.18%	Italy: £62
	others: £4

The Times Projection (Bartholomew)

The Receivers:

Those receiving over £10 million: totals received £ million and per cent of Gross Domestic Product and average per person

TO LATIN AMERICA
£575 million   **1.01%**   **£2**

1	£59	French Territories	25.50%	£8?
2	£55	Chile	2.16%	£?
3	£22	Dominican Republic	3.93%	£?
4	£73	Columbia	2.31%	£?
5	£17	Bolivia	4.42%	£?
6	£22	Venezuela	0.53%	£?
7	£10	Ecuador	1.62%	£?
8	£23	Peru	1.15%	£?
9	£58	Mexico	0.46%	£?
10	£89	Brazil	0.65%	£?
	£147	to other Latin American countries		

Map labels: 1 Guadeloupe, Martinique 1, 1 Guyane

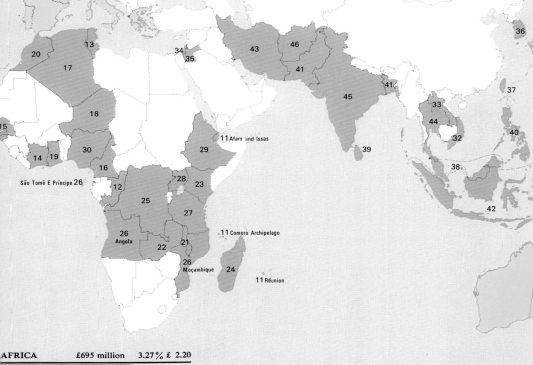

In 1970 the total net flow of economic assistance to the developing countries was over £6 500 million, with just half representing official government aid and the rest private investment. Of this official aid, some 80 per cent was bilateral aid given directly to the developing country and often tied to the purchase of the donor's goods and services. The rest represented untied multilateral aid channelled through United Nations bodies like the World Bank and the International Development Association. Financial aid is, however, not the sole solution to the problems of the 'Third World' and most of the developing countries desperately need expert technical advice to ensure that scarce resources are put to the most effective use to foster economic growth. Despite definite increases in aid, the gap between rich and poor worlds has hardly changed.

AFRICA	£695 million	3.27%	£ 2.20
45	French Territories	25.00%	£56.00
12	Congo	12.40%	£13.00
45	Tunisia	9.01%	£9.00
20	Ivory Coast	3.49%	£4.80
18	Senegal	5.06%	£4.70
19	Cameroun	4.20%	£3.30
46	Algeria	2.77%	£3.30
12	Niger	7.45%	£3.10
26	Ghana	2.72%	£3.10
43	Morocco	3.28%	£2.90
12	Malawi	10.03%	£2.80
1	Zambia	1.65%	£2.70
7	Kenya	4.35%	£2.50
6	Malagasy Republic	4.41%	£2.40
44	Zaïre	4.56%	£1.60
2	Portuguese Territories	1.80%	£1.50
8	Tanzania	3.59%	£1.40
1	Uganda	2.25%	£1.20
9	Ethiopia	2.80%	£0.80
3	Nigeria	2.10%	£0.80
06	to other African countries		

TO ASIA AND THE PACIFIC	£1572 million	2.24%	£ 1.40
31 £55	Papua New Guinea	19.00%	£23.30
32 £187	South Vietnam	12.00%	£10.50
33 £27	Laos	19.00%	£ 9.30
34 £26	Israel	1.34%	£ 9.20
35 £19	Jordan	7.97%	£ 8.50
36 £148	South Korea	5.06%	£4.80
37 £33	Taiwan	1.63%	£2.40
38 £22	Malaysia	1.40%	£2.20
39 £21	Sri Lanka	2.58%	£1.70
40 £58	Philippines	1.64%	£1.60
41 £186	Pakistan & Bangladesh	3.30%	£1.50

42 £161	Indonesia	3.69%	£1.40
43 £38	Iran	0.91%	£1.40
44 £42	Thailand	1.63%	£1.30
45 £367	India	2.69%	£0.70
46 £10	Afghanistan	2.30%	£0.60
£172	to other Asian and Pacific countries		

Official aid is channelled to the Less Developed Countries through multinational agencies like the World Bank.
In any one year there is inevitably, therefore, a timing delay and the amount of aid given does not exactly correspond with the total aid received.

The United Nations

Headquarters of UN
Organisations 1973

Main operations only

SANTIAGO
ECLA: Economic
Commission for Latin America

WASHINGTON
THE WORLD BANK
IBRD: International
Bank for Reconstruction
and Development

IFC: International
Finance Corporation

IDA: International
Development Association

IMF: International
Monetary Fund

MONTREAL
ICAO: International
Civil Aviation Organisation

NEW YORK
HEADQUARTERS AND
GENERAL ASSEMBLY
of 135 member states

The Secretariat

Economic and Social Council

Security Council
15 members

Trusteeship Council

UNICEF: UN
Children's Fund

UNITAR: UN Institute
for Training and Research

UNDP: UN Development
Programme

UNCDF: UN Capital
Development Fund

UNFPA: UN Fund
for Population Activities

THE HAGUE
ICJ: International
Court of Justice
15 judges elected
for 9 year terms.
International Court cases
at The Hague

*LONDON
IMCO: Inter-Governmental
Maritime Consultative
Organisation

*PARIS
UNESCO: UN Educational
Scientific and Cultural
Organisation

*GENEVA
ECE: Economic
Commission for Europe

GATT: General Agreement
on Tariffs and Trade

WHO: World
Health Organisation

UNCTAD: UN Conference
on Trade and Development

UNHCR: UN High
Commissioner for Refugees

VIENNA
IAEA: International
Atomic Energy Agency

UNIDO: UN Industrial
Development Organisation

ROME*
FAO: Food and
Agricultural Organisation

UN-FAO: WFP: World
Food Programme

BERNE
UPO: Universal
Postal Union

ILO: International
Labour Organisation

WMO: World Meteorological
Organisation

ITU: International
Telecommunications Union

UNRISD: UN Research
Institute for Social Development

UNDRO: UN Disaster
Relief Office

BANGKOK
ECAFE: Economic
Commission for Asia
and the Far East

DACCA
UNROD: UN Relief
Operation Dacca

NAIROBI
UNES: UN
Environment Secretariat

ADDIS ABABA
ECA: Economic
Commission for Africa

BEIRUT
UNWRAP: UN Relief
and Works Agency
for Palestine

NICOSIA
UNFICYP: UN Force
in Cyprus

UNMEM: UN Middle
East Mission

*Cities in Western Europe
with UN Information Centres
plus Athens and Copenhagen

KEY
BASIC UN
ORGANISATION

Inter-Governmental
Agencies related to UN

Regional Economic
Commissions

Other UN units
and operations

© Bartholomew/Warne 1974

Western Europe and the UN

THE BACKGROUND

1914
1915
1916
1917
1918

January 1920: The League of Nations founded. 12 countries of Western Europe are founder members and Austria, Finland and Luxembourg join shortly afterwards. Headquarters: Palais des Nations, Geneva. As a forum of nations working towards international co-operation it has considerable success, but in its wider aims of preserving world peace it fails.

September 1939: With the outbreak of World War II The League of Nations ceases to exist, although it is not officially superceded until 1946.

June 1941: The Inter-Allied Declaration calls for the willing co-operation of free peoples in a world relieved of the menace of aggression. **August:** USA and Great Britain agree on the basic principles of peace in the Atlantic Charter.

January 1942: 26 nations pledged to defeat the Axis accept the principles of the Atlantic Charter. Franklin D. Roosevelt names the 'United Nations'.

1939
1940
1941
1942
1943
1944
1945

October 1943: The Moscow Declaration by the Soviet Union, China, Great Britain and USA agrees to set up an international organization to keep the peace.

August 1944: The Dumbarton Oaks Conference in Washington outlines initial proposals for this general international organization for the maintenance of peace and security.

February 1945: Roosevelt, Stalin and Churchill meet at Yalta, USSR, to renew their proposals for a world peace-keeping organization. **April:** A meeting at San Francisco drafts the United Nations Charter. Of the 51 original members, only eight are from Western Europe.

October 24 1945: The United Nations officially comes into existence. Its headquarters are established in New York. The first Secretary-General is Trygve Lie, Norway. Subsequent holders of the post: Dag Hammarskjold, Sweden, 1953-61; U Thant, Burma, 1961-71; Dr Kurt Waldheim, Austria, 1971-

January 1974: The United Nations has grown to 135 members. 17 are from Western Europe.

The Contribution by Western Europe to the UN Budget of £66.6 mn in 1970

The Proposed Rate of Contribution to the UN: 1974 to 1976

	Total contribution £ thousands	pence per person	per cent share of total UN expenses each year
France £3 990		8p	5.86
United Kingdom £4 400		8p	5.31
Italy £2 150		4p	3.60
Sweden £830		10p	1.30
Netherlands £770		6p	1.24
Belgium £730		8p	1.05
Spain £610		2p	0.99
Denmark £410		8p	0.63
Austria £380		5p	0.56
Norway £290		7p	0.43
Finland £330		7p	0.42
Greece £190		2p	0.32
Ireland £110		4p	0.15
Portugal £110		1p	0.15
Luxembourg £30		10p	0.04
Iceland £30		13p	0.02
West Germany not a member until September 1973			7.10
Switzerland not a member but contributes to some activities			0.82

The UN Budget does not include contributions to UN Agencies and development funds etc., these are mainly included in official aid flows (see pages 86 and 87). The main expenditure is on staff, their travel, premises and conferences and the support of missions and services.

The UN and agencies employed over 36 thousand staff in 1973. The UN over 12 000.
The seven largest agencies:
FAO: 5 000   ILO: 3 000
UNESCO: 4 000   World Bank: IBRD & IDA: 3 200
WHO: 3 500   IAEA: 1 000   IMF: 1 300

1970 16 countries made up	1974 to 1976 16 countries plus West Germany

Western Europe's Share of the UN Regular Budget

22.70% 29.17%

© Bartholomew/Warne 1974

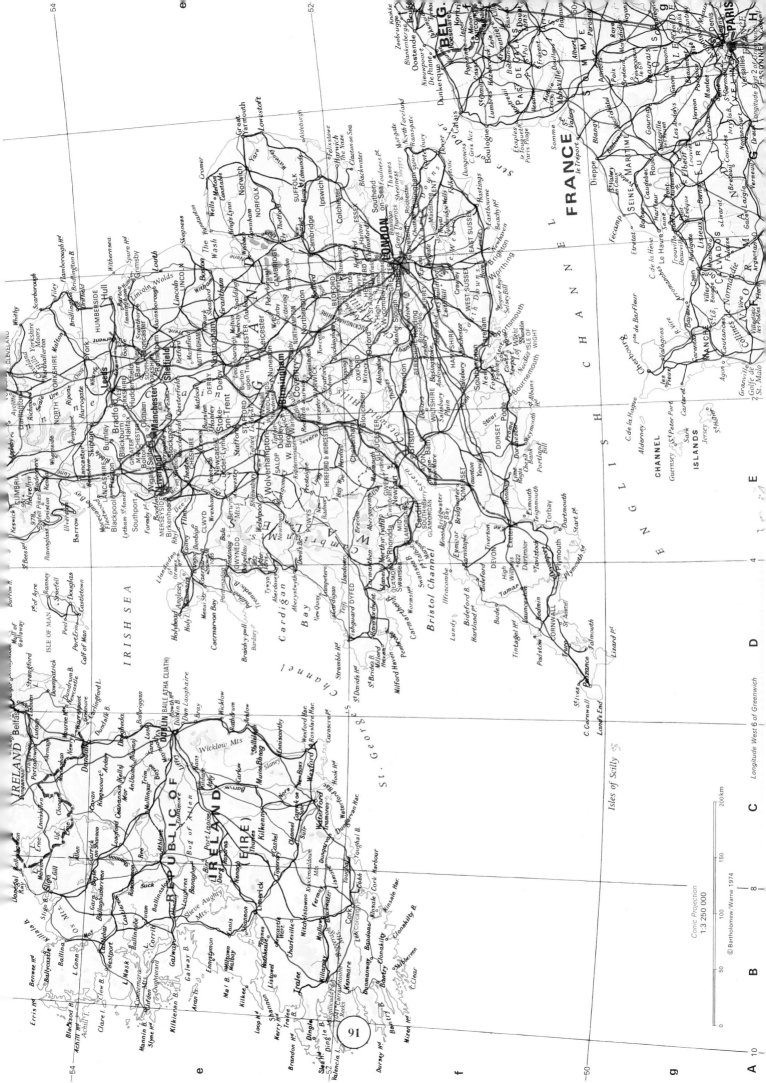

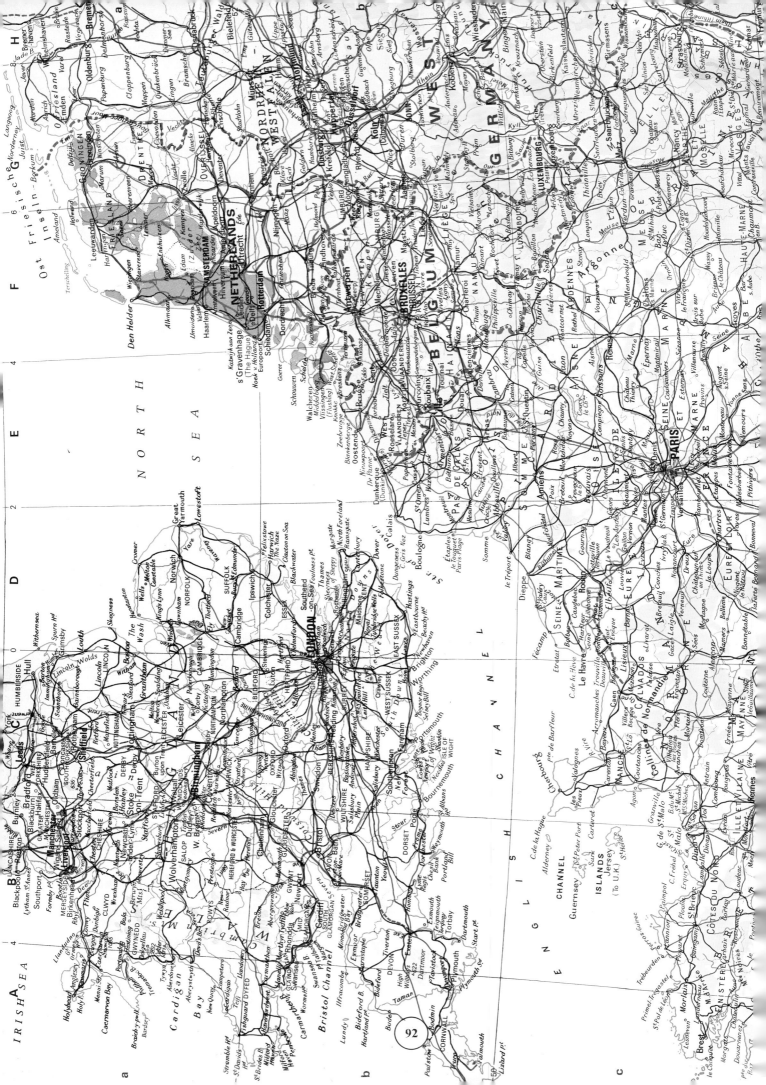

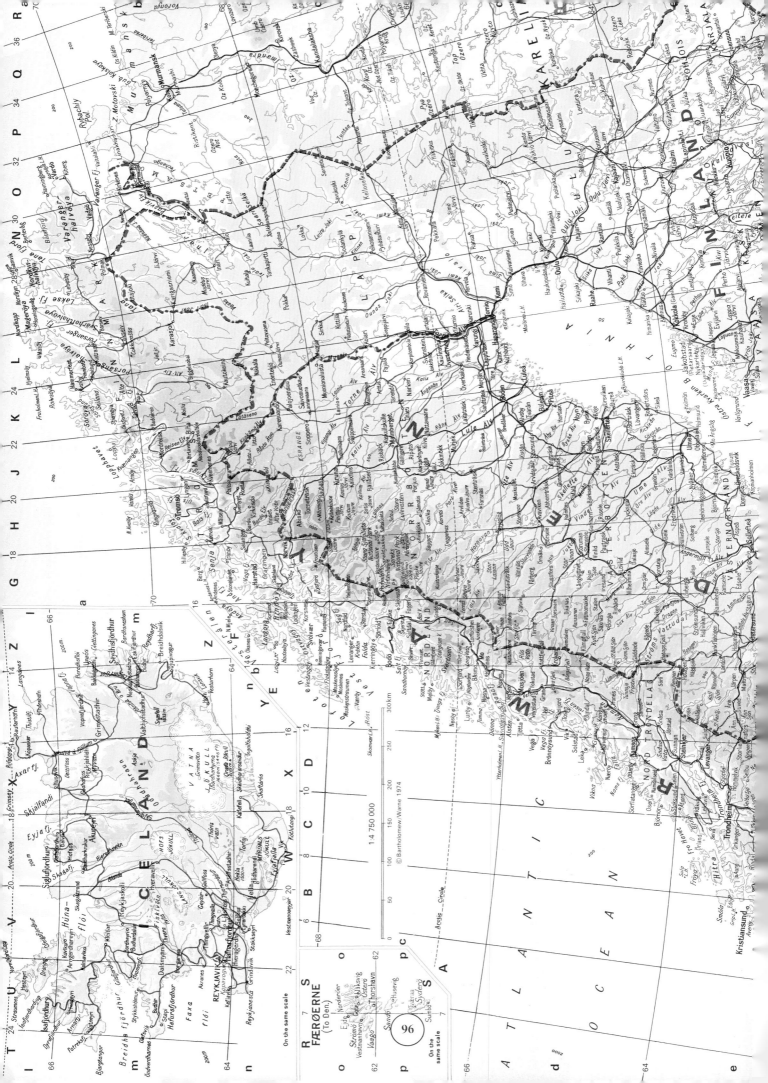

FÆRØERNE
(To Den.)

On the same scale

96

© Bartholomew/Warne 1974

1:4 750 000

0   50   100   150   200   250   300 km

On the same scale

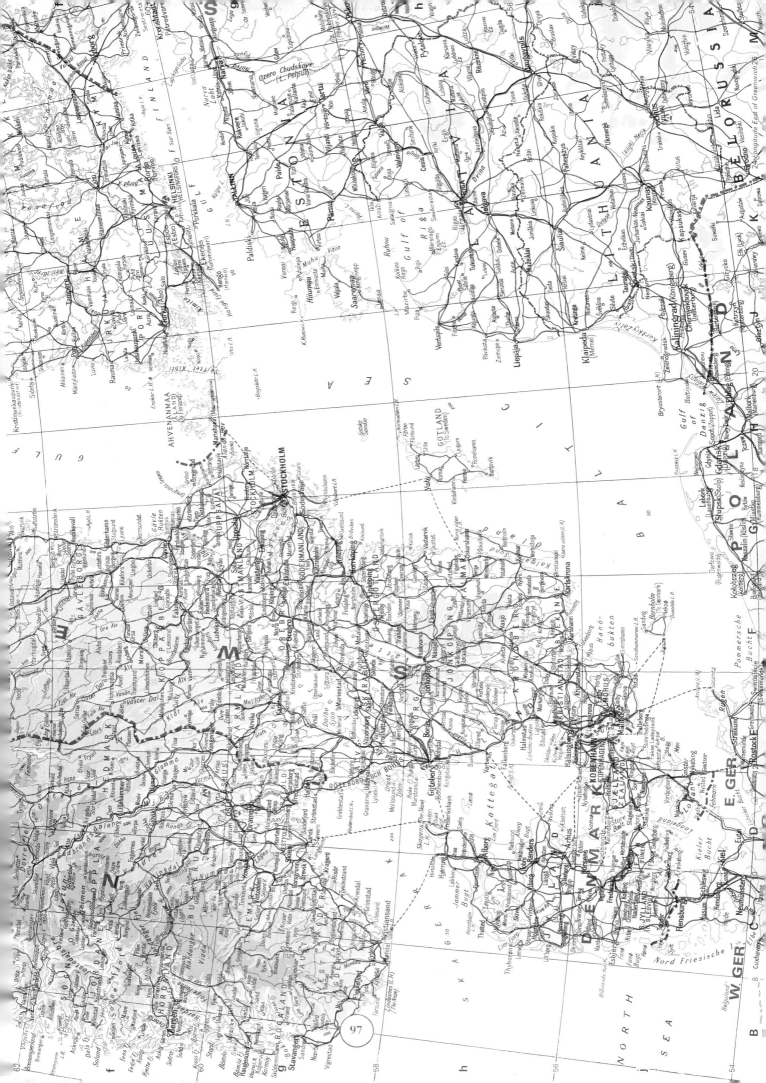

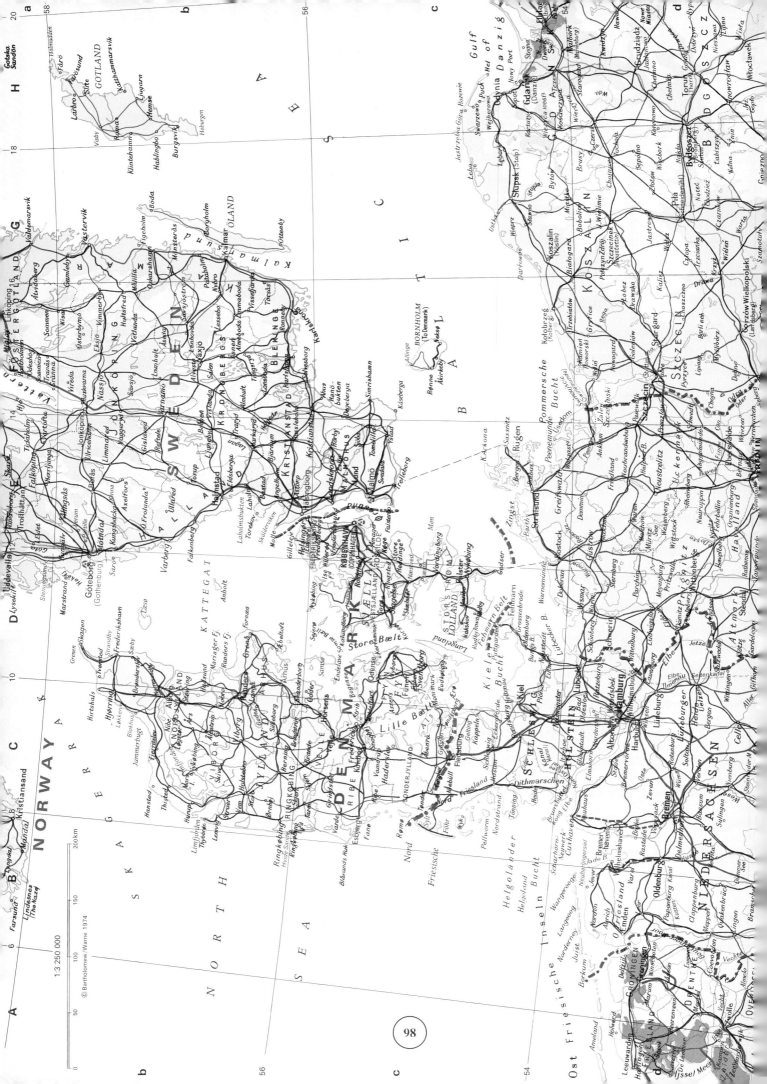

99

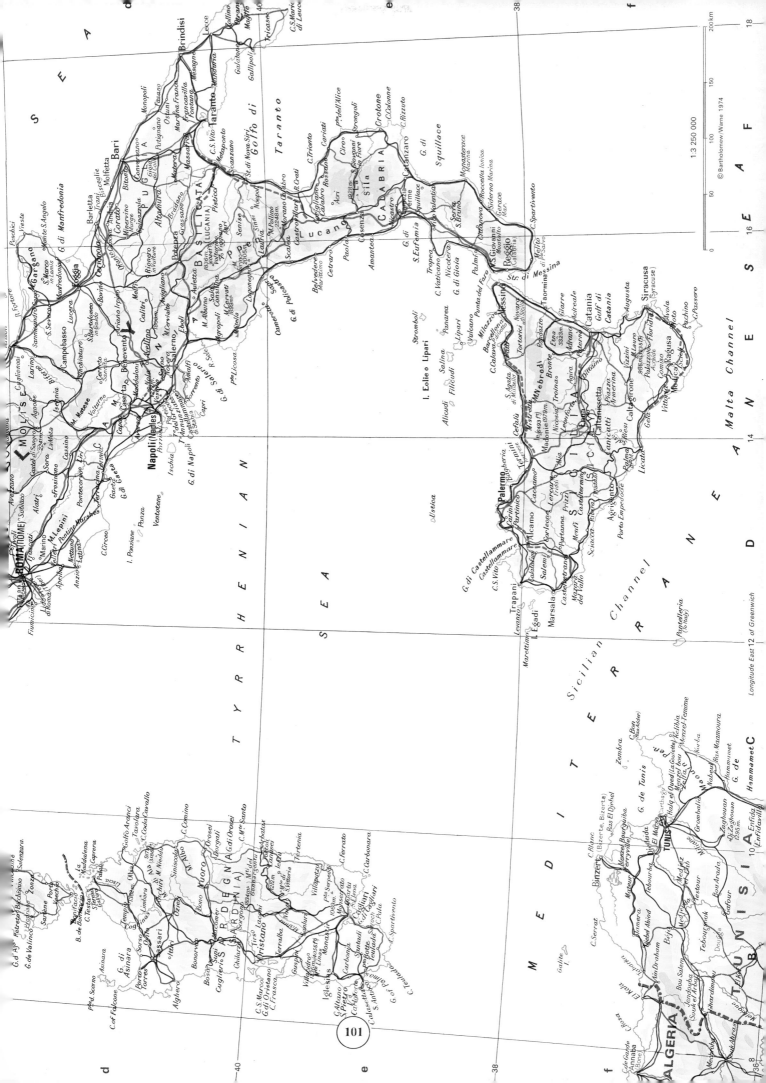

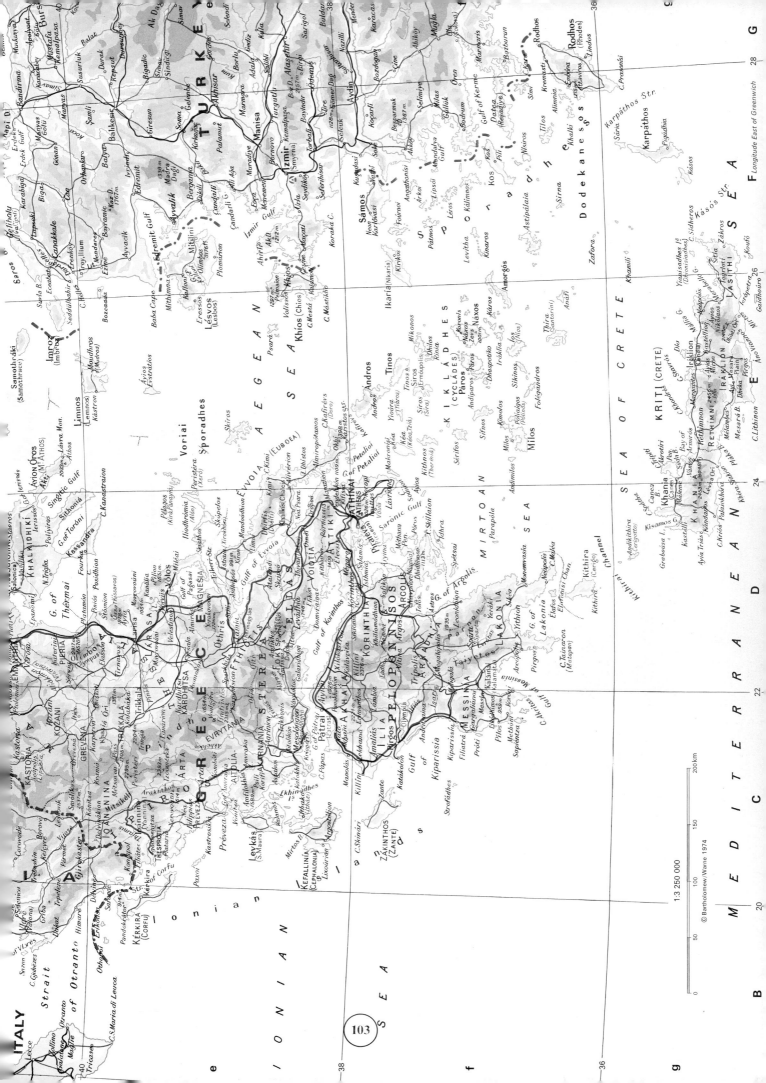

The Small
States and Island
Territories

The Small States

① Co-Principality of Andorra
area: 453 km²
population: 21425 = 47 per km²
currency: French Francs and Pesetas
languages: French and Spanish/Catalan
main town: Andorra la Vella

② Malta
area: 316 km²
population: 322000 = 1019 per km²
currency: £M: Maltese Pound
languages: Maltese and English
main town: Valletta

③ Principality of Liechtenstein
area: 157 km²
population: 22000 = 140 per km²
currency: Swiss Francs
language: German (Alemannish dialect)
main town: Vaduz

④ Principality of Monaco
area: 1.5 km²
population: 24000 = 15700 per km²
currency: French Francs
language: French/Monégasque
main town: Monte Carlo

⑤ Republic of San Marino
area: 61 km²
population: 18000 = 294 per km²
currency: Lire
language: Italian
main town: San Marino

⑥ Vatican City State
area: 0.44 km², 44 hectares
population: 1000 = 2273 per km²
currency: Papal issued Lire
language: Italian and Latin
main town: Città del Vaticano

The Island Territories of Western Europe

⑦ Azores: Açores
district of Portugal: Ilhas Adjacentes
area: 2335 km²
population: 291028 = 125 per km² (1970)
currency: Escudos
language: Portuguese
main town: Vila do Porto

⑧ Madeira
district of Portugal: Ilhas Adjacentes
area: 796 km²
population: 253220 = 318 per km²
currency: Escudos
language: Portuguese
main town: Funchal

⑨ Canary Islands: Islas Canarias
*provinces of Spain; Las Palmas and
Santa Cruz de Tenerife*
area: 7273 km²
population: 1170224 = 161 per km² (1970)
currency: Pesetas
language: Spanish
main towns: Santa Cruz de Tenerife
Las Palmas de Gran Canaria

⑩ Gibraltar (*isthmus*)
British Colony
area: 6.5 km²
population: 28694 = 4414 per km² (1971)
currency: £ Gibraltar/£ Sterling
languages: English and Spanish

⑪ Channel Islands
British Crown dependency
area: 195 km²
population: 126363 = 648 per km² (1971)
currency: £ issued locally/£ Sterling
languages: English and French
main town: St. Helier

⑫ Isle of Man
British Crown dependency
area: 572 km²
population: 56289 = 98 per km² (1971)
currencies: £ Sterling, £ Manx, £ Irish
language: English (some Manx revival)
main town: Douglas

⑬ The Faeroe Islands: Faeröerne
county of Denmark
area: 1399 km²
population: 40000 = 29 per km²
currency: Danish Kroner
languages: Faeroese and Danish
main town: Thorshavn

⑭ Greenland
county of Denmark
area: 2175600 km², 341700 km² ice-free
population: 47000 = 1 per 50 km², 1 per 7 km² ice-free
currency: Danish Kroner
language: Danish/Eskimo
main town: Godthåb

⑮ Svalbard: Spitsbergen, Jan Mayen and associated Islands
area: 62730 km²
population: 1052 Norwegian 1943 Russian =
total 1 per 20 km² (1971)
currencies: Norwegian Kroner and Russian Roubles
languages: Norwegian and Russian
camps inhabited only during winter season

Constitutions and Governments

The eighteen countries of Western Europe are listed in order of the size of their total populations in 1972. The same order is followed in the Statistical Profile on pages 108 to 115.

West Germany: Bundesrepublik Deutschland

A federal republic with a President elected by the Federal Assembly. The central government headed by the Chancellor consists of the Federal Diet (Bundestag) elected by popular vote for four years on a mixed proportional representation system and the Federal Council (Bundesrat) which is made up from representatives of the ten states (Länder). Voting age is 18. **Each Land** has its own parliament with wide legislative powers in such matters as education and the police. Local administration is effected through locally elected counties (Landkreise) and communes (Gemeinden). **After the defeat of Germany** in 1945 the territory was occupied by the allied powers and divided into four control zones. The Federal Republic became an independent sovereign state in May 1955, but recognition of a Germany divided into East and West was not agreed until 1972. A founder member of the EEC. **Language:** German. **Religion:** The population is equally divided between Protestants and Roman Catholics. **Capital city:** Bonn. **Currency:** Deutsche Mark: 100 Pfennig = 1 DM.

United Kingdom of Great Britain & Northern Ireland

A constitutional monarchy with the sovereign acting on the advice of a Privy Council. Parliament is divided into the House of Lords consisting of hereditary and life peers and the House of Commons which is elected by direct vote for terms of up to five years. In practice executive power is in the hands of the Prime Minister and his Cabinet which is dependent on the support of a majority in the House of Commons. The voting age is 18. **Local government** is carried out by locally elected county, district and parish councils each of which has set specialised functions to perform. Certain variations apply in Northern Ireland, Scotland and Wales. **Since the war** Britain has granted independence to most of her extensive empire, but has worked to retain strong links through the Commonwealth of Nations. A founder member of EFTA, Britain's commitment to European integration has only recently been strengthened by joining the enlarged EEC in 1973. **Language:** English is the national language although Welsh is commonly spoken in Wales. **Religion:** The Church of England is the established church. **Capital city:** London. **Currency:** Pounds Sterling: 100 pence = £1.

Italy: Repubblica Italiana

A democratic republic since 1946. Parliament consists of the Chamber of Deputies elected for 5-year terms by popular vote and a Senate elected on a regional basis. The President is elected by Parliament and delegates from Regional Councils for a term of seven years. The voting age is 21. **Italy is** administered through 20 autonomous regions, 94 provinces and at local level by communes headed by a mayor. **First united** only a hundred years ago, Italy was ruled by the House of Savoy until the declaration of the republic in June 1946. After the war Italy was required to give up all colonies and to cede territory to France, Greece and Yugoslavia. Acceptance of Marshall Aid and membership of the EEC helped economic and social recovery although the enormous differences between the rich North and the poor South have continued to create internal problems. **Language:** Italian is mostly spoken but there are German and Albanian-speaking minorities. **Religion:** Article 7 of the Constitution makes Roman Catholicism the only religion of the State. **Capital city:** Roma (Rome). **Currency:** Lire: 100 centesimi (not in current use) = 1 L.

France: République Française

A republic with a President as head of state. The new constitution of the Fifth Republic came into force in October 1958. The President, elected by popular vote for a term of seven years, has wide powers to ensure the proper functioning of government. Parliament consists of the National Assembly elected by direct and universal suffrage and the Senate elected to 9-year terms by an electoral college. Voting age is 21. **The administrative organisation** consists of 99 départements headed by a Prefect and 21 regional activity divisions (circonscriptions d'action régionale) for dealing with economic problems. The main unit of local government is the commune headed by a mayor who is both a local representative and an agent of central government. **France's colonial possessions** were granted independence by the 1960s although economic links are retained through membership of the Franc Zone. Particularly following the election of President de Gaulle France made rapid economic progress and has become a significant force in the political development of the Common Market. **Language:** French. **Religion:** There is no officially recognised religion although the dominant church is the Roman Catholic Church. **Capital city:** Paris. **Currency:** French Francs: 100 centimes = 1 F.

Spain: Estado Español

Ruled by a Head of State (Caudillo) although the Law of Succession provides for the restitution of the monarchy. The Leader is assisted by a Council of Ministers. The Parliament (Cortes) is composed of various representatives from the government, the National Council, the trade unions, universities and learned societies, local councils and 100 deputies elected by the heads of families. Heads of families and their wives are entitled to vote. **Local government** is administered through provinces each headed by a civil governor and municipalities whose councils are locally elected. **The Spanish state** was established by General Franco in 1936 and there followed a civil war until April 1939. In 1969 Prince Don Juan Carlos de Borbon was declared successor to the Head of State bearing the title HRH Prince of Spain until such time as he becomes king. **Languages:** Spanish, Catalan and Basque especially in the North. **Religion:** The established church is Roman Catholic. **Capital city:** Madrid. **Currency:** Pesetas: 100 centimos = 1 Pta.

The Netherlands: Koninkrijk der Nederlanden

A constitutional monarchy with a hereditary sovereign. The Parliament (Staen-Generaal) consists of an Upper Chamber (Eerste Kamer) elected by members of the Provincial States and a Lower Chamber (Tweede Kamer) who are elected directly for a term of four years. The sovereign also presides over a Council of State. Voting age is 18. **Local government** is organised through 11 provinces and 863 municipalities each headed by a Burgomaster and a locally elected council. **After the last war** the Netherlands abandoned its policy of neutrality, relinquished its colonies in South-east Asia and became a strong supporter of European integration. Her domestic economy has been boosted by vigorous commercial activity that has made the Netherlands the 'Gateway to Europe'. **Language:** The official language is Dutch although German and English are widely spoken. **Religion:** The population is mixed Protestant and Catholic and the royal family belong to the Dutch Reformed Church. **Capital city:** Amsterdam, with the seat of the Court and Parliament at Den Haag (The Hague). **Currency:** Dutch Guilder or Florin: 100 cents = 1 Gulden.

Belgium: Royaume de Belgique-Koninkrijk België

A constitutional and hereditary monarchy with legislative power in the hands of the King, Senate and Chamber of Deputies. Election to both chambers is by popular vote on the basis of proportional representation. The voting age is 18. **Local government** is through the elected councils of provinces and communes which enjoy a wide measure of independence. **An independent state** since 1830, Belgium was subsequently occupied in both world wars. In 1960 it relinquished its African colony and became one of the leaders of international co-operation in Europe. Brüssel has emerged as the Common Market capital. A recurring issue since the war has been the language dispute and since 1971 all Belgians are now officially recognised as either Walloons or Flemings (except for the German speaking Belgians) and each of these three communities has the right to preserve its own special identity. **Languages:** Flemish, French and German are official languages. **Religion:** A majority profess to the Roman Catholic faith. **Capital city:** Brüssel, Bruxelles (Brussels). **Currency:** Belgian Francs: 100 centimen-centimes = 1 F.

Greece: Vasileion tis Ellados

A republic since the referendum of 1973 which abolished the monarchy and substituted a self-appointed President as head of state. A national Government with a civilian cabinet is headed by the Prime Minister who is appointed by the President. Greek citizens over the age of 21 can vote, but free general elections have been superceded since the 1968 constitution. **Local government** is based on prefectures (Nomoi) although widespread reforms and reorganisation are promised by the present government. **During the last war** Greece was occupied by the Germans until 1944. After the war British and American help prevented the country from becoming communist along with most of the Balkans, although civil war lasted until 1949. A bloodless military coup in 1967 forced the king to leave the country and a military junta ruled in his absence. In 1969 Greece withdrew from the Council of Europe. **Language:** There are two forms of modern Greek: katharevoussa (used for official purposes and newspapers) and demotiki (spoken language). **Religion:** The Greek Orthodox Church is the established church of Greece. **Capital city:** Athínai (Athens). **Currency:** Drachmai: 100 leptai = 1 Drachma.

Portugal: Republica Portuguesa

A unitary and corporative republic with a President as head of state who is elected for 7-year terms by an electoral college. The single chamber National Assembly (Assembleia Nacional) is elected for four years by direct vote and a consultative Corporative Chamber, made up of representatives of the professions, functions alongside it. The President is advised by a State Council. Literate, registered citizens over the age of 21 are eligible to vote. **For local government purposes:** Portugal and its island territories are divided into provinces and districts. **Until 1910** Portugal was a monarchy. The present constitution dates from a national plebiscite in 1933. Portugal unlike the other European powers has retained much of its colonial empire although since 1951 its status has been that of overseas territories and it has been permitted a good deal of financial and administrative independence. **Language:** Portuguese. **Religion:** The people are mostly Roman Catholic. **Capital city:** Lisboa (Lisbon). **Currency:** Portuguese Escudos: 100 centavos = 1 Esc (1$00).

Finland: Suomen Tasavalta-Republiken Finland

A republic since 1919 headed by a President who serves for six years and is chosen by a college of electors representing the people. A single chamber parliament (Eduskunta) is chosen by direct and proportional election for 4-year terms. The Council of State is appointed by the President. The voting age is 20. **For local government** Finland is divided into twelve provinces (lääni) run by a governor and local elected sheriffs. **Once part of Sweden,** Finland became an autonomous Grand Duchy of Russia until it declared itself independent in 1917. During the second world war territory was ceded to the USSR, including parts of Karelia and the Petsamo area, but subsequently treaties of non-aggression and mutual assistance have been regularly agreed between the two countries. **Languages:** Finnish and Swedish are official languages. **Religion:** The national churches are the Lutheran National Church representing 92 per cent of the population and the Greek Orthodox Church of Finland. **Capital city:** Helsinki. **Currency:** Finnmarks: 100 penni = 1 Markkaa.

Sweden: Konungariket Sverige

A constitutional monarchy with the sovereign acting on the advice of a Council of State. The constitutional reforms of 1974 mean that, in all but name, Sweden is effectively a republic. Parliament consists of a single chamber (Riksdag) elected by universal suffrage for periods of three years. Voters must have reached the age of 19 a calendar year before the date of the election. **For administrative purposes,** Sweden is divided into 24 counties (län) and some 270 commune councils (kommunfullmaktige). All elections are conducted on the proportional system. **An independent state** for centuries, Sweden has previously ruled both Norway and Finland. Sweden remained neutral during both world wars and was a founder member of the Council of Europe, the Nordic Council and EFTA. **Language:** Swedish with Finnish and Lappish minorities. **Religion:** The Evangelical Lutheran is the established church. **Capital city:** Stockholm. **Currency:** Swedish Kroner: 100 öre = 1 Kr.

Norway: Kongeriket Norge

A limited and hereditary monarchy with the sovereign exercising authority through a Council of State (Statsrad). The Parliament (Stortinget), elected by popular vote, meets annually and is divided into an Upper Chamber (Lagting) and a Lower Chamber (Odesting) each of which has its own president. Citizens may vote on reaching the age of 20. **The country is administered** through 19 counties (fylker) and at local level by publicly elected district councils (kommunestyre). **Previously ruled** by Denmark and Sweden, Norway remained in independent union with Sweden until 1905. Occupied by Germany in 1940, Norway was not liberated until 1945. A founder member of EFTA and planned to join the enlarged EEC but withdrew at the last moment after a national referendum. **Language:** The official languages are Bokmål and Nynorsk. **Religion:** The Evangelical Lutheran is the established church of the country. **Capital city:** Oslo. **Currency:** Norwegian Kroner: 100 øre = 1 Kr.

Austria: Republik Osterreich

Federal republic with a President as head of state elected by direct popular vote for a term of six years. Two legislative chambers form the National Assembly; the Bundesrat (Federal Council) representing the nine federal provinces and the Nationalrat (National Council) elected by proportional representation. The voting age is 20. **Local government** is through an elected Provincial Assembly (Landtag) and commune councils headed by a burgomaster. **Boundaries** were formally established by the Treaty of St. Germain in 1919. In March 1938 Austria was forcibly incorporated into the German Reich and not liberated by the Allies until the spring of 1945. A provisional government was supervised by the Four-Power Allied Control Council until independence in October 1955. Austria became a member of EFTA in 1960. **Languages:** 98 per cent are German speaking. **Religion:** Over 90 per cent are Roman Catholic. **Capital city:** Wien (Vienna). **Currency:** Schillings: 100 Groschen = 1 S.

Republic of Ireland: Eire

A republic exercising control over 26 of the 32 counties of Ireland. The President is elected by direct popular vote for 7-year terms. The National Parliament (Oireachtas) comprises a House of Representatives (Dail Eireann) elected by adult suffrage and a nominated Senate (Seanad Eireann). Voting is by all citizens over 18. **Local government** is organised by county councils and urban councils elected under a system of proportional representation. **The republic** was proclaimed in April 1916 following an insurrection against British rule. The border between Northern Ireland and the Irish Free State was fixed in 1925. Ireland adopted a policy of neutrality during the last war and relinquished its membership of the Commonwealth in 1949. A national referendum in 1972 approved the decision to join the EEC with Britain and Denmark. **Language:** The official languages are Irish and English. **Religion:** 95 per cent of the population are Roman Catholic. **Capital city:** Dublin. **Currency:** Irish Pounds: 100 pence = £1.

Switzerland: Schweiz-Suisse-Svizzera

A democratic republic. The electorate vote representatives to Parliament and can also vote to change the Constitution. Parliament consists of a Council of States (Standerat) representing the cantons of the Confederation and a National Council (Nationalrat) elected by proportional representation for a period of four years. The President of the Confederation is elected by the Federal Assembly (Bundesrat) which consists of seven members elected by a joint session of both chambers. The voting age is 20. **Local administration** gives wide powers to the cantonal councils and public participation in local and national affairs is encouraged by common use of referendum. **In 1815** perpetual neutrality was guaranteed to Switzerland by the Great Powers and it has been jealously guarded ever since. The headquarters of many international organisations, Switzerland still has not joined the United Nations although she takes part in the work of several of its agencies. **Languages:** German, French, Italian and Romansch. **Religion:** There is a mixed Catholic and Protestant population. **Capital city:** Bern (Berne). **Currency:** Swiss Francs: 100 Rappen, centimes, centesimi = 1 F.

Luxembourg: Grand-Duché de Luxembourg

A hereditary monarchy with a constitution that leaves wide powers of control to the sovereign. Parliament consists of a Council of State chosen by the sovereign and a Chamber of Deputies elected for five years by popular vote. Citizens may vote on reaching the age of 18. **For local government** purposes the country is divided into 12 cantons. **Luxembourg** has formed an economic union with Belgium since 1922 and in addition to the customs union, Belgian currency is legal tender in Luxembourg. A founder member of the EEC, Luxembourg has become the second capital of the Common Market and is the administrative centre of the European Parliament and the seat of the EEC Court of Justice. **Language:** The national language is Letzburgish; French, German and English are also widely used. **Religion:** The majority of the population are Roman Catholics. **Capital city:** Luxembourg City. **Currency:** Luxembourg and Belgian Francs: 100 centimes = 1 F.

Denmark: Kongeriget Danmark

Constitutional monarchy with the sovereign exercising executive power through the Statsraadet (State Council). The parliament (Folketing) consists of a single chamber elected by popular vote. The Faeroes and Greenland enjoy equal status with the rest of the kingdom. Danish nationals of over 20 may vote. **Local government** is through counties, municipalities and district councils elected directly for 4-year terms. The counties and København are supervised by a governor appointed by the monarch. **Occupied** during the last war Denmark became a founder member of NATO and the Nordic Council in 1952. The 1953 constitution revision abolished the upper house of the parliament, changed the law of succession to allow a female to succeed to the throne and made Greenland part of the kingdom. A founder member of EFTA and negotiated with Britain and Ireland to join the enlarged EEC in 1973. **Language:** Danish. **Religion:** The established church is the Danish Lutheran Church. **Capital city:** København (Copenhagen). **Currency:** Danish Kroner: 100 øre = 1 Kr.

Iceland: Lyoveldio Island

A republic with a President who is elected by popular vote for a 4-year term of office. The parliament (Athing) consists of an Upper and a Lower House with the members mostly elected by proportional representation but others apportioned to the parties according to their total vote. The voting age is 20. **Administration** is through provincial and municipal councils, but for economic planning purposes the country is divided into seven districts (kjödaemi). **An independent** free state from 874 until 1264 when it fell under Norwegian rule. From 1381 it was ruled by Danish kings until acknowledged a sovereign state in 1918. The republic was declared after a referendum in 1944. **Language:** Icelandic is the national language. **Religion:** The national church is the Evangelical Lutheran Church. **Capital city:** Reykjavik. **Currency:** Icelandic Kronur: 100 aurar = 1 Kr.

Statistical Profile 1

1972 figures unless otherwise noted　　　　Metric units

	West Germany	United Kingdom	Italy
AREA Total: km²] km² per thousand people	248 577] 4	244 047] 4	301 243] 6
POPULATION Total: thousands] average per km²	61 669] 248	55 798] 229	54 344] 180[f]
Rate per thousand people: Births] Deaths	11.4] 11.8	14.9] 12.1	16.3] 9.6
CAPITAL:	Bonn	London	Roma
	279	7 345 (12 762)	2 755[b]
MAIN TOWNS: Population in thousands (Agglomeration total in brackets)　1	West Berlin 2 084	Birmingham 1 008 (2 367)	Milano 1 708[b]
2	Hamburg 1 782	Glasgow 862 (1 698)	Nápoli 1 277[b]
3	München 1 338	Liverpool 591 (1 247)	Torino 1 184[b]
EMPLOYMENT: Working population: thousands	26 802[a]	25 159	19 028
Per cent of civilian workforce in: agriculture] manufacturing	8.2[a]] 38.9[a]	2.7[a]] 36.0[a]	17.5] 31.1
UNEMPLOYMENT: average, thousands] per cent of workforce	246] 1.1	885] 3.8	697] 3.6
INDUSTRIAL STOPPAGES: total working days lost	66 045	23 909 000	19 497 143
AGRICULTURAL PRODUCTION Important produce: thousand tons　MAJOR CROPS A	Wheat 6 608	Barley 9 244	Wheat 9 423
B	Barley 5 997	Wheat 4 780	Maize 4 802
C	Rye 2 914	Oats 1 255	Grapes 9 369
D	Potatoes 15 036	Potatoes 6 550	Tomatoes 3 361
MAJOR ANIMAL PRODUCTS A	Meat 3 890	Meat 2 708	Meat 2 592
B	Eggs 948	Eggs 870	Eggs 570
C	Cheese 540	Cheese 182	Cheese 485
D	Milk 21 318	Milk 14 200	Milk 9 180
SEA FISHING Total landed catch: thousand tons	755[b]	1050	391[a]
ENERGY COAL PRODUCTION[c]: thousand tons] tons per head	138 908] 2.252	121 843] 2.184	583] 0.011
GAS PRODUCTION[d]: mn cubic metres] cubic metres per head	34 926] 566	36 012] 645	17 068] 314
ELECTRICITY PRODUCTION: mn kWh] kWh per head	274 774] 4456	265 982] 4767	134 700] 2479[g]
CRUDE OIL IMPORTED: thousand tons] tons per head	100 230] 1.635[a]	107 706] 1.937	115 705] 2.147[a]
MEDIA TELEVISION: thousand licences] per thousand people	17 673] 299[a]	16 982] 305	10 344] 191[a]
PRESS: dailies circulation, thousands] copies per thousand people	19 701] 319[b]	25 609] 463 (1968)	7 899] 146[a]
TRANSPORT ROADS: total km] km of motorway	440 059] 4461	359 622[a]] 1662	287 447[a]] 4615
PASSENGER CARS: total in use, thousands	16 324	13 044	12 475
COMMERCIAL VEHICLES: buses and lorries, thousands	1 274	1 808	1 022
RAIL: total km of track] per cent electrified	32 838] 28.2	18 738] 16.9[e]	20 116] 46.7
TOTAL RAIL TRAFFIC: million passenger km	39 065	28 349[e]	35 370
TOTAL RAIL TRAFFIC: million freight ton km	64 865	20 471[e]	17 097
TOTAL AIR TRAFFIC: million passenger km	10 452	22 168	9 502[a]
TOTAL AIR TRAFFIC: million freight ton km	701	783	324[a]
SEA: international cargoes thousand tons: loaded] unloaded	22 462] 102 009	49 539] 206 446[a]	35 875] 220 407
PIPELINES: total km	2 086	1 898	1 875

[a] 1971　[b] 1970　[c] including coal equivalent of lignite　[d] manufactured and natural

France	Spain	Netherlands	Belgium	Greece	Portugal
France	**Spain**	**Netherlands**	**Belgium**	**Greece**	**Portugal**
547026 ❙ 11	504750 ❙ 15	40844 ❙ 3	30514 ❙ 3	131944 ❙ 15	92082 ❙ 11
51615 ❙ 94	34365 ❙ 68	13330 ❙ 326	9711 ❙ 318	8890[g] ❙ 67	8590 ❙ 93
16.9 ❙ 10.6	19.4 ❙ 8.2	16.1 ❙ 8.5	13.8 ❙ 12.0	15.9 ❙ 8.3[a]	20.3 ❙ 10.5
Paris	Madrid	Amsterdam	Brüssel	Athínai	Lisboa
2591 (8197)[b]	3302	808 (1029)	1075[a]	867 (2540)[a]	782 (1651)[b]
Marseille	Barcelona	Rotterdam	Antwerpen	Thessaloníki	Oporto
889 (964)[b]	1773	670 (1064)	223 (673)[a]	346 (557)[a]	310 (836)[b]
Lyon	Valencia	Den Haag	Gent	Pátrai	Coimbra
528 (1075)[b]	679	525 (702)	148 (225)[a]	112 (121)[a]	46[b]
Toulouse	Sevilla	Utrecht	Liège	Iraklion	Vila Nova de Gaia
371 (440)[b]	565	275 (463)	145 (440)[a]	78 (85)[a]	46[b]
21860	12957	4784[a]	3969	3284[a]	3284[a]
12.3 ❙ 26.3	24.9[a] ❙ 52.6[a]	6.9[a] ❙ 26.0[a]	4.0[a] ❙ 31.7	40.4[a] ❙ 16.4[a]	31.1 ❙ 26.8[a]
383 ❙ 1.8	191 ❙ 1.5	108 ❙ 2.7	87 ❙ 3.5	30 ❙ 4.5[a]	77 ❙ 2.4 (1960)
3755343	586616	134187	354086	nil	not available
Wheat 18123	Wheat 4562	Wheat 673	Wheat 863	Wheat 1919	Wheat 585
Barley 10426	Barley 4358	Apples 470	Barley 653	Grapes 1620	Tomatoes 910
Maize 8610	Grapes 4250	Sugar 763	Sugar 667	Tomatoes 1100	Grapes 1050
Grapes 8938	Olives 2300	Potatoes 5360	Potatoes 1150	Olives 1090	Potatoes 1200
Meat 3850	Meat 1260	Meat 1475	Meat 930	Meat 286	Meat 275
Cheese 863	Eggs 422	Cheese 322	Eggs 247	Cheese 137	Eggs 38
Eggs 672	Cheese 81	Eggs 270	Butter 95	Eggs 110	Cheese 17
Milk 29177	Milk 4400	Milk 8860	Milk 3680	Milk 540	Milk 470
742[a]	1500[a]	321[a]	60[a]	125[a]	498[a]
31541 ❙ 0.611	12535 ❙ 0.365	2812 ❙ 0.211	10510 ❙ 1.082	3769 ❙ 0.424	252 ❙ 0.029
13113 ❙ 254[g]	2455 ❙ 71	59214 ❙ 4442	3026 ❙ 313[a]	8 ❙ 1	129 ❙ 15
160080 ❙ 3101	68140 ❙ 1983	49550 ❙ 3717	36908 ❙ 3801	12035 ❙ 1354	8676 ❙ 1010
104749 ❙ 2.029[a]	35132 ❙ 1.029[a]	71568 ❙ 5.426[a]	30581 ❙ 3.162[a]	4857 ❙ 0.549[a]	3987 ❙ 0.462[a]
11655 ❙ 227[a]	4520 ❙ 132[a]	3776 ❙ 283	2200 ❙ 228[a]	250 ❙ 28	529 ❙ 62
11957 ❙ 238 (1969)	3396 ❙ 99[a]	4100 ❙ 311[a]	2500 ❙ 260 (1968)	682 ❙ 76	674 ❙ 71 (1967)
790000[g] ❙ 1713[a]	139881 ❙ 307	97519 ❙ 1209[b]	94500 ❙ 898	35515 ❙ 65	42525 ❙ 75
13920	3255	3117	2247	302	660
1930	852	356	237	142	83
35277 ❙ 26.3	1631 ❙ 23.2	3147 ❙ 52.3	4144 ❙ 29.7	2571 ❙ none	3563 ❙ 11.7
43093	14393	8114	8168	1635[a]	3760
68493	10221	3071	7454	748[a]	829
17458	8083	7857	3093	2965	3323
696	175	480	233	47	62
22845 ❙ 149905[a]	16267 ❙ 65959[a]	77219 ❙ 232800	32454 ❙ 54338	5929 ❙ 17771	3400 ❙ 9636
4129	267	476	317	not available	not available

[e]state railways only [f]resident population [g]estimated

Statistical Profile 2

1972 figures unless otherwise noted   Metric units

		West Germany	United Kingdom	Italy
PRODUCTION	CRUDE STEEL: thousand tons **∎ kg per head**	43 705 ∎ **709**	25 321 ∎ **454**	19 689 ∎ **362**
	MAN MADE FIBRES: thousand tons **∎ kg per head**	799 ∎ **13**	626 ∎ **11**	492 ∎ **9**
	TV SETS: thousands made **∎ per thousand people**	2 538 ∎ **41**[a]	2 397 ∎ **43**[a]	2 028 ∎ **38**[b]
	PASSENGER CARS: thousands made **∎ per thousand people**	3 514 ∎ **57**	1 921 ∎ **34**	1 732 ∎ **32**
	SHIPS LAUNCHED thousands GRT **∎ GRT per thousand people**	1 632 ∎ **26**	1 242 ∎ **222**	949 ∎ **17**
TRADE	IMPORTS: £ million **∎ average per head**	16 063 ∎ **£260**	11 155 ∎ **£200**	7 707 ∎ **£142**
	EXPORTS: £ million **∎ average per head**	18 665 ∎ **£303**	9 746 ∎ **£175**	7 413 ∎ **£136**
	NET INVISIBLE EARNINGS £ million **∎ average per head**	—632 ∎ **—£10**	+932 ∎ **+£17**	+667 ∎ **+£12**
	TOURISM, INCOME: £ million **∎ per cent of GDP**	741 ∎ **0.7**	547 ∎ **0.9**	869 ∎ **1.8**
IMPORTS Per cent of total imports	from the EEC of 9	54	32	49
	from the rest of the 18	12	16	8
	from the USA	11	11	8
	from centrally planned economies	4	4	6
	from less developed countries	16	22	24
PRODUCTS IMPORTED Per cent of total imports	Top five groups 1.	Food 15	Machinery 14	Machinery 14
	2.	Machinery 13	Oil & products 10	Oil & products 13
	3.	Oil & products 8	Chemicals 6	Chemicals 8
	4.	Chemicals 6	Meat 5	Cattle 5
	5.	Iron & steel 5	Vehicles 4	Vehicles 5
EXPORTS Per cent of total exports	to the EEC of 9	48	30	50
	to the rest of the 18	22	17	13
	to the USA	9	12	10
	to centrally planned economies	5	3	5
	to less developed countries	13	23	17
PRODUCTS EXPORTED Per cent of total exports	Top five groups 1.	Machinery 32	Machinery 28	Machinery 24
	2.	Vehicles 14	Chemicals 10	Fabric & yarn 13
	3.	Chemicals 12	Vehicles 9	Chemicals 7
	4.	Iron & steel 7	Fabric & yarn 6	Vehicles 9
	5.	Fabric & yarn 4	Iron & steel 4	Iron & steel 4
GOVERNMENT SPENDING[g]	HEALTH: £ million **∎ per head**	3 529 ∎ **£58**[b]	2 053 ∎ **£37**[a]	442 ∎ **£8**[b]
	EDUCATION: £ million **∎ per head**	1 827 ∎ **£31** (1969)	2 037 ∎ **£37**[a]	1 459 ∎ **£27**[a]
	DEFENCE: £ million **∎ per head**	2 765 ∎ **£45**[a]	2 739 ∎ **£49**[a]	1 391 ∎ **£26**[b]
	OVERSEAS AID: £ million **∎ per head**	321 ∎ **£5.20**[a]	220 ∎ **£3.90**[a]	114 ∎ **£2.10**[a]
LIVING STANDARDS	HOUSEHOLDS: thousands **∎ average size**	22 230 ∎ **2.8**[g]	19 335 ∎ **2.9**	16 100 ∎ **3.4**[g]
	NATIONAL INCOME: £ million **∎ average per head**	92 162 ∎ **£1 494**	56 262 ∎ **£1 008**	43 199 ∎ **£795**
	CARS: per thousand people	263	233	229
	TELEPHONES: per thousand people	268	314	208
	HOUSING: thousand homes built **∎ per thousand people**	661 ∎ **10.7**	331 ∎ **5.9**	240 ∎ **4.4**
COST OF LIVING Per cent increase 1970 to 1972	FOOD: retail prices	10	21	11
	MANUFACTURES: wholesale prices	8	14	7

[a] 1971 [b] 1970

France	Spain	Netherlands	Belgium	Portugal	Greece
24054 ▌466	9533 ▌277[g]	5587 ▌419	14538 ▌1497	210 ▌24[b]	425 ▌49
347 ▌7	173 ▌5	144 ▌11[a]	57 ▌6	5 ▌1	22 ▌3
1471 ▌29[a]	660 ▌19[a]	not available	514 ▌53[b]	45 ▌5[b]	46 ▌5 (1969)
2993 ▌58	610 ▌18	73 ▌5	905 ▌93[j]	nil	66 ▌8[j]
1129 ▌58	1134 ▌33	752 ▌56	238 ▌25	97 ▌11	11 ▌1
10792 ▌£209	2691 ▌£78	6963 ▌£522	6237 ▌£620	937 ▌£105	874 ▌£102
10561 ▌£205	1515 ▌£44	6707 ▌£503	6427 ▌£639	348 ▌£39	514 ▌£60
+220 ▌+£4	+820 ▌+£24	+319 ▌+£24	+116 ▌+£12	+249 ▌+£28	+65 ▌+£8
648 ▌0.8	1042 ▌6.0	259 ▌1.7[a]	173 ▌1.3	157 ▌3.2	156 ▌5.0
56	42	62	71	55	46
8	8	6	6	7	15
8	16	8	5	6	9
3	2	2	2	5	1
19	26	18	12	14	22
Machinery 19	Machinery 22	Machinery 17[a]	Machinery 15	Machinery 25	Machinery 22
Food 11	Oil & products 12	Food 11[a]	Vehicles 11	Food 10	Food 13
Oil & products 10	Chemicals 11	Oil & products 10[a]	Food 11	Chemicals 10	Chemicals 10
Chemicals 8	Food 11	Chemicals 8[a]	Chemicals 8	Oil & products 9	Vehicles 8
Iron & steel 6	Iron & steel 4	Vehicles 56[a]	Oil & products 7	Ships 9	Oil & products 6
56	45	74	74	52	47
12	9	8	8	6	17
5	16	4	6	10	11
4	3	2	2	14	1
19	21	9	8	14	20
Machinery 18	Fruit & veg 16	Machinery 15[a]	Iron & steel 15	Fruit 21	Fabric & yarn 18
Food 14	Machinery 10	Chemicals 13[a]	Fabric & yarn 11	Tobacco 13	Food 10
Vehicles 11	Footwear 7	Meat & dairy prod. 10[a]	Machinery 11	Fabric & yarn 9	Clothing 10
Chemicals 10	Ships 7	Oil & products 10[a]	Vehicles 10	Chemicals 7	Machinery 10
Iron & steel 7	Iron & steel 5	Fabric & yarn 8[a]	Chemicals 10	Cotton 5	Wine 7
4358 ▌£86[b]	205 ▌£6 (1969)	32 ▌£2[b]	560 ▌£58[a]	42 ▌£5[a]	65 ▌£8[a]
1727 ▌£34 (1969)	179 ▌£5[b]	534 ▌£41[b]	628 ▌£65[a]	69 ▌£8[b]	46 ▌£5[a]
2070 ▌£41[b]	250 ▌£7[b]	543 ▌£41[a]	306 ▌£32[a]	201 ▌£23[b]	195 ▌£23[a]
452 ▌£8.80[a]	not applicable	87 ▌£6.50[a]	59 ▌£6.10[a]	not applicable	48 ▌£6.00[a]
16950 ▌3.0[g]	8590 ▌4.0[g]	4020 ▌3.3[g]	3210 ▌3.0[g]	2267 ▌3.9[g]	2147[a] ▌4.0[g]
70935 ▌£1374	16135 ▌£470	16838 ▌£1263	10793 ▌£1111[a]	4706 ▌£529	2643 ▌£306[a]
269	94	232	231	34	77
199	164	299	237	163	99
667 ▌12.9[a]	190 ▌5.5[i]	153 ▌11.5	53 ▌5.5	179 ▌20.1	29 ▌3.4
15	18	11	9	9	20
10[h]	13	5	3	10	8

Total trade figures include Luxembourg (page 115)

Statistical Profile 3

1972 figures unless otherwise noted   Metric units

		Sweden	Austria	Switzerland
AREA	Total: km² **‖ km² per thousand people**	449 964 **‖ 55**	83 850 **‖ 11**	41 293 **‖ 6**
POPULATION	Total: thousands **‖ average per km²**	8 122 **‖ 18**	7 487 **‖ 89**	6 385 **‖ 155**
	Rate per thousand people: Birth **‖ Deaths**	13.8 **‖ 10.3**	13.9 **‖ 12.8**	14.4 **‖ 8.7**
	CAPITAL:	Stockholm	Wien	Bern
		699 (1351)	1615 (1859[a])	159 (285)
MAIN TOWNS:	1	Göteborg	Graz	Zürich
Population in thousands		442 (688)	248 (314[a])	416 (718)
(Agglomeration total in brackets)	2	Malmö	Linz	Basel
		259 (452)	203 (357[a])	208 (380)
	3	Uppsala	Salzburg	Genève
		133	129 (196[a])	172 (320)
EMPLOYMENT:	Working population: thousands	3 568	3 027[a]	3 005[b]
Per cent of civilian workforce in: agriculture **‖ manufacturing**		7.7 **‖ 28.6**	16.4 **‖ 29.8**	7.6 **‖ 48.4**[bk]
UNEMPLOYMENT: average, thousands **‖ per cent of workforce**		107 **‖ 2.7**	49 **‖ 1.9**	0.1 **‖ 0.0**
INDUSTRIAL STOPPAGES: total working days lost		10 507	15 104	2 002
AGRICULTURAL PRODUCTION	MAJOR CROPS A	Oats 1 909	Barley 928	Wheat 378
Important produce: thousand tons	B	Barley 1 883	Wheat 791	Potatoes 1 000
	C	Wheat 1 150	Maize 750	Apples 270
	D	Potatoes 1 213	Potatoes 2 341	Sugar Beet 270
	MAJOR ANIMAL PRODUCTS A	Meat 429	Meat 497	Meat 373
	B	Eggs 100	Eggs 90	Cheese 96
	C	Cheese 70	Cheese 68	Eggs 39
	D	Milk 2 700	Milk 3 200	Milk 3 213
SEA FISHING	Total landed catch: thousand tons	237[a]	nil	nil
ENERGY	COAL PRODUCTION[c]: thousand tons **‖ tons per head**	nil	1 877 **‖ 0.251**	nil
GAS PRODUCTION[d]: mn cubic metres **‖ cubic metres per head**		511 **‖ 64**[b]	2 592 **‖ 346**	386 **‖ 60**
ELECTRICITY PRODUCTION: mn kWh **‖ kWh per head**		70 673 **‖ 8701**	29 366 **‖ 3922**	31 443 **‖ 4925**
CRUDE OIL IMPORTED: thousand tons **‖ tons per head**		11 267 **‖ 1.391**[a]	4 480 **‖ 0.601**[a]	5 186 **‖ 0.821**[a]
MEDIA	TELEVISION: thousand licences **‖ per thousand people**	2 619 **‖ 323**[a]	1 586 **‖ 213**[a]	1 520 **‖ 238**
PRESS: dailies circulation, thousands **‖ copies per thousand people**		4 324 **‖ 534**[b]	2 187 **‖ 293**[a]	2 360 **‖ 374**[a]
TRANSPORT	ROADS: total km **‖ km of motorway**	175 220 **‖ 605**	95 388[a] **‖ 585**	60 305 **‖ 450**
PASSENGER CARS: total in use, thousands		2 457	1 460	1 561
COMMERCIAL VEHICLES: buses and lorries, thousands		161	145	157
RAIL: total km of track **‖ per cent electrified**		12 181 **‖ 61.7**	6 546[b] **‖ 40.1**	5 000[a] **‖ 99.5**
TOTAL RAIL TRAFFIC: million passenger km		4 125[a]	6 703[a]	8 302
TOTAL RAIL TRAFFIC: million freight ton km		15 658[a]	9 912[a]	6 703
TOTAL AIR TRAFFIC: million passenger km		3 006	477	5 783
TOTAL AIR TRAFFIC: million freight ton km		134	6	219
SEA: international cargoes thousand tons: loaded **‖ unloaded**		33 533 **‖ 47 801**	nil	nil
PIPELINES: total km		not available	597	222

[a]1971   [b]1970   [c]including coal equivalent of lignite   [d]manufactured and natural

Denmark	Finland	Norway	Republic of Ireland	Luxembourg	Iceland
43070 ▌9	337032 ▌73	323886 ▌82[em]	70283 ▌23	2586 ▌7	103000 ▌493
4992 ▌116	4624 ▌14	3933 ▌12	3014 ▌43	347 ▌134	209 ▌2
15.2[a] ▌10.1	12.7 ▌9.6	16.3 ▌10.0	22.4 ▌11.2	11.9 ▌11.9	19.7 ▌7.1[b]
København	Helsinki	Oslo	Dublin	Luxembourg-Ville	Reykjavik
626 (1344)[a]	520 (804[b])	473	566 (670)[a]	78	82
Århus	Tampere	Bergen	Cork	Esch-sur-Alzette	Kópavogur
238[a]	165 (217[b])	214	128 (132)[a]	28	11
Odense	Turku	Trondheim	Limerick	Differdange	Akureyri
166[a]	158 (220[b])	131	57 (60)[a]	18	11
Ålborg	Espoo	Stavanger	Dun Laoghaire	Dudelange	Hafnarfjördhur
155[a]	104	83	53 (95)[a]	15	10
2424	2199	167	1119	151	82[a]
9.7 ▌27.0[al]	20.6[a] ▌25.8[al]	11.9 ▌24.9[al]	26.5[a] ▌20.9[a]	10.2 ▌47.4[an]	14.8[a] ▌20.1[a]
30 ▌3.6	55 ▌2.5	15 ▌1.0	48 ▌8.1	0.04 ▌0.0	0.6 ▌0.7[a]
21800	473100	12402	206 955	nil[b]	12 037
Barley 5589	Oats 1197	Barley 522	Barley 935	Barley 54	Hay 310
Oats 638	Barley 1054	Oats 268	Wheat 260	Oats 37	Potatoes 11
Wheat 602	Wheat 424	Potatoes 634	Potatoes 1300	Wheat 36	Turnips 1
Potatoes 700	Potatoes 820	Apples 50	Sugar Beet 186	Potatoes 53	Tomatoes 1
Meat 1038	Meat 271	Meat 158	Meat 473	Meat 22	Meat 16
Butter 136	Butter 83	Cheese 57	Butter 76	Butter 7	Cheese 4
Cheese 131	Eggs 75	Eggs 38	Eggs 43	Eggs 4	Eggs 2
Milk 4500	Milk 3344	Milk 1780	Milk 3750	Milk 220	Milk 125
1401[a]	82[b]	3075[a]	74[a]	nil	685[a]
nil	nil	455 ▌0.166	74 ▌0.025	nil	nil
380 ▌76	47 ▌10	29 ▌7	257 ▌85	12 ▌35	nil
18500 ▌3706	26279 ▌5683	67522 ▌17168	6675 ▌2215	2220 ▌6398	1767 ▌8455
10664 ▌2.150[b]	8859 ▌1.922[a]	6404 ▌1.628	3110 ▌1.047[a]	*with Belgium*	Petroleum: 522 ▌2559[b]
1375 ▌277[a]	1177 ▌254	920 ▌234	486 ▌164[a]	85 ▌246	42 ▌196[a]
1829 ▌368[a]	1836 ▌392 (1968)	1548 ▌396[a]	694 ▌234[a]	191 ▌560	96 ▌449[a]
63925 ▌240	78000[b] ▌130	73112 ▌88	87202[b] ▌none	4962 ▌20	11137 ▌none
1229	818	854	418[a]	111	47[a]
179	130	170	49[a]	10	6[a]
2890[b] ▌2.9[b]	5968 ▌1.1	4240 ▌57.5	2189 ▌none	271 ▌50.2	nil
3487[ae]	2580	1600[a]	818	262	nil
1926[e]	6508	2518[a]	500	783	nil
1808	935	2526	1623	119[a]	1940
86	27	90	80	0.2[a]	20
7370 ▌30590[a]	11882 ▌21649	37493 ▌20384	not available	nil	258 ▌1040[a]
not available	not available	not available	not available	not available	not available

[e] state railways only   [g] estimated   [k] includes construction and utilities   [l] includes mining and utilities   [m] excludes Svalbard and islands   [n] includes mining, construction and utilities

Statistical Profile 4

1972 figures unless otherwise noted   Metric units

		Sweden	Austria	Switzerland
PRODUCTION	CRUDE STEEL: thousand tons **⌶ kg per head**	5 233 ⌶ 644	4 069 ⌶ 543	532 ⌶ 84[a]
	MAN MADE FIBRES: thousand tons **⌶ kg per head**	14 ⌶ 2	106 ⌶ 14[a]	69 ⌶ 11
	TV SETS: thousands made **⌶ per thousand people**	188 ⌶ 23[a]	324 ⌶ 43[a]	not available
	PASSENGER CARS: thousands made **⌶ per thousand people**	323 ⌶ 40	0.4 ⌶ 0.05	19 ⌶ 3[j]
	SHIPS LAUNCHED thousands GRT **⌶ GRT per thousand people**	1 810 ⌶ 223	nil	nil
TRADE	IMPORTS: £ million **⌶ average per head**	3 222 ⌶ £397	2 085 ⌶ £278	3 383 ⌶ £530
	EXPORTS: £ million **⌶ average per head**	3 497 ⌶ £431	1 552 ⌶ £207	2 725 ⌶ £427
	NET INVISIBLE EARNINGS £ million **⌶ average per head**	—64 ⌶ —£8	+371 ⌶ +£50	+729 ⌶ +£114
	TOURISM, INCOME: £ million **⌶ per cent of GDP**	72 ⌶ 0.4	671 ⌶ 8.1	424 ⌶ 3.6
IMPORTS Per cent of total imports	from the EEC of 9	55	65	69
	from the rest of the 18	19	12	11
	from the USA	7	3	7
	from centrally planned economies	5	9	2
	from less developed countries	10	7	7
PRODUCTS IMPORTED Per cent of total imports	Top five groups 1.	Machinery 22	Machinery 23	Machinery 19
	2.	Oil & products 9	Vehicles 12	Food 10
	3.	Food 9	Chemicals 9	Chemicals 10
	4.	Chemicals 9	Food 7	Fabric & yarn 9
	5.	Vehicles 7	Fabric & yarn 7	Vehicles 8
EXPORTS Per cent of total exports	to the EEC of 9	50	49	46
	to the rest of the 18	24	21	16
	to the USA	7	5	9
	to centrally planned economies	4	12	4
	to less developed countries	10	10	17
PRODUCTS EXPORTED Per cent of total exports	Top five groups 1.	Machinery 26	Machinery 22	Machinery 31
	2.	Vehicles 10	Iron & steel 10	Chemicals 22
	3.	Paper & products 9	Fabric & yarn 9	Watches & clocks 11
	4.	Iron & steel 8	Chemicals 6	Fabric & yarns 7
	5.	Woodpulp 7	Wood 5	Instruments 3
GOVERNMENT SPENDING[g]	HEALTH: £ million **⌶ per head**	161 ⌶ £20[b]	252 ⌶ £34[a]	415 ⌶ £67[b]
	EDUCATION: £ million **⌶ per head**	804 ⌶ £99[a]	218 ⌶ £29[a]	253 ⌶ £41 (1969)
	DEFENCE: £ million **⌶ per head**	549 ⌶ £68[a]	68 ⌶ £9[a]	170 ⌶ £27[b]
	OVERSEAS AID: £ million **⌶ per head**	63 ⌶ £7.70[a]	6 ⌶ £0.70[a]	11 ⌶ £1.80[a]
LIVING STANDARDS	HOUSEHOLDS: thousands **⌶ average size**	3 010 ⌶ 2.7[g]	2 497 ⌶ 3.0[g]	2 060 ⌶ 3.1[g]
	NATIONAL INCOME: £ million **⌶ average per head**	15 142 ⌶ £1 864	7 340 ⌶ £980	10 745 ⌶ £1 683[g]
	CARS: per thousand people	302	195	243
	TELEPHONES: per thousand people	593	227	539
	HOUSING: thousand homes built **⌶ per thousand people**	104 ⌶ 12.8	43 ⌶ 5.7[a]	28 (92 cities only)
COST OF LIVING Per cent increase 1970 to 1972	FOOD: retail prices	19	10	13
	MANUFACTURES: wholesale prices	9	9	6

Denmark	Finland	Norway	Republic of Ireland	Luxembourg	Iceland
498 ∎ 100	1456 ∎ 315	916 ∎ 233	82 ∎ 28[b]	5458 ∎ 15729	nil
8 ∎ 2[a]	40 ∎ 9[a]	28 ∎ 7	nil	nil	nil
73 ∎ 15[a]	146∎32[bo]	103 ∎ 27[b]	86 ∎ 29[b]	nil	nil
12 ∎ 2[aj]	0.3∎0.07[b]	nil	52 ∎ 17[j]	nil	nil
905 ∎ 181	203∎44	829 ∎ 211	3 ∎ 1[a]	nil	nil
2026 ∎ £406	1278 ∎ £276	1731 ∎ £440	843 ∎ £280		94∎£447
1765 ∎ £354	1178 ∎ £255	1297 ∎ £330	641 ∎ £213	*All trade figures are included with Belgium (page 111)*	76∎£365
+159 ∎ +£32	+62 ∎ +£13	+372 ∎ +£95[a]	+85 ∎ +£28		+2∎+£9[b]
196 ∎ 2.3	45 ∎ 0.8	80 ∎ 1.4	71 ∎ 3.3		3.3∎1.1[g]
46	42	45	69		53
30	26	26	7		19
7	4	6	8		8
3	16	3	2		10
10	7	9	8		5
Machinery 19	Machinery 23	Machinery 18	Machinery 19		Machinery 21
Oil & products 10	Oil & products 10	Ships 12	Food 11		Food 9
Chemicals 9	Chemicals 10	Chemicals 8	Chemicals 10		Chemicals 8
Food 8	Vehicles 8	Food 7	Oil & products 6		Vehicles 8
Iron & steel 6	Food 7	Oil & products 7	Vehicles 6		Oil & products 8
43	44	50	77		33
33	27	26	3		20
8	5	7	9		31
3	16	4	1		12
10	6	10	3		2
Machinery 22	Paper & board 28	Ships 16	Meat 13		Fish 65
Meat 17	Machinery 11	Machinery 10	Cattle 11		Aluminium 16
Chemicals 6	Timber 9	Paper & pulp 9	Fabric & yarn 10		Fishmeal 7
Dairy produce 6	Woodpulp 8	Aluminium 9	Machinery 6		Meat 2
Fish 5	Clothing 6	Fish 8	Chemicals 5		Hides & skins 2
348 ∎ £70[a]	180 ∎ £39[a]	31 ∎ £8[b]	31 ∎ £11 (1969)	20 ∎ £60[b]	8 ∎ £40[b]
431 ∎ £87[a]	234 ∎ £51[a]	196 ∎ £51 (1969)	57 ∎ £19 (1969)	14 ∎ £40[b]	4 ∎ £21 (1969)
172 ∎ £35[a]	73 ∎ £16[a]	158 ∎ £41[b]	18 ∎ £6[b]	3 ∎ £10[b]	5 ∎ £23[b]
33 ∎ £6.60[a]	not available	20 ∎ £5.20[a]	not available	not available	not available
1745 ∎ 2.9[g]	1392 ∎ 3.3[g]	1269 ∎ 3.1[g]	750 ∎ 4.0[g]	104 ∎ 3.3	50 ∎ 4.2[g]
7663 ∎ £1535	4816 ∎ £1041	4929 ∎ £1253	2042 ∎ £678	397 ∎ £1145[g]	215 ∎ £1040[a]
245	176	216	141[a]	319	226[a]
379	305	320	113	364	371
50 ∎ 10.0	50 ∎ 10.8	44 ∎ 11.2	21 ∎ 7.0	2.0 ∎ 5.8[g]	1.4 ∎ 6.7
16	14	14	20	10	19
9	14	8	16	not available	not available

[g]estimated   [j]assembly only   [o]includes some assembly

Glossary

Act of Accession, the Treaty signed 22 November 1972 by Denmark, the Republic of Ireland, Norway and the United Kingdom which committed them, subject to ratification, to join the Common Market on 1 January 1973. Subsequently, Norway withdrew its agreement after a referendum.

Agglomeration, an extensive urban area. In Britain the term **conurbation** is more widely used. The agglomeration is a more realistic definition of the built up area of large cities than the official municipal boundaries. Agglomerations often include several individual towns and their suburbs.

Air mass, an extensive area of the lower atmosphere having uniform characteristics of temperature and humidity. The following types are generally recognized: **A:** Arctic; **AA:** Antarctic; **P:** Polar; **T:** Tropical; **E:** Equatorial. The prefix **m** or **c** indicates whether the source area was over sea (maritime) or over land (continental). It is at the boundaries of contrasting air masses that fronts develop with characteristically changeable weather – *see Fronts.*

ATGW(s), anti-tank guided weapon(s).

Balance of Payments is an account of the total transactions in goods, services and capital movements between one country and the rest of the world.

Benelux Treaty was signed in November 1960 and aims to achieve the complete economic union of Belgium, Luxembourg and the Netherlands. A free labour market already exists and there is a commitment to continuous co-ordination of economic and social policies.

CAP is the Common Market Agricultural Policy which seeks to establish common trading, prices and budgeting for farm produce among EEC members. The main objectives of the **CAP** as set out in article 39 of the Rome Treaty are to increase agricultural productivity, to ensure a fair standard of living for farmers, to stabilize markets, guarantee regular supplies and to ensure reasonably priced supplies for consumers. Under the **CAP** Community farm prices are maintained at annually fixed target levels by the operation of intervention prices to support the internal market and import levies to keep out cheap world food. The cost of supporting farm prices and modernizing agriculture is met by the **CAP** budget provided by member states and organized by the Agricultural Guidance and Guarantee Fund (FEOGA). Special arrangements exist for new entrants to the Common Market so that wide differences in price levels are phased out over a transitional period. Temporary distortions in market prices due to changes in the value of currencies are prevented by the imposition of special export rebates and border taxes.

Cassa per il Mezzogiorno. The Development Fund for Southern Italy created in 1950 to rehabilitate the physical and human environment of the South and reduce the economic contrasts with the more prosperous North. State-owned industrial enterprises are required to allocate 40 per cent of new investment in the South and low interest loans are available for industrialists planning to open factories there. The life of the Fund has since been prolonged to 1980.

CCT, Common Customs Tariff, also known as the **CET,** Common External Tariff. This trade barrier was established around EEC countries so that goods from the rest of the world pay the same customs duty regardless of port of entry into the EEC. For the original six the **CCT** was based on the average of the customs duties applied by them on goods from the rest of the world on 1 January 1957. The Act of Accession requires new members to progressively introduce the **CCT** by 1977.

Centrally Planned Economies are those in countries where the means of production and trade are in public ownership and are subject to state direction and control.

Channel Tunnel plans have been promoted since 1802 but following completion of financial and technical feasibility studies in 1973 the decision to begin the first phase of a bored rail tunnel under the Channel was agreed by the British and French governments. It is intended that the 50 kilometre tunnel will provide ferry train services for road vehicles in addition to through rail services. Construction work began early in 1974 and is expected to be finished by 1980.

Coal equivalent expresses the thermal value of other fuels in terms of coal for comparison purposes. For lignite the conversion factor varies between 0.6 and 0.33.

Company titles. European abbreviations are: **AB** (Sweden), **AG** (Austria, Germany), **AS** (Denmark, Norway), **SpA** (Italy) = joint stock company; **GmbH** (Germany), **NV** (Netherlands), **SA** (Belgium, France) = company with limited liability.

Death Rate. Total number of deaths per 1 000 of population. The crude death rate figures do not take into account the age and sex structure of population and are only a rough measure of mortality.

Durable goods, a category of consumer expenditure consisting mainly of motor cars, furniture and carpets, radio and electrical goods.

EEC Budget. All Community members contribute to a common budget which is used for specific purposes like FEOGA. Contributions come from customs revenue, import levies, part of the income from standard value-added tax rates and proportional contributions from member states which reflect the share of each country in total Community GNP.

EEC Institutions. The Common Market works through a **Commission** of 13 members appointed by member states to initiate and draw up policies which reconcile national viewpoints and to present to a **Council of Ministers** who represent member States' governments and are the decision-making body on major questions of policy and direction. The work of both the Commission and the Council of Ministers is monitored by the **European Parliament** which also acts in a consultative capacity and has the power to dismiss the Commission on a two-thirds majority. The European **Court of Justice** rules on interpretations and applications of the various treaties. The Communities are a compromise between a federal and a functional organization and progress in achieving aims and objectives is seen in terms of collaboration and co-operation by members.

Eur is the unit of account of the European Communities for standardized prices. It is equal to the pre-1971 US dollar valued at $35 a fine ounce of gold, and acts as a measure for international comparison purposes. Thus support prices for agricultural goods are fixed in units of account and the amount paid to individual farmers is then determined by the prevailing rates of exchange between the dollar and their own national currencies. In this atlas the use of the **Eur** for the period 1960–70 is equivalent to using US dollar values.

The European Communities. ECSC, The European Coal and Steel Community, **EEC,** the European Economic Community also known as the Common Market and **Euratom,** the European Atomic Energy Community. Set up by different treaties the three communities are legally separate but now share centralized common institutions. The ECSC was created in 1951 by the Paris Treaty to pool coal and steel production and to promote rational expansion and modernization of members' coal and steel industries and was an initial step towards the wider Common Market. The EEC came into force on 1 January 1958 to foster growing unity amongst European peoples, improve their working and living standards, progressively abolish all trade restrictions by the creation of a common customs union, establish the free movement of labour, capital and services and extend preferential aid to associated overseas countries. Progress towards these objectives is seen in terms of common policies for trade, social welfare, energy, the regions and the environment. **Euratom** was established in 1957 to co-ordinate growth in members' nuclear industries. It is in no way concerned with the military uses of nuclear energy. A common market for all nuclear materials and equipment is in force and basic standards for health protection throughout the Community have been drawn up. It controls research centres at Geel (Belgium), Ispra (Italy), Karlsruhe (Germany) and Petten (Netherlands). The Merger Treaty of 1967 established a single Council and a single Commission instead of separate ones for each Community and the 1970 Budget Treaty created a common budget.

FEOGA. Fonds Européen d'Orientation et de Garantie Agricole, the European Agricultural Guidance and Guarantee Fund. The support-buying agency of the Common Agricultural Market. The Guidance section of FEOGA is concerned with the modernization and restructuring of agriculture in the Common Market countries.

Fishing limits restrict fishing by other countries within what are held to be national waters. Most European countries operate a 12 nautical mile limit although there are widespread special arrangements for favoured nation fishing within these limits. The use of base lines between headlands has extended the fishing limits of many countries and the decision by Iceland to extend its territorial waters to 50 miles has once more thrown open the whole question of fishing limits. Agreements with Iceland now mean that waters between 12 and 50 miles from Iceland's coast are divided into six areas, five of which are open at any time to international fishing. Each area will be closed at different times during the season for two months at a time and fishing will be totally restricted in three special conservation areas. Final agreement on fishing rights has yet to be negotiated in Western Europe although for EEC countries the Common Fisheries Policy proposes to allow member states to fish within each others' 6-12 mile limits.

Flags of convenience. Each country's merchant fleet must be registered which involves legal requirements relating to taxation, insurance, construction and use regulations and manning agreements. These vary considerably from country to country and ship owners may register their fleets under any national flag which best serves their interests. Where a ship owner registers his fleet under the flag of another nation this is called using a flag of convenience. The financial attractions to ship owners of flags of convenience have to some extent been matched by the variety and size of tax incentives offered by the major maritime nations e.g. Greece, and the wider adoption of international safety conventions and manning regulations by the free flags. Such has been the attraction of free flags that Liberia now has the world's largest merchant fleet although in 1948 it only had two ships totalling under a thousand tons.

Front, Arctic. The boundary separating cold dry air blowing outwards from Polar latitudes from warmer, moist air originating over the Atlantic Ocean. It is in this zone that cyclonic disturbances develop making it one of the principal winter depression tracks of the Northern Hemisphere.

GDP, Gross Domestic Product is an economic indicator used particularly by the United Nations for international comparison purposes. It measures the total value of a country's home production of goods and services before providing for the consumption and depreciation of fixed capital. It differs from Gross National Product (GNP) which includes the c.i.f. value of imported goods and services and net factor income from abroad. Both indices on a per head basis give an approximate average income for international comparisons. The use of **GDP** requires very accurate knowledge of economic activity in quantitative terms in all sectors of the economy and reliable data are not always available even in the developed countries of Western Europe. In countries where many of the people live wholly or partly outside the cash economy, money figures are not fully indicative of relative prosperity and national income is vulnerable to the vagaries of climate and world markets. International comparison is also made difficult since each country devises its own formula for collecting data on national income. Within Western Europe **GDP** can be accepted as a reasonable indicator of national wealth for comparison purposes.

GMP, Gross Material Product is used as an economic indicator for centrally planned countries instead of **GDP.** It measures the gross output of goods and material services but excludes many other economic activities not directly contributing to material production such as insurance, public administration, community services and defence.

Golden Triangle describes that area of the EEC bounded by Paris, the Ruhr and Milan and containing many of the Community's economic growth centres.

Great Circle Routes are the shortest possible between any two places in the world. They lie along Great Circles which are lines spanning the full circumference of the earth. For political and operational reasons most scheduled air routes do not exactly follow Great Circles.

GRT, Gross Registered Tonnage of a ship is its total inside capacity or volume measured in tons, each of which represents 2.83 cubic metres.

ICBM(s), intercontinental ballistic missile(s) able to deliver a nuclear warhead over a range between 9 000 and 13 000 km.

Industrial population. The definition used in this atlas includes workers engaged in manufacturing, mining and quarrying, construction and utilities (electricity, gas and water supplies).

International Monetary Fund, an independent international organization established in 1945 to promote monetary co-operation and exchange stability between member nations and assist generally in funding their economic development. *See page 88.*

IRBM(s), intermediate range ballistic missile(s) able to deliver a nuclear warhead over a range between 3 000 and 6 400 km.

Isolines or isopleths are lines on a map along which values or quantities are equal and which separate areas with different values.

LDC's, less developed countries. This atlas uses the expression less developed countries in line with UN practice implying poor nations with low levels of per head income, little industrial development and limited economic and social infrastructure. Such countries are variously described as being undeveloped, under-developed, the developing, the less developed and the Third World.

Metric units. The metric system of weights and measures was adopted in France in 1799 and widely accepted by other European countries during the next hundred years. It is now in common use throughout the world with several nations in the process of completing the changeover. Some common relationships used in this atlas include:

1 millimetre, **mm** = 0.03937 inches	1 kilogramme, **kg** = 2.20462 lbs
1 metre, **m** = 3.281 feet	1 metric ton, **tonne** = 0.98 long tons
1 kilometre, **km** = 0.621 miles	
1 square kilometre, **km**² = 247.105 acres	*temperature conversion:* °C to °F
(1 square mile = 640 acres)	9/5 Degrees Centigrade + 32
1 hectare, **ha** = 2.47105 acres	= degrees Fahrenheit

PAL derives from phase alternation line, a German colour TV system developed from the American NTSC (National Television Systems Committee) by W. Bruch of AEG Telefunken. **PAL** was adopted generally in Western Europe during the 1960s in preference to the French **SECAM** system when it proved impossible to get international agreement on a common European colour standard.

Passenger km = the number of passengers transported multiplied by the distance they were carried. This indicates the total distance travelled by all passengers and is a measure of traffic density.

Primary occupations include activities directly concerned with collecting and extracting natural resources e.g. agriculture, fishing, forestry, hunting and mining. *See Secondary and Tertiary occupations.*

Quaternary period is the name given to the last two million years of geological history during which repeated glaciation occurred over much of Western Europe and North America and great ice sheets accumulated on at least four occasions. Much of the landscape of Western Europe reflects the extensive modifications that the ice caused both in terms of the erosion of the mountain areas and the laying down of glacial drift deposits. Oscillations of the sea level resulting from ice melt and the readjustment of land depressed by the huge weight of the ice sheets have considerably altered the coastlines of Western Europe in post-glacial times.

Reserves are a nation's holdings of gold and foreign currencies. The pound and the dollar act as international reserve currencies and individual countries exchange net earnings of gold and convertible currencies for sterling and dollar balances. Another source of reserves to meet balance of payments difficulties is available to members from the International Monetary Fund in the form of fixed loans and Special Drawing Rights (SDRs)

Rhine, Central Commission for the Navigation of. A central authority established by the Congress of Vienna in 1815 to ensure free movement of traffic and equal river facilities for the vessels of all nations having access to the Rhine. The administrative offices of the Commission are in the Palais du Rhin, Strasbourg.

Romansch is a group of Romance related dialects spoken by about half a million people in the Alpine region of SE Switzerland and N Italy. **Rumantsch** is widely spoken in the Grisons canton of eastern Switzerland and since 1938 has been officially recognised as one of the national languages of Switzerland. **Ladin** is spoken in parts of the Alto Adige region of north Italy and **Friulan** is common in the Udine province of northeast Italy.

Rome, Treaty of. The Treaty setting up the European Community on 25 March 1957 was the culmination of negotiations between Belgium, France, Italy, Luxembourg, the Netherlands and West Germany chaired by the Belgian Foreign Minister, M. Paul-Henri Spaak. The Preamble signed by the heads of state determines "*to establish the foundations of an ever closer union among the European people . . . to ensure by common action the economic and social progress of their countries by eliminating the barriers which divide Europe . . . and calls upon the other people of Europe who share their ideal to join in their efforts.*" A 12-year target was set for the creation of a customs union with the long-term intention of establishing a more far-reaching economic union. **The Treaty of Rome** has been termed an 'outline treaty' in the sense that it leaves the institutions of the Community to work out the finer details of the general objectives. This gives the members the right to negotiate the character and the evolution of the Community within the framework of a fair balance between the different national interests involved.

SAM, surface-to-air missile.

SDRs, Special Drawing Rights have a fixed value in terms of gold which members of the International Monetary Fund can draw on a quota basis for buying foreign currency. **SDRs** are not loans and form a permanent addition to international reserves.

SECAM, the French colour TV system developed by Henri de France and now widely used in Eastern Europe and the USSR. **SECAM** is a contraction from the expression *sequentiel à memoire* (*see also* **PAL**).

Secondary occupations involve the processing of raw materials into manufactured articles. *See Primary and Tertiary occupations.*

Special Development Areas are those regions of Great Britain with high levels of unemployment which have been designated as needing preferential government assistance to encourage industrial development. They include the Glasgow area, Ayrshire, the Workington-Whitehaven district, Tyneside and the coal mining valleys of South Wales.

Standard International Trade Classification (SITC) is a standard list of trade commodity categories used by governments on the recommendation of the UN Economic and Social Council (1950) to make trade statistics internationally comparable. A revised list drawn up in 1960 is based on 625 sub-groups which are classified into 177 groups, 56 divisions and 10 sections.

Sterling Area, those countries which based their currencies on sterling rather than gold and maintained a significant proportion of their currency reserves in the Bank of England. The Sterling Area ceased to be of real practical importance when the pound was floated in 1972.

Taiga is a belt of natural coniferous forest extending across northern latitudes of Scandinavia and USSR.

Tertiary occupations include mainly the service industries. *See Primary and Secondary occupations.*

Ton km. An index of traffic density calculated by multiplying the tonnage of revenue load carried by the actual distance carried. For comparison purpose an index of ton-kilometres per kilometre of length can be calculated to give a value of traffic density flow or 'work done' over specific routes and parts of routes.

Tourist arrivals refers to persons travelling for pleasure, domestic reasons, health and business and stopping in another country for a period of more than 24 hours. They do not include immigrants, residents in frontier zones and travellers or transport crews in transit across a country.

Wholesale price index is derived from a representative list of commodities priced at the wholesale stage of distribution. The index gives a measure of the charges of manufacturers and importers before distributive margins are added.

World Bank or International Bank for Reconstruction and Development is an agency of the United Nations and began work in June 1946. It lends money for economic development schemes and offers technical advice on financing such projects. In 1970 about 12 per cent of its lending was directed to Europe. The Bank has close contacts with other UN agencies such as FAO and UNESCO and also works through the Development Assistance Committee of the OECD. Affiliated to the World Bank are the International Finance Corporation which aims to stimulate the flow of capital to the private sectors of developing states' economies and the International Development Association which finances economic growth in less developed countries at special low rates of interest. *See page 88.*

Xerophytes are plants adapted to live where arid conditions normally prevail. Their structure is modified to conserve moisture losses from transpiration.

Sources

This list of sources is intended to help the reader to take his own research further and it illustrates the extent of the reference material available for European studies.

MAIN SOURCES

A. Statistical Yearbook, UN, New York, *annual.*

B. Statistical Yearbooks, and Census Reports *published by each country at various intervals.*

C. Demographic Yearbook, UN, New York, *annual.*

D. Monthly Bulletin of Statistics, UN, New York, *monthly.*

E. The Statesman's Yearbook, Macmillan, London, *annual.*

F. The Europa Yearbook, Europa Publications, London, *annual.*

G. Statistical Yearbook, UNESCO, Paris, *annual.*

H. Road Atlas Europe, Bartholomew, Edinburgh, 1974.

I. Labour Force Statistics 1960-1971, OECD, Paris, 1971.

J. Production Yearbook, FAO, Rome, *annual.*

K. Monthly Bulletin of Agricultural Economics and Statistics, FAO, Rome, *monthly.*

L. Annual Bulletin of General Energy Statistics for Europe, UN, Geneva, *annual.*

M. Statistics of Foreign Trade, Series A, B and C, OECD, Paris, *quarterly.*

N. Annual Bulletin of Transport Statistics for Europe, UN, New York, *annual.*

O. International Tourism and Tourism Policy, OECD, Paris, *annual.*

P. The Economist Diary, The Economist Newspaper Ltd., London, *annual.*

Q. Yearbook of National Accounts Statistics, UN, New York, *annual.*

R. National Accounts of OECD Countries 1960-1971, OECD, Paris, *annual.*

S. Balance of Payments Yearbook Volume 24, IMF, Washington, *annual.*

T. Yearbook of International Trade Statistics, UN, New York, *annual.*

PAGE REFERENCES

Endpapers: A, B. 9: A; B; C.

☐ 10-11: A; C; Air Distances Manual, International Aeradio Ltd., London, *annual.*

☐ 12-13: Physical Geographic Atlas of the World, Moscow, 1964; Bioclimatic Map of the Mediterranean Region, UNESCO, Paris, 1962; Vegetation Map of the Mediterranean Region, UNESCO, Paris, 1968.

☐ 14-17: E; Calendario Atlante Agostini, Novara, 1974; Cartactual Cartographia, Budapest, *bimonthly;* information from the Department of the Environment, London, and Scottish Development, Department, Edinburgh.

☐ 18-19: Atlas zur Weltgeschichte, Westermann, Braunschweig, 1963; The New Cambridge Modern History Volume XIV Atlas, Cambridge, 1970.

☐ 20-21: European Studies Teachers' Series No 2, European Community Information Service, London, 1968.

☐ 22-23: E; F.

☐ 24: A; G; information from newspapers and London embassies.

☐ 25: A; European Broadcasting Union (Network map), EBU, Brussels, 1972.

☐ 26: A; B; C. ☐ 27: A; B; C.

☐ 28-31: A; B; C; Densité de la Population en Europe Occidental (map), edited by Professor I. B. F. Kormoss, Collège d'Europe, Brugge, 1972.

☐ 32: A; B; C. ☐ 33: A; B.

☐ 34: A; B; Census 1971 Great Britain Advanced Analysis, HMSO, London, 1972.

☐ 35: A; B.

☐ 36-37: H; Meteorological Office Climatic Data, HMSO, London, 1967.

☐ 38: I. ☐ 39: B; J; K.

☐ 40-41: B; J; K.

☐ 42: B; Review of Fisheries in OECD Member Countries, OECD, Paris, 1969; Fishing Fleet Statistics, FAO, Rome, *annual;* Limits and Status of the Territorial Sea, Exclusive Fishing Zones, Fishery Conservation Zones and the Continental Shelf, FAO, Rome, 1969; Yearbook of Fishery Statistics, FAO, Rome, *annual.*

☐ 43: Licences in the North Sea, Celtic Sea and British Coastal Waters (map), PB, London, 1972; Petroleum and Petrochemical International (map), London, 1972; information from major oil companies exploring the North Sea.

☐ 44: L; M.

☐ 45: information from the Welsh Office, Department of Trade and Industry, Development Corporation of Wales and National Coal Board, Cardiff; Siedlungsverband Ruhrkohlenbezirk, Essen.

☐ 46-47: A; L; M; International Directory of Electrical Supplies, Power and Research Reactors in Member States, IAEA, Vienna, 1972; Electrical Supply Handbook, Electrical Times, London, *annual.*

☐ 48-49: A; I; The Growth of World Industry, UN, New York, *annual.*

☐ 50-51: B; I; Yearbook of Labour Statistics, ILO, Geneva, *annual;* information from the International Confederation of Free Trade Unions, Brussels.

☐ 52: H; E-Route System (map), International Road Federation, Geneva, 1973; Motorway Progress Reports, Touring Club Suisse, Geneva, *published at regular intervals;* AA Continental Handbook, London, 1972-73; information from national road touring organisations.

☐ 53: N; World Road Statistics, International Road Federation, Geneva, *annual.*

☐ 54-55: N; Union International des Chemins de Fer (map), British Rail, London, 1974; Jane's World Railways, London, *annual.*

☐ 56-57: O; Digest of Statistics: Airport Traffic, ICAO, Montreal, *annual;* ABC World Airways Guide Map Supplement, London, *bi-annual.*

☐ 58-59: N; Canals and Inland Waterways of Europe (map), Economic Commission for Europe, Geneva, 1973; Rapport Annuel Intérimaire, Central Commission for the Navigation of the Rhine, Strasbourg, *annual;* Lloyd's Register of Shipping Statistical Tables, London, *annual;* information from various national waterways departments.

☐ 60: A.

☐ 61: A; D; P; International Financial Statistics, IMF, Washington, *monthly;* national holidays checked with London embassies.

☐ 62: A; D; Q; R. ☐ 63: A.

☐ 64: C; World Health Statistics Volume III, Health Personnel and Hospital Establishments, WHO, Geneva, *annual.*

☐ 65: Q; R; World Health Statistics Volume I, Vital Statistics and Causes of Death, WHO, Geneva, *annual.*

☐ 66: A; G.

☐ 67: F; The World of Learning, Europa Publications, London, 1972-73.

☐ 68: A; O; R; International Travel Statistics, IUOTO, Geneva, *annual.*

☐ 69: O. ☐ 70: D; J.

☐ 71: J; List of National Parks and Equivalent Reserves, UNESCO, Paris, 1972.

☐ 72: A; Report on the Regional Problems in the Enlarged Community (The Thomson Report), Brussels, 1973; EEC Regional Statistics Yearbook, Brussels, *annual;* UK Annual Abstract of Regional Statistics, HMSO, London, *annual.*

☐ 73: Information from individual companies and annual lists: The Times 1 000, Fortune and Vision.

☐ 74: Q; S; Financial Statistics, OECD, Paris, *annual.*

☐ 75: S.

☐ 76-77: A; T; Destination Europe, Exporters' Guide to Europe, British Overseas Trade Board, London, 1973; Eurostat, Statistical Office of the European Communities, Luxembourg, *annual.*

☐ 78-79: A; M.

☐ 80-81: M; Policy Perspectives for International Trade and Economic Relations, OECD, Paris, 1972; Bank for International Settlements, Basle, *annual report.*

☐ 82-83: A; E.

☐ 84-85: A; I; The Military Balance 1973-74, International Institute of Strategic Studies, London, 1973; Allied Defence in the Seventies, NATO, Brussels, 1972.

86-87: A.

☐ 88-89: E; P; UN Yearbook, New York, *annual;* information from United Nations Information Centre. London.

☐ 105: A; E; F.

☐ 106-107: E; F; information from London embassies.

☐ 108-115: Each entry in the Statistical Profile employs the same sources as those used to document the subject in the main part of the atlas. Subsequent editions have been used to extend the 1970 base date of the atlas to 1972.

Acknowledgement is also made to the many other references that were consulted in the compilation and checking of this atlas but are not specifically listed above. Every effort has been made to obtain permission from owners of copyrights and the authors and the publishers take this opportunity of tendering their apologies to any owners whose rights have been unwittingly infringed.

Subject Index

This index supplements and expands the list of contents which is on pages 6 - 7. The list of references below is intended to provide a quick alphabetical guide to subject areas within the atlas and is not a comprehensive index. Place names can be located by reference to the Reference Map Index on pages 120-128.

General Reference Map Index

NOTE: This is a selective index for names shown on the *General Reference Maps* (pp. 90-104). For Belgium, England, France, Italy, Netherlands and West Germany all towns of over 50,000 have been included; for the other countries in Western Europe, towns of over 25,000 have been added. Further categories listed are: first-tier administrative divisions (for second-tier divisions, see pp. 14-17), principal mountain ranges, mountain peaks, islands, rivers, canals, growth towns, new towns, university towns, holiday resorts, airports, and specific industrial centres.

Where a name cannot be shown on the map, reference is made to a nearby centre. Conventional names are referred to local forms as used on the map.

Abbreviations

Adm: Administrative
Anc: Ancient
Aut: Autonomous
Auth: Authority

B: Bahia, Baia, Bay, Bjerge
Br: Burnu, Burun, Bridge

C: Cabo, Cap, Cape
Chan: Channel
Co: County

Dep: Dependency, Dependent

Dep: Département
Dist: District
Div: Division

E: East, Étang
Emb: Embalse

Fed: Federal
Fj: Fjord

G: Golfe, Golfo, Gulf
Geb: Gebirge
Geog: Geographical

Gr: Grosse

Har: Harbour
Hd: Head

I: Île, Island, Isle, Isole
Ind: Independent
Is: Islands, Islas

J: Jezioro

K: Kanal, Kanaal
King: Kingdom

L: Lac, Lago, Lake, Limni, Loch, Lough

M: Monte
Mt: Mont, Mount, Mountain
Mte: Monte
Mtes: Montes
Mts: Monts, Mountains

N: Noord, Nord, Nordre, Nörre, Nørre, North
Nat: National

O: Oost, Ost, Oude
Ö: Öster, Östra, Östre
Ø: Øster, Østre

P: Pass
Pen: Peninsula, Peñisola
Pl: Planina
Plat: Plateau
Pnte: Pointe
Princ: Principality
Prom: Promontory
Prov: Province
Pt: Point, Port
Pta: Ponta, Punta
Pto: Puerto

R: Rio, River
Reg: Region, Regional
Rep: Republic
Res: Reservoir

S: See, Sör, Sør, South, Sur, Syd
Sa: Sierra
Sd: Sound
St: Saint
Sta: Santa
Ste: Sainte
Str: Strait
Sv: Sveti

Terr: Territory

V: Väster, Vest, Vester, Vestre
W: West, Wester

A

Aachen *W. Germany* **104Ec**
Aalen *W. Germany* **99Df**
Aalsmeer *Netherlands* **104Ca**
Aarau *Switzerland* **100Ba**
Aargau, canton *Switzerland* **16**
Åbenrå *Denmark* **98Cc**
Aberdare=Merthyr Tydfil
Aberdeen *Scotland* **90Ec**
Aberystwyth *Wales* **91De**
Åbo=Turku
Åbo-Björneborg=Turku ja Pori
Abruzzi, reg. *Italy* **100Dc**
Achill I. *Ireland, Rep.* **91Ae**
Adamello, mt. *Italy* **100Ca**
Adige, R. *Italy* **100Cb**
Adour, R. *France* **93Cf**
Æbeltoft=Ebeltoft
Aegina, I.=Aíyina I.
Ærø, I. *Denmark* **98Dc**
Afragola=Nápoli
Agder=Aust-Agder, Vest-Agder
Agrigento *Italy* **101Df**
Agrínion *Greece* **103Ce**
Ahvenanmaa=Åland
Ahvenanmaa, lääni *Finland* **97Hf**
Aigaleo=Athínai
Aigion=Aiyion
Ain, dép. *France* **93Fd**
Aisne, dép. *France* **92Ec**
Aisne, R. *France* **92Ec**
Aitolía kai Akarnanía, nomos *Greece* **103Ce**
Aix-en-Provence *France* **93Ff**
Aix-la-Chapelle=Aachen
Aíyina, I. *Greece* **103Df**
Aiyion *Greece* **103De**
Ajaccio *France* **100Bb**
Akershus, fylke *Norway* **97Df**
Akhaïa, nomos *Greece* **103Ce**
Akranes *Iceland* **96Um**
Akureyri *Iceland* **96Wm**
Ål *Norway* **97Cf**
Åland=Ahvenanmaa
Åland, I. *Finland* **97Hf**
Alava, prov. *Spain* **95Da**
Albacete *Spain* **95Ec**
Albacete, prov. *Spain* **95Dc**
Albert Kanaa. *Belgium* **104Db**
Ålborg *Denmark* **98Cb**
Albufeira *Portugal* **94Ad**
Alcalá de Guadaira=Sevilla
Alcala de Henares *Spain* **94Db**
Alcantara, Embalse de, res. *Spain* **94Bc**
Alcira *Spain* **95Ec**
Alcobaça *Portugal* **94Ac**
Alcobendas=Madrid
Alcorcón=Madrid
Alcoy *Spain* **95Ec**
Aldeburgh *England* **91Ge**
Aldridge-Brownhills=Walsall
Alentejo=Alto Alentejo, Baixo Alentejo
Alessandria *Italy* **100Bb**

Ålesund *Norway* **97Be**
Alexandria=Balloch
Alexandroúpolis *Greece* **102/103Ed**
Alfeite=Lisboa
Algarve, reg. *Portugal* **94Ad**
Algeciras *Spain* **95Ec**
Alghero *Italy* **101Bd**
Alicante *Spain* **95Ec**
Alicante, prov. *Spain* **95Ec**
Alkmaar *Netherlands* **104Fa**
Allier, dép. *France* **93Ed**
Allier, R. *France* **93Ee**
Allinge *Denmark* **98Fc**
Almelo *Netherlands* **104Ea**
Almeria *Spain* **95Dd**
Almería, prov. *Spain* **95Dd**
Almuñecar *Spain* **94Dd**
Alpes-de-Haute-Provence, dép. *France* **93Fe**
Alpes de Savoie, mts *France, etc.* **93Ge**
Alpes, Hautes-, dép. *France* **93Ge**
Alpes-Maritimes, dép. *France* **93Gf**
Alta *Norway* **96Kb**
Altamira, Cuevas de=Santillana
Alto Alentejo, reg. *Portugal* **94Bc**
Älvadalen *Sweden* **97Ff**
Älvsborg, län *Sweden* **97Dg**
Amadora *Portugal* **94Ac**
Amalfi *Italy* **101Ed**
Amaroúsion=Athínai
Amboise *France* **93Dd**
Amersfoort *Netherlands* **104Da**
Amiens *France* **92Ec**
Amstelveen *Netherlands* **104Ca**
Amsterdam *Netherlands* **104Ca**
Ancona *Italy* **100Dc**
Åndalsnes *Norway* **97Be**
Andermatt *Switzerland* **100Ba**
Andernach *W. Germany* **104Fc**
Andorra, co-princ. **95Fa**
Andorre=Andorra
Andri *Italy* **101Fd**
Andritsaina *Greece* **103Cf**
Andujar *Spain* **94Cc**
Angelholm *Sweden* **98Eb**
Angers *France* **93Cd**
Anglesey, I. *Wales* **91De**
Angouleme *France* **93De**
Antequera *Spain* **94Cd**
Antibes *France* **93Gf**
Antony=Paris
Antrim *N. Ireland* **91Cd**
Antwerp=Antwerpen
Antwerpen *Belgium* **104Cb**
Antwerpen, prov. *Belgium* **104Cb**
Anvers=Antwerpen
Anzio *Italy* **101Dd**
Apeldoorn *Netherlands* **104Da**
Appennino Ligure, mts *Italy* **100Bb**
Appenzell *Switzerland* **100Ba**
Appenzell, canton *Switzerland* **16**
Appledore=Bideford
Arachova=Delphi
Arakhova=Arachova

Aranjuez *Spain* **94Db**
Arbatax *Italy* **101Be**
Arbon *Switzerland* **100Ba**
Arbroath *Scotland* **90Ec**
Arcachon *France* **93Be**
Arcadia=Arkadhía
Arcos *Spain* **94Cd**
Årdal *Norway* **97Bf**
Ardèche, dép. *France* **93Fe**
Ardeer=Ardrossan
Ardennes, dép. *France* **92Fc**
Ardennes, mts *Belgium* **92Fb**
Ardersier=Nairn
Ardrossan *Scotland* **90Dd**
Åre *Sweden* **96Ee**
Arendal *Norway* **98Ca**
Arezzo *Italy* **100Cc**
Argeles Gazost *France* **93Cf**
Argenteuil *France* **92Ec**
Argentière, I'=Briançon
Argolís, nomos *Greece* **103Df**
Argonne, mts *France* **92Fc**
Argostolion, Kefallinía I. *Greece* **103Ce**
Argovie=Aargau
Århus *Denmark* **98Db**
Århus, reg. *Denmark* **98Db**
Ariège, dép. *France* **93Df**
Arkadhía, nomos. *Greece* **103Df**
Arklow *Ireland, Rep.* **91Ce**
Arkösund *Sweden* **97Gg**
Arles *France* **93Ff**
Armentières *France* **92Eb**
Arnhem *Netherlands* **104Db**
Arosa *Switzerland* **100Ba**
Arran, I. *Scotland* **90Dd**
Arras *France* **92Eb**
Arrecife *Spain* **95Lf**
Árta, nomos *Greece* **103 Ce**
Arucas=Las Palmas
Arvika *Sweden* **97Eg**
Aschaffenburg *W. Germany* **99Cf**
Ascoli Piceno *Italy* **100Dc**
Ascq *France* **104BC**
Asnières-sur-Seine=Paris
Assisi *Italy* **100Dc**
Asúa=Bilbao
Athens=Athínai
Athínai *Greece* **103Df**
Athlone *Ireland, Rep.* **91Ce**
Áthos, mt. *Greece* **103Ed**
Athos, Mount=Áyion Óros
Aube, dép. *France* **92Fc**
Aubervilliers=Paris
Aude, dép. *France* **93Ef**
Augsburg *W. Germany* **99Df**
Augusta *Italy* **101Ef**
Aulanko=Hämeenlinña
Aulnay-sous-Bois=Paris
Aune, R. *France* **92Bc**
Aurland=Flåm
Ausser Rhoden=Appenzell
Aust-Agder, fylke *Norway* **97Bg**
Austria, fed. rep. **99**
Auzat=Foix

Aveiro *Portugal* **94Ab**
Avellino *Italy* **101Ed**
Avernakke=Nyborg
Aveyron, dép. *France* **93Ee**
Aviemore *Scotland* **90Ec**
Avignon *France* **93Ff**
Avila *Spain* **94Cb**
Avila, prov. *Spain* **94Cb**
Aviles *Spain* **94Ca**
Avon, co. *England* **91Ef**
Avonmouth=Bristol
Axel *Netherlands* **104Bb**
Aycliffe *England* **91Fd**
Áyion Óros, nomos *Greece* **103Ed**
Áyios Nikólaos, *Kriti, Greece* **103E**
Ayr *Scotland* **90Dd**

B

B.R.D.=Germany, W.
Bacharach=St Goar
Bad Godesburg=Bonn
Bad Hersfeld *W. Germany* **99Ce**
Badajoz *Spain* **94Bc**
Badajoz, prov. *Spain* **94Bc**
Badalona *Spain* **95Gb**
Baden-Baden *W. Germany* **99Cf**
Baden-Württemberg, land *W. Germany* **99Cf**
Badgastein *Austria* **99Eg**
Bærum *Norway* **97Dg**
Bagenkop=Langeland
Baglan=Port Talbot
Bagur *Spain* **95Gb**
Baile Atha Cliath=Dublin
Baixo Alentejo, reg. *Portugal* **94A**
Bâle=Basel
Baleares, prov. *Spain* **95Gc**
Baleares, Islas, Is. *Spain* **95Gc**
Balearic Is.=Baleares
Balestrand *Norway* **97Bf**
Ballater *Scotland* **90Ec**
Ballerup-Målov=København
Ballina *Ireland, Rep.* **91Bd**
Balloch *Scotland* **90Dc**
Ballycastle=Portrush
Ballymena *N. Ireland* **91Cd**
Ballyshannon *Ireland, Rep.* **91Bd**
Bamberg *W. Germany* **99Df**
Bangor *N. Ireland* **91Dd**
Bangor *Wales* **91De**
Bantry *Ireland, Rep.* **91Bf**
Bantry Bay *Ireland, Rep.* **91Bf**
Baracaldo *Spain* **94Da**
Barbizon=Fontainebleau
Barcelona *Spain* **95Gb**
Barcelona, prov. *Spain* **95Fb**
Bardu *Norway* **96Hb**
Bardufoss=Bardu
Bari *Italy* **101Fd**
Barking=London
Barletta *Italy* **101Fd**
Barnet=London

The Cities of Europe

Towns with populations of over 100 thousand in 1970
in the Eighteen Countries of Western Europe

Populations in thousands

Where towns are centres of agglomerations this larger total is also shown

France 1968, Austria, Greece, Republic of Ireland and the United Kingdom 1971

The largest towns in Iceland and Luxembourg are Reykjavík 82 and Luxembourg City 76 thousand

The 292 towns shown total 95·4 million: 28 per cent of total population

London 7418
1st: 1st in the United Kingdom
12762: as an agglomeration

Madrid 3146
2nd: 1st in Spain

Roma 2731
3rd: 1st in Italy

Paris 2591
4th: 1st in France: 8197

Berlin 2134
5th: 1st in West Germany

Hamburg 1817
6th: 2nd in W. Germany

Barcelona 1745
7th: 2nd in Spain

Milano 1702
8th: 2nd in Italy

Wien 1603
9th: 1st in Austria

München 1326
10th: 3rd in W. Germany

Napoli 1277
11th: 3rd in Italy

Torino 1177
12th: 4th in Italy

Bruxelles 1071
13th: 1st in Belgium: 1071

Birmingham 1013
14th: 2nd in the UK: 2369

Glasgow 894
15th: 3rd in the UK: 1723

Marseille 889
16th: 2nd in France: 964

Athinai 867
17th: 1st in Greece: 2540

Köln 866
18th: 4th in W. Germany

Genova 842
19th: 5th in Italy

Amsterdam 831
20th: 1st in Neth: 1040

Lisboa 782
21st: 1st in Portugal: 1651

Stockholm 740
22nd: 1st in Sweden: 1345

Essen 705
23rd: 5th in W. Germany

Rotterdam 687
24th: 2nd in Neth: 1061

Düsseldorf 681
25th: 6th in W. Germany

Frankfurt am Main 660
26th: 7th in W. Germany

Palermo 659
27th: 6th in Italy

Valencia 654
28th: 2nd in Spain

Venèzia 368
59th: 10th in Italy

Belfast 360
60th: 11th in the UK

Bari 352
61st: 11th in Italy

Kassel 213
109th: 24th in the UK

Gelsenkirchen 349
62nd: 15th in W. Germany

Bochum 347
63rd: 16th in W. Germany

Basel 213
112th: 2nd in Switz: 373

Thessaloniki 346
64th: 2nd in Greece: 557

Brescia 206
113th: 18th in Italy

Coventry 333
65th: 12th in the UK

Linz 205
114th: 3rd in Austria

Mannheim 331
66th: 17th in W. Germany

Münster 205
115th: 28th in the UK

Palma de Mallorca 234
97th: 13th in Spain

Århus 233
98th: 2nd in Denmark

Krefeld 229
99th: 24th in W. Germany

Antwerpen 227
100th: 2nd in Belgium: 673

Padova 226
101st: 15th in Italy

Braunschweig 225
102nd: 25th in W. Germany

Càgliari 223
103rd: 16th in Italy

Newcastle upon Tyne 221
104th: 21st in the UK: 804

Táranto 219
105th: 17th in Italy

Derby 219
106th: 22nd in the UK

Sunderland 216
107th: 23rd in the UK

Augsburg 214
108th: 26th in W. Germany

Southampton 214
109th: 24th in the UK

Sabadell 159
159th: 21st in Spain

Ferrara 156
160th: 23rd in Italy

Tampere 155
161st: 2nd in Finland: 217

Turku 155
162nd: 3rd in Finland: 220

Bolton 154
163rd: 36th in the UK

Oviedo 154
164th: 22nd in Spain

West Bromwich 167
146th: 31st in the UK

Réggio di Calàbria 166
147th: 22nd in Italy

Freiburg im Breisgau 166
148th: 36th in W. Germany

San Sebastian 166
149th: 19th in Spain

Odense 164
150th: 3rd in Denmark

Brighton 164
151st: 32nd in the UK

Warley 163
152nd: 33rd in the UK

Badalona 163
153rd: 20th in Spain

Southend on Sea 162
154th: 34th in the UK

Bern 162
155th: 4th in Switz: 259

Montpellier 162
156th: 14th in France: 171

Grenoble 162
157th: 15th in France: 332

Luton 161
158th: 35th in the UK

Vitoria 137
195th: 29th in Spain

Cádiz 136
196th: 30th in Spain

Reading 133
197th: 41st in the UK

Limoges 133
198th: 21st in France: 148

Arnhem 133
199th: 11th in Neth: 270

Oldenburg 131
200th: 42nd in W. Germany

Salford 131
201st: 42nd in the UK

Ravenna 131
202nd: 27th in Italy

Saarbrücken 131
203rd: 43rd in W. Germany

Huddersfield 131
204th: 43rd in the UK

Basildon 130
205th: 44th in the UK

La Spèzia 129
206th: 28th in Italy

Angers 129
207th: 22nd in France: 163

Cork 128
208th: 2nd in Ireland: 132

Tours 128
209th: 23rd in France: 202

Regensburg 128
210th: 44th in W. Germany

Salzburg 127
211th: 4th in Austria

Uppsala 127
212th: 4th in Sweden

Reggio nell' Emilia 127
213th: 29th in Italy

Örebro 116
244th: 7th in Sweden

Innsbruck 115
245th: 5th in Austria

Göttingen 115
246th: 51st in W. Germany

Roubaix 115
247th: 30th in France

Almería 115
248th: 34th in Spain

Besançon 113
249th: 31st in France: 116

Vicenza 112
250th: 34th in Italy

Pátrai/Patras 112
251st: 5th in Greece: 121

Newport 112
252nd: 49th in the UK

Leverkusen 112
253rd: 52nd in W. Germany

Oxford 111
254th: 56th in the UK

Caen 110
255th: 28th in France: 152

Ancona 109
256th: 35th in Italy

Boulogne-Billancourt 109
257th: 33rd in France

Havant & Waterloo 109
258th: 51st in the UK

Baracaldo 109
259th: 35th in Spain

Bottrop 108
260th: 53rd in W. Germany

Monza 108
261st: 36th in Italy

Jönköping 108